D1539115

Number 2 in the series *North American Beethoven Studies*, edited by William Meredith

Letters to Beethoven
and Other Correspondence
VOLUME 2: 1813–1823

Beethoven in 1814. Engraving by
Blasius Höfel, after a drawing by Louis Letronne.
Source: Vienna: Artaria & Co., 1814.

LETTERS TO

BEETHOVEN

and Other Correspondence

ॐ

Translated and Edited by
Theodore Albrecht

VOLUME 2: 1813–1823

Published by the *University of Nebraska Press*,
Lincoln & London, in association
with the *American Beethoven Society* and
the *Ira F. Brilliant Center for
Beethoven Studies*, San Jose State
University

♾ The paper in this book meets the minimum
requirements of American National
Standard for Information Sciences – Permanence
of Paper for Printed Library Materials,
ANSI Z39.48-1984.

Library of Congress
Cataloging-in-Publication Data
Letters to Beethoven and other correspondence /
translated and edited by Theodore Albrecht
p. cm. – (North American Beethoven studies; no.2)
Includes bibliographical references (p.   ) and index.
ISBN 0-8032-1033-7 (cloth: alkaline paper) (v.1)
ISBN 0-8032-1039-6 (cloth: alkaline paper) (v.2)
ISBN 0-8032-1040-x (cloth: alkaline paper) (v.3)
1. Beethoven, Ludwig van, 1770–1827 – Correspondence.
2. Composers – Austria – Correspondence.
I. Albrecht, Theodore. II. Series.
ML410.B4L5338 1996 780'.92–dc20 [B]
95-43793 CIP MN

CONTENTS

LETTERS AND DOCUMENTS

ILLUSTRATIONS

Frontispiece: Beethoven in 1814

NOTE ON CURRENCY VALUES

The nature of the currencies used in Beethoven's day—spanning from a period of variously enlightened monarchies, through the Napoleonic wars, to an uneasy period when the monarchy was restored in France—is complicated, both in terminology and in purchasing power. In general, however, the following relative values applied to the various denominations (using the Austrian kreuzer [or kreutzer] as the lowest practical value):

1 groschen = ca. 3 kreuzer
1 gulden = 60 kreuzer
1 gulden = 1 florin[1]
1 gulden = ca. 2 shillings (British)
1 ducat (#) = ca. 4½ gulden (or 4½ florins)
2 ducats = ca. 1 louis d'or (French, variable)
8 gulden = 1 friedrich d'or (Prussian)
9 gulden = 1 carolin (German)
10 gulden = ca. £1 (British)

Less frequently encountered in this volume is the Thaler:

1 Reichsthaler = 90 kreuzer
1 Rheinthaler = 120 kreuzer (2 gulden)

After Austria officially went bankrupt as a result of inflation during the Napoleonic Wars, the government initiated a *Finanz-Patent* on February 20, 1811, and ultimately a number of reforms in currency values, with figures given in *Convenzions-münze* (*C.M.:* convention coinage, called "Assimilated Coinage" by Anderson) and in local paper currency, *Wiener Währung* (*W.W.:* called "Viennese Currency" by Anderson).

1. The two terms were virtually interchangeable, sometimes within the same letter or similar document.

Emily Anderson's "Notes on Money Values" in her 1961 *Letters of Beethoven*, I, xlvii–xlviii, provides a concise and generally comprehensible account of the situation, without attempting to equate early currencies with modern purchasing power.

In consultation with Eduard Holzmair, director of the Vienna Coin Cabinet, George Marek (*Beethoven*, pp. xvii–xviii) attempted to equate Austrian currency in Beethoven's day with the approximate American purchasing power of 1969; his success was moderate but short-lived, as inflation became a daily factor in the 1970s.

Mary Sue Morrow covered "Business and Financial Aspects . . ." through roughly 1810 in her *Concert Life in Haydn's Vienna* (1989), pp. 109–139. Similarly, Alice Hanson discussed economic circumstances faced by Vienna's musicians, especially late in Beethoven's lifetime, in her *Musical Life in Biedermeier Vienna* (1985), pp. 3, 14–33. Although it does not consider all aspects of Beethoven's income (notably the Thomson folk song commissions in his middle years), Julia Moore's 1987 dissertation, "Beethoven and Musical Economics," presents the most thorough discussion of this thorny subject to date. Barry Cooper fills the aforementioned lacuna in his chapter "Economics and Logistics: Beethoven's Earnings," in *Beethoven's Folksong Settings* (1994), pp. 93–101. A concise overview of the whole subject appears in Cooper's "Economics," in *Beethoven Compendium*, ed. Barry Cooper (1991), pp. 68–70.

ABBREVIATIONS

As noted in the preface, this collection employs very few abbreviations. Abbreviated citations of published source materials are given as complete names and/or key words in the notes and thus can be located in the bibliography with little difficulty.

Anderson
The Letters of Beethoven, trans. and ed. Emily Anderson, 3 vols. (London: Macmillan; New York: St. Martin's, 1961; reprint, New York: W. W. Norton, 1985). Citations generally by letter number (Anderson No. 35); in the case of prefatory material or the roughly 82 letters in nine appendixes, citations by volume and page numbers (Anderson, III, 1428–1429).

Grove
Grove's Dictionary of Music and Musicians, most commonly the 5th edition, ed. Eric Blom, 9 vols. & suppl. (London: Macmillan, 1954, 1959). Earlier editions, extending back to 1889, are also valuable for details necessarily omitted as the chronology expanded later. See also *New Grove* (below) for the 6th edition.

Hess
Numbers assigned to incomplete, previously unrecognized or recently discovered works in Willy Hess, *Verzeichnis der nicht in der Gesamtausgabe veröffentlichten Werke Ludwig van Beethovens* (Wiesbaden: Breitkopf & Härtel, 1957).

MacArdle & Misch
New Beethoven Letters, trans. and ed. Donald W. MacArdle and Ludwig Misch (Norman: University of Oklahoma Press, 1957). Citations generally by letter number (MacArdle & Misch No. 67).

MGG
Die Musik in Geschichte und Gegenwart, ed. Friedrich Blume, 17 vols. (Basel

and Kassel: Bärenreiter, 1949–1986). Its index (in vol. 17) renders it especially indispensable for verifying details.

New Grove
The New Grove Dictionary of Music and Musicians, ed. Stanley Sadie, 20 vols. (London: Macmillan, 1980). Actually the 6th edition of *Grove* (above), which it does not entirely supersede in many details.

P.P.
Praemissis Praemittendis (premising what is to be premised; i.e., with the necessary introduction, Dear Sir or Dear Madam), a form of heading, address or salutation occasionally used in business letters. Beethoven used this formula less frequently after 1810, but its use in the present collection is almost exclusively confined to the years 1802–1804. Another combination of the same letters is *pp.* (lowercase, usually with a period following), meaning "the aforementioned," "the said," "selfsame" or a similar intensification. Härtel used it occasionally, other business correspondents only rarely. In the present collection, it is translated directly into English or sometimes simply omitted if the context warrants.

WoO
Werk(e) ohne Opuszahl. Work(s) without an opus number, in order of organization in Georg Kinsky, *Das Werk Beethovens: Thematisch-bibliographisches Verzeichnis seiner sämtlichen vollendeten Kompositionen,* completed by Hans Halm (Munich: G. Henle, 1955).

1813

168. Archduke Rudolph to Beethoven

[Vienna; Tuesday, January 5, 1813][1]

Dear Beethoven,

On the day after tomorrow, Thursday, at 5:30 o'clock[2] in the evening, there will again be a concert[3] at Prince Lobkowitz's, and I shall repeat the Sonata with Rode then,[4] if your health and affairs allow it; thus I would like to see you tomorrow at my residence in order to play through the Sonata.

If Rode perhaps wants to play through the violin part, let me know, and I could send it; but this, too, depends upon if and when you can come to me tomorrow.[5]

Your friend,

Rudolph

1. This undated note is answered by Anderson No. 402, which seems to date from January 6, 1813, if Thayer is correct in assuming that the evening of music at Lobkowitz's palace took place on Thursday, January 7.

2. Nohl and Frimmel read the autograph correctly and give the time as "½ 6 Uhr abends" (5:30 P.M.).

3. Rudolph uses the term *Musik*.

4. The Sonata for Violin and Piano, Op. 96, had recently been composed for the famous French violinist Pierre Rode (1774–1830), although it may originally have been inspired by Giovanni Battista Polledro, with whom Beethoven played a concert in Carlsbad on August 6, 1812 (see No. 164 above). While Polledro had studied with Gaetano Pugnani in Turin, Rode had studied with Giovanni Battista Viotti (1755–1824), Pugnani's most prominent pupil. Thus Rode and Polledro to some degree shared the same violinistic heritage. The Sonata, Op. 96, was first performed by Rode and Rudolph at Lobkowitz's on December 29, 1812. Rode's first public appearance in Vienna was on January 6, 1813. The archduke here consistently spells the violinist's name "Rhode."

5. Such an engagement would have subjected Rode to both a refresher rehearsal and a public concert of different music on the same day.

Incipit: Übermorgen Donnerstags ist um ½ 6 Uhr abends. . . .

Sources: Nohl, *Neue Briefe Beethovens* (1867), p. 68; Theodor Frimmel, "Verzeichnisse," *Beethoven-Jahrbuch* 1 (1908), 110; Thayer, III (1879), 225; Thayer-Deiters-Riemann, III, 351–352; Kastner (1910), pp. 266–267. Legible facsimile in Franz Grasberger, ed., *Beethoven, the Man and His Time* (Guelph: University of Guelph, 1970), pp. 53–54. In 1867, the letter was in the possession of the artist Friedrich von Amerling (1803–1887), Vienna. By 1908, it was in the Städtische Sammlungen of the Bibliothek und Museum der Stadt Wien (today's Stadt- und Landesbibliothek).

169. Beethoven to Countess Maria Eleonora Fuchs[1]

[Vienna; after January 6, 1813][2]

My dear Countess!

How sorry I am not to be able to accept your invitation, but at the moment I have something very pressing to write, for unfortunately this is the only thing that remains to me, despite all the sacrifices that I have made, if I do not want to die of hunger[3] — and if I do not want to have one of my brothers, who is unfortunate and sick, do the same.[4] In such an undeserved position, one is not inclined to mingle among people. Give Rode my best, only tell him that I must reproach him that he has not asked me for something new or still unknown from among my compositions. I did not want to offer any to him, because I believed that, since he gave his concert in the Grosser Redoutensaal, he had already made his choice with other works by other masters, in order to fill out his concert, for *in his case* I would have made an exception to this above all else.[5] My head is tirelessly trying to improve my situation again, and once this has been accomplished, then you will see me at your house once again. Society cannot deal with a person who suffers from a thoroughly wounded heart and is forced to rely upon himself.

Your friend,

Beethoven

[Exterior:]
   For Countess Fuchs
   née Countess Gallenberg

1. Maria Eleonora Gallenberg (born April 25, 1786) married Imperial Chamberlain Count Franz Xaver von Fuchs on July 13, 1801. On November 3, 1803, her brother, Count Wenzel Robert von Gallenberg, married Julie (Giulietta) Guicciardi (see Beethoven to Countess Susanna Guicciardi, January 23, 1802, No. 36 above). As Otto Biba notes, the intimate tone of this letter implies frequent contact with Countess Fuchs, although this is the only Beethoven letter to her that is known. Sieghard Brandenburg, Beethoven-Archiv, Bonn, has indicated that the countess's first name is Maria, not "Marka," as previously reported.

2. This undated letter probably derives from the period between Rode's two public concerts in Vienna, January 6 and January 31, 1813.

3. The work in progress was possibly the Symphonies Nos. 7 and 8, which were given a reading rehearsal at Archduke Rudolph's palace on ca. April 21, 1813 (see Beethoven to Zmeskall, April 22, 1813, No. 172 below). In hopes of using new works for projected benefit concerts for himself in the spring, Beethoven would certainly have placed considerable economic importance on finishing the symphonies during the winter.

4. Beethoven's brother Carl suffered from consumption and ultimately died on November 15, 1815 (see Carl's declaration, April 12, 1813, No. 171 below). Although Beethoven's original actually translates as "one of my unfortunate, sick brothers," there is no indication that brother Johann was either unfortunate or sick at this time.

5. French violinist Pierre Rode gave the first performance of Beethoven's Violin Sonata, Op. 96, with Archduke Rudolph as pianist, on December 29, 1812, at Prince Lobkowitz's palace. His first public appearance in Vienna took place in the Grosser Redoutensaal on January 6, 1813, with a program consisting of a concerto and variations of his own, operatic arias by Giovanni Simone Mayr and Ferdinando Paer, and the first movement of Beethoven's Fourth Symphony. Beethoven's complaint, then, is to be taken at face value: that Rode did not include any *new* or *unknown* works of his. Rode's second concert, this time in the Kleiner Redoutensaal, on January 31, included a repeat of his own violin concerto, complemented by operatic arias and Beethoven's *Egmont* Overture. See *Allgemeine musikalische Zeitung* 15 (1813), cols. 114, 117.

Incipit: Wie leid thut es mir nicht. . . .

Sources: Transcribed and edited by Otto Biba in Staehelin, "Unbekannte . . . Schriftstücke," pp. 39–42. Autograph in a private Austrian collection in 1982.

170. George Thomson to Beethoven

Edinburgh; March 27, 1813

Monsieur Louis van Beethoven[1]
Vienna, Austria

Monsieur,

I have written you several letters since the month of August last, and I have sent twenty-one airs to be harmonized by you. But since I have not yet had the pleasure of receiving a reply,[2] and since I do not know if any of these letters have reached you, I take this opportunity to send you, enclosed, another *correct* copy, containing twenty-three airs, for which I request you to make ritornellos and accompaniments.

$$\frac{x}{2}$$

In the piano parts, I entreat you to make a simplicity prevail that is apparent even to the eye, and is as easy and as accommodating as possible for the fingers. Such simplicity is of the utmost importance to the success of my work, for it is only the simple style in these airs that accommodates itself to the taste in this country.

I have finally received your ritornellos and accompaniments for sixty-four airs, which in general are truly excellent and are, indeed, masterpieces: I was delighted by them. But, my dear Monsieur, there are a small number of them that are much too difficult for *our* public. I believe, then, that you will not be offended if I beg you, as a very great favor, to revise the ritornellos and accompaniments of eight airs[3] that I have indicated to you at the end of the enclosed sheet.[4]

In this country, there is not one pianist in a hundred who would like the ritornellos and accompaniments that I wish you would revise. It will be easy for you to revise these; it will oblige me greatly, and I will gladly pay you for them. Your great predecessor Haydn would ask me to indicate to him frankly everything that would not please the national taste in the ritornellos and accompaniments, and he would change most willingly all of those in which I found fault.

4

You will find enclosed a note to Messrs. Fries & Co. that you will present to them with the ritornellos and accompaniments.[5] For the twenty-three ritornellos and accompaniments (and for the six others,[6] revised), they will pay you *eighty ducats* in cash.

I assure you that Haydn never asked for more than two ducats for each air, and not a *sou* for those that he revised.

Be so kind as to write me soon that you have received this letter,[7] to save me the trouble of preparing and sending other copies of the music. It is truly with a great deal of shame and vexation that I trouble Messrs. Fries so often. I would very much like to know your own address so that I can write to you without giving them trouble.[8]

I am beginning to hope that, before long, our correspondence will be more free than it has been for some years past.[9]

I have the honor, Monsieur, to be, with great esteem,

Your friend and very obliging servant,

(signed) George Thomson

1. Below the address, Thomson noted to himself that he sent this letter in an envelope to Fries & Co., Bankers, Vienna, and transmitted it through John Hunter, 43 Beaumont Street, Marybone [*sic*], to Mr. Broughton, Secretary of State's Office, to be sent "by the first safe opportunity or courier going to Vienna."

2. Thomson had written to Beethoven on August 5, October 30 and December 21, 1812 (Nos. 163, 166 and 167 above), but had not yet received Beethoven's reply of February 19, 1813 (Anderson No. 405). Beethoven also wrote several receipts to Thomson through Fries at about this time, listed in MacArdle, "Beethoven and George Thomson," pp. 36–38; two are given in MacArdle & Misch (Nos. 117 and 119).

3. The number 6 is crossed out and replaced with an 8 in this copy.

4. The enclosure's contents were not registered in the copybook copy.

5. The note to Fries, adjacent in the copybook, instructs the bankers to pay Beethoven 80 ducats for twenty-three airs and eight revisions.

6. Thomson inconsistently crossed out the 8 here and inserted "6 others."

7. Beethoven's next letter to Thomson seems to be one in Italian dated September 15, 1814 (Anderson No. 496), apologizing for his long delay in writing.

8. Beethoven never seems to have entrusted Thomson with his own address(es).

9. Thomson is anticipating the end of the Napoleonic Wars.

Incipit: Je vous ai écrit plusieurs lettres. . . .

Sources: Summarized in MacArdle, "Beethoven and George Thomson," p. 38, and very briefly in Hadden, *George Thomson,* p. 327. Copy in Thomson's copybook, British Library, Add. MS 35267, pp. 72v–73v.

171. Carl van Beethoven, Declaration to the Court[1]

Vienna; April 12, 1813

Declaration

Since I am convinced of the openhearted disposition of my brother Ludwig van Beethoven, I desire that, after my death, he undertake the guardianship of my surviving minor son, Karl Beethoven.[2] I therefore request the honorable court to appoint my said brother to this guardianship upon my death, and beg my dear brother to undertake this office and, like a father,[3] to assist my child with word and deed in all circumstances. In witness of my preparation:

Vienna; April 12, 1813

Carl v. Beethoven
I.R. Cashier

Ludwig van Beethoven

Baron Joh[ann] v. Pasqualati
I.R. priv. Wholesale Merchant
as solicited witness

Fr[anz] Oliva
as requested witness

Peter v. Leber[4]

1. Although Carl uses the term *Abhandlungs-Instanz* for the court in this document, Beethoven ultimately submitted it to the Imperial Royal Landrecht (a court for the privileged classes) on November 28, 1815 (Anderson, III, 1360–1361). In Beethoven's petition to the Landrecht, this declaration is cited as "Document B." In a rare lapse, Anderson was not aware of its publication in Thayer and declared that "Document B has not been recovered."

2. Beethoven had been concerned about Carl's health for some time and felt compelled to work doubly hard to provide him with income (see Beethoven to Countess Fuchs, after January 6, 1813, No. 169 above). Carl's consumption worsened

early in March 1813, prompting this declaration of guardianship. His condition improved with the coming of spring, and he lived until November 15, 1815. Young Karl, an only child, was born on September 4, 1806.

3. Solomon (*Beethoven,* pp. 235, 238–240, 253–254) has attached great negative significance to Beethoven's later regarding himself as a "father" to his nephew Karl. In fact, Carl seems here to be the first to use the term in reference to Ludwig.

4. The document was signed and sealed by all concerned. Pasqualati and Leber were co-owners of the house on the Mölkerbastei where Beethoven lived; Oliva was a businessman and a friend of the composer's. To what extent these witnesses were also friends of Carl's is unknown. Thayer transcribes Carl's signature as "Karl v. Beethoven."

Incipit: Da ich von den offenherzigen Gesinnungen. . . .

Sources: Thayer, III (1879), 231; Thayer-Deiters-Riemann, III, 363–364; Thayer-Krehbiel, II, 241; Thayer-Forbes, p. 550. Another English translation is in Richard Sterba and Editha Sterba, *Beethoven and His Nephew: A Psychoanalytic Study of Their Relationship,* trans. Willard R. Trask (New York: Pantheon, 1954), p. 42, citing the German transcription in Thayer-Deiters-Riemann.

172. Beethoven to Nikolaus Zmeskall von Domanovecz

[Vienna; April 22, 1813][1]

I was already at your place, dear Z. Although your servant said that you did not go to the Chancellery at all, I took this to be an error. Do you already know something? Could I speak with you? I would appreciate it, especially because of yesterday and the especially bad playing,[2] in connection with which Herr Kraft[3] very much takes first place.

Entirely your

Beethoven

1. This one-page letter bears no place or date in Beethoven's hand, but Zmeskall indicated the date of receipt in the lower margin.

2. Beethoven's letter to Zmeskall on April 19, 1813 (Anderson No. 416), concerns his search for a hall in which to hold two benefit concerts and refers to a possible rehearsal of two symphonies—surely a reading rehearsal to try out the Symphonies Nos. 7 and 8—at Archduke Rudolph's the next day. For similar rehearsals in connection

with the Symphony No. 3 and the Triple Concerto, see Anton Wranitzky's bill, June 11, 1804 (No. 81 above).

An undated letter from Beethoven to Rudolph (Anderson No. 330, almost surely misplaced in the chronology) indicates that Beethoven was ill the previous day, and was still ill that day, but projects the rehearsal for the next day. If the present letter is correct, that rehearsal took place on Wednesday, April 21; thus, undated Anderson No. 330 was probably written on Tuesday, April 20. For that reading rehearsal Beethoven requested 4 first violins, 4 second violins, 4 violas (a slip of the pen notwithstanding), 2 violoncellos and 2 contrabasses. As part of a fairly standard complement of winds, the symphonies (Nos. 7 and 8) required only 2 horns each (see Schlemmer's receipt of February 28, 1814, No. 182 below, concerning additional parts required for public performance). Beethoven told Rudolph that, if he (Rudolph) desired two overtures rehearsed as well, 4 horns would be required. Although the *Egmont* Overture required four horns, it was nearly three years old by this time and fairly well established. The most likely works are the Overtures to *King Stephan* and *The Ruins of Athens,* premiered in Pest a little over a year before, and therefore relatively unfamiliar to the Viennese.

Beethoven's next letter to Zmeskall, April 23, 1813 (Anderson No. 417), deals with the composer's trouble in securing his stipend payment from Prince Lobkowitz and possible intervention on his behalf by Archduke Rudolph. By the time he wrote to Zmeskall again on April 26 (Anderson No. 418), Beethoven's hopes of securing an auspicious date for a concert had dwindled to virtually nil, for which he blamed Prince Lobkowitz's ineffective advocacy. In any case, the Symphony No. 7 remained one of Archduke Rudolph's favorite works, as he wrote the composer on March 25, 1820 (No. 268 below), after a performance in Olmütz.

3. Nikolaus Kraft (1778–1853) or his father, Anton Kraft (1749–1820), both virtuoso violoncellists long associated with Beethoven's music. After playing in Haydn's Esterházy orchestra, Anton entered Prince Lobkowitz's service in 1795. As Lobkowitz's fortunes declined after 1811, Beethoven's stipend payments from the prince became more irregular, and, when Lobkowitz turned Anton Kraft out of his house in 1813, Beethoven wrote to Archduke Rudolph on his behalf (Anderson No. 445), describing him as a "poor, old and deserving man," and asking the archduke to provide him lodging.

Although the elder Kraft is reputed to have performed in the premiere of the Symphony No. 7 and *Wellington's Victory* (on December 8, 1813), Beethoven's complaint might be directed at Nikolaus. In any case, note that Beethoven does not rail loudly about the orchestra or Kraft but instead seeks to discuss his disappointment somewhat confidentially.

Incipit: Ich war schon bej ihnen. . . .

Sources: Stargardt, *Autographen aus verschiedenem Besitz: Katalog 577* (Marburg, November 29–30, 1966), p. 136, item 583. Quoted briefly in Hans Schmidt, "Die Beethovenhandschriften des Beethovenhauses in Bonn," *Beethoven-Jahrbuch* 7 (1971), 198–199. Autograph in the Beethoven-Archiv, Bonn, BH 478, since 1966.

173. *Archduke Rudolph to Beethoven*

Baden; June 7, 1813[1]

Dear Beethoven!

With great pleasure I learned from your letter of the 27th of last month, which I just received the evening before last, of your arrival in my beloved Baden. I hope to see you tomorrow morning in my residence, if your time allows, because my stay here of a few days has already been so favorable to my health that, without fearing any ill effects on it, I may listen to music and even perform it again myself. If your stay in this healthful and beautiful region brings about the same effect on your condition, my intention in taking care of your lodging will be completely fulfilled.

Your friend,
Rudolph

1. Answers Beethoven's letter of May 27, 1813 (Anderson No. 426).

Incipit: Mit vielem Vergnügen habe ich aus Ihrem Briefe. . . .

Sources: Schindler (1860), p. 186 (correct date); Schindler-MacArdle, p. 164 (with the incorrect date of "July 7" given); Thayer, III (1879), 247; Thayer-Deiters-Riemann, III, 379; Theodor Frimmel and Edward Speyer, "Verzeichnis . . . ," *Beethoven Jahrbuch* 2 (1909), 310; Kastner (1910), pp. 285–286; Hellinghaus (1922), p. 98; Kobald, *Beethoven* (1927), pp. 284–285; Brenneis, "Fischhof-Manuskript," p. 59. Schindler (1860) noted that the autograph was to be found in the collection of Franz Gräffer, Vienna; by 1909, it was in Edward Speyer's collection; it is now in the Bodmer Collection, Beethovenhaus, Bonn. A copy in the hand of Aloys Fuchs is in the Staatsbibliothek zu Berlin–Preussischer Kulturbesitz.

174. Beethoven to Prince Franz Joseph Lobkowitz (?)[1]

Vienna; July 24, 1813[2]

Pro Memoria

In the year 1809, I received from the Court of Westphalia the offer of a position with the annual [salary] of 600 ducats in gold. His Imperial Highness, the Archduke Rudolph, and the Princes Kinsky & Lobkowitz voluntarily made me an offer, to assure me of a lifelong stipend of Four Thousand Gulden, if I would turn down this position and remain in Austria.

The Archduke Rudolph committed himself to contribute	1,500 fl[orins]
Prince von Kinsky " " " "	1,800
Prince von Lobkowitz " " " "	700
	4,000 fl[orins]

according to the contract dated March 1, 1809. Even though this sum at that time was not comparable with that offered me in Westphalia, I resolved myself, however, out of preference for Austria, to accept this offer, and drew my stipend from the interested parties according to their share. When the Finance Patent appeared, I requested the Archduke Rudolph to pay me his portion of the stipend (now reduced in value) fully in redemption notes, and raised by an insignificant amount, according to the exchange rate.[3] He granted my request immediately; Prince Kinsky also did the same.[4] When, during my absence in Bohemia, I had my friend here apply to Prince Lobkowitz about it, this person then sent me word that the 700 fl[orins] in question would be paid in redemption notes, and repeated this promise to me in person upon my return.[5]

Nevertheless, it was not possible, at the Prince's Cashier's Office, despite my numerous inquiries there and the repeated written requests that I had delivered to the Prince, to receive my stipend, which had been in arrears since September 1, 1811.

Pressed by all manner of unfavorable family circumstances[6] and by the unforeseen death of Prince Kinsky (also in this regard hindered in the correct payment of my stipend),[7] I had to accept the payment of the depreciated portion from Prince Lobkowitz. I gave receipts for the payments and did not doubt the correct payment of the same in the future. Since, however, the lender still could not get any money for such a long time, he sued me legally for repayment of the loaned sum, and I, unable to repay it, had to take legal action against Prince Lobkowitz concerning the matter.[8]

After the conference[9] that took place on the 21st of this month, Doctor Frischherz,[10] the attorney for Prince von Lobkowitz, declared that, in the absence of the Prince, he had questioned the Cashier Damm[11] concerning this matter, and learned from him that the Prince had indeed given the instruction earlier for the payment of this stipend, 700 florins, in full *Wiener Währung*,[12] calculated from the day of the Patent forward, but that the Prince had later revoked it. Concerning the oath that my lawyer friend[13] imposed upon the Prince for that purpose, Dr. Frischherz said that he wanted to turn to Prince Lobkowitz in order to obtain further procedural instructions. Convinced that the Prince will not delay a moment in repeating his promise, whose revocation at the Cashier's Office was surely only a misunderstanding, I now take the liberty of requesting Your Highness, as soon as this matter is resolved, most graciously to order the speedy payment of the same.

Your Highness cannot fail to notice that this stipend does not fit into the same category as so many of the outstanding princely debts. It is voluntarily offered compensation for a very significant sum and is designated for my life's subsistence. Through the receipt of the decree concerning the difficulty of making a living, it was intended to make my life trouble free, a purpose that has completely failed because of the present way in which it is being handled.

After the proofs of noble humanity that Your Highness has had the graciousness to give me upon several occasions, I confidently hope that I will not be turned down, and have the honor, with my great esteem, to be

Your Highness's most devoted servant,

Ludwig van Beethoven

1. On the basis of the form of address (*Euer Durchlaucht*) employed here, Gutiérrez-Denhoff concludes that the recipient was a prince with whom Beethoven had previously had dealings, possibly an administrator of one of Prince Lobkowitz's

estates. Despite the switch from third to second person three-quarters of the way through the document, the memorandum may actually have been intended for the eyes of Prince Lobkowitz himself.

2. In addition to the present memorandum, in the hand of bank clerk Franz Oliva, Beethoven also wrote a letter to Archduke Rudolph on July 24 (Anderson No. 429), indicating his frustration over the delays he was experiencing in receiving his stipends from Prince Lobkowitz and the estate of Prince Kinsky. Lobkowitz himself was in the midst of a severe financial crisis at this time, although on a much less life-threatening level than Beethoven's dilemma. Several letters from the first half of 1813 also indicate Beethoven's growing vexation with Lobkowitz: to Zmeskall (March, Anderson No. 409), to Johann Baptist Pasqualati (undated, spring, Anderson No. 412), to Zmeskall (April 23 and May 10, Anderson Nos. 417 and 421), and to Joseph Varena (July 4, Anderson No. 428).

3. Beethoven's letter to Lobkowitz, January 4, [1814, possibly 1815] (Anderson No. 457), indicates that the prince's representative tried to induce the composer to accept his stipend according to a (variable) scale, rather than in Viennese currency.

4. Beethoven described this event, which took place on June 8, 1812, to Princess Karoline Kinsky, in a letter of December 30, 1812 (Anderson No. 393), two months after the prince's death.

5. Beethoven spent from early July through the third week in September 1812 in Bohemia, visiting several spas, and possibly crossing paths with Antonie Brentano (probably the "Immortal Beloved") and her family for the last time. The friend in Vienna was probably Franz Oliva, who wrote out the present memo, and who is mentioned by name in Beethoven's letter to Lobkowitz, January 4, [1814 or 1815] (Anderson No. 457).

6. Having returned to Vienna briefly, Beethoven journeyed to Linz in October 1812 to break up his brother Johann's unwedded liaison with Therese Obermayer; as a result of this fraternal fracas, Johann simply married her. Brother Carl's consumption also seems to have worsened at about this time (see Beethoven to Fuchs, after January 6, 1813, and Carl's declaration, April 12, 1813, Nos. 169 and 171 above).

7. Prince Kinsky had died on November 3, 1812, as a result of a riding accident.

8. Gutiérrez-Denhoff could locate no background material concerning this assertion.

9. *Tagsatzung* (National Assembly).

10. Since 1807, Dr. Ferdinand Frischherz had been Lobkowitz's attorney in Prague.

11. Kaspar Wenzel Damm (spelled *Dann* here), Lobkowitz's assistant bookkeeper and chief cashier in Vienna between 1812 and 1823.

12. Viennese currency.

13. Possibly Dr. Carl von Adlersburg, who had assisted Beethoven since early 1813 in his dealings with the overdue Kinsky payments. The oath was a *Haupteid*.

Incipit: Im Jahre 1809 erhielt ich. . . .

Sources: Gutiérrez-Denhoff, " 'o Unseeliges Dekret': Beethovens Rente," pp. 123–125, with extensive discussion. Autograph in the Beethoven-Haus, Bonn, BH 42 a–b, with an accompanying copy of the contract of March 1, 1809 (see Thayer-Forbes, p. 457).

175. *Clemens Brentano to Beethoven*

[probably Vienna; probably late Summer 1813][1]

Dear very beloved Beethoven!

Through the individual expressions of your art, you have become for me such a living and yet eternal comfort, that the moment when I first saw you had to be noteworthy. To reveal a heart full of love and sincere veneration at a coffeehouse is an act as mad as any in life, but I have done as much in the worst places, for I dare say that nothing in the world can deter me from doing what I feel necessary. Nonetheless I had heard as much spoken about your eccentricities from sleek and polished people as the rabble always did about the hound of Alcibiades,[2] and for that reason I had profound concern, for some minutes, that through my awkwardness I might be bothersome to you. But I would not act this way, for I acknowledge the inner necessity of ideal solitude for every creative spirit, which is necessarily lonely, as is God himself, because it is omnipresent, as is God.

Pardon me, then, for the way I was, or for perhaps having talked too much. Believe me that, while I had many more thoughts, in my relationship with you I would rather remain forever silent than be deprived of hearing your tones.[3] I cannot speak to you in anything other than superlatives, that I love you as much as the few for whom you have composed, and among whom I could hardly place myself in another world; for, other than my very dear Bettina,[4] I know of no one who hears your music with more spiritual inspiration than

Yours truly,

Clemens Brentano

[P.S.] I am coming to you soon, and will make my muse available to you for any purpose!

1. Beethoven may have met poet Clemens Brentano (1778–1842), the brother of Bettina Brentano, in Teplitz during the summer of 1811, although there is no contemporary evidence for such a meeting. On January 10, 1811, Brentano had sent his sister-in-law, Antonie Brentano in Vienna, a text for a "Cantata on the Death of Queen Luise," with hopes that Beethoven might set it to music. Clemens Brentano spent the period from July 1813 to July 1814 in Vienna. While this undated letter, written shortly after their first meeting (seemingly a chance encounter rather than a formal introduction), may have been written in Teplitz in 1811, it more likely dates from Vienna in the late summer of 1813. Beethoven seems to have spent much of July in Vienna ("It is a torment for me to stay in the city in the summertime," he wrote to Archduke Rudolph on July 24 [Anderson No. 429]) and most of August and early September in Baden (with occasional trips to the city), moving back to Vienna between September 15 and 20.

2. Alcibiades (ca. 450–404 B.C.), unscrupulous Athenian general and statesman who, after an adventurous and politically checked career, was murdered at the behest of the Spartans.

3. It seems that Beethoven may have exhibited impatience with the garrulous, mentally unstable Brentano.

4. Elisabeth (Bettina) Brentano, 1785–1859, poetess and sculptress, was, like her brother, slightly unbalanced and given to exaggeration. Married to Achim von Arnim in 1811, she was on friendly terms with both Goethe and Beethoven at various times.

Incipit: Sie sind mir durch einzelne Äusserungen. . . .

Sources: Heinz Amelung, "Beethoven und die Brentanos," *Rheinischer Beobachter* 2 (1923), 501–503; "Beethoven und Clemens Brentano," *Deutsche Musiker-Zeitung* 60 (1929), 352. The letter, from the estate of Bettina Brentano, was auctioned by Karl Ernst Henrici, Berlin, on March 23, 1929. The unidentified author of 1929 presented extensive excerpts from the letter that seem, on the whole, more plausibly transcribed than Amelung's full text.

176. George Thomson to Beethoven

Edinburgh; September 1813

Monsieur Beethoven,

Last April, I received, in duplicate, your letter of the previous February 2, and I paid then the 90 ducats that you have received upon my account from Messrs. Fries for the 30 airs.[1] But alas! to my great vexation these airs have not appeared! It will be necessary, then, for you to have another copy made, as you see fit, to be sent to me by *mail*. To this end, be sure that this copy is written in a very compact manner, but at the same time very distinct and legible, without abbreviations, and on a paper of the same type that you have sent me before.

You will excuse me if I evince my surprise that you have rewritten nine of your ritornellos and accompaniments, and that you have had me pay 27 ducats for them, when only three of them needed to be redone. I would never have imagined that you would have qualms about making the very small changes that I wished for the other six airs. There does not exist a man to whom I would give the money with greater pleasure than to Monsieur Beethoven; but in truth, the music and the poetry of this work, and the [engraving] plates, will cost me more money than I shall ever be able to derive from it.

I am sending you, enclosed, four other Irish airs, and I ask you to be so kind as to compose ritornellos and accompaniments for them in a simple and easy style principally for the piano, and for the violin and violoncello ad libitum. The first two are to be found, perhaps, among the most recent 30 airs—I am not certain about that. If they turn out to be there, do only Nos. 3 and 4.

I find, from what you say, that you have never seen the work that Haydn did for me. Each air has its ritornellos and accompaniments for piano, violin and violoncello, and several of the airs are arranged as duets, precisely like yours.

I still desire to have some songs of your composition for the English verses, and I shall give you twenty ducats in cash for six of the songs, if you will really compose them for me con amore. I shall not risk more at this time, considering the hazards and the difficulty of obtaining the manuscript. But, if the public appreciates them, I shall take a greater number afterward. You will recall that I am offering now the same price that you at first set yourself, in your letter of July 17, 1810,[2] and I assure you that I cannot give you more.

If, therefore, it is agreeable to you, you will compose six songs for the English subjects, of which five are in your hands, in my letters of February 10 and September 17, 1810.[3]

Here are the words that I have chosen for the six songs:[4]

[1.]   "The Battle of Hohenlinden"—grand and sublime, beginning "On Linden when the sun was low."

[2.] "On May Morning"—description of the delights, the gaiety and the beauty of May, beginning "Now the bright morning star."

[3.] "The farewells of a lover to his charming mistress"—full of tenderness, beginning "Once more, enchanting girl, adieu."

[4.] "The Happy Italian Shepherdess," singing the pleasures and beauties of the valley of her birth, beginning "Dear is my little native vale."

[5.] "Song of Norman," a young warrior, who was obliged to tear himself from the arms of his beloved Marie at the moment of their marriage—very pathetic, beginning "The heath this night must be my bed."

[6.] The sixth song expresses the despair of a [female] lover; it is as follows:

> *Recitative*
> Raving winds around her blowing,
> Yellow leaves the woodlands showing,
> By a river hoarsely roaring,
> Isabella stray'd deploring.

> *Air*
> Farewell, hours that late did measure
> Sunshine days of joy and pleasure:
> Hail, thou gloomy night of sorrow,
> Cheerless night that knows no morrow.
> O'er the past too fondly wand'ring,
> On the hopeless future pond'ring,
> Chilly grief my life blood freezes,
> Fell despair my fancy seizes.

> Life, thou soul of ev'ry blessing,
> Load to misery most distressing,
> Oh! how gladly I'd resign thee
> And to dark oblivion join thee.

You will compose the airs for one voice, or some for two or three, as it pleases you alone; and with the accompaniment for the piano alone; and, in order that the airs accommodate most voices, I believe that they should not go any higher than G, or at most A.

If you do not understand English, you would do well to ask some Englishman in Vienna to read you the verses, and to acquaint you not only with the meaning, but also the true accentuation of the words.

I am extremely desirous of seeing some more of your charming quartets and sonatas. I spent some days recently in the country with a small select coterie of amateur friends, where among other things, we played your first Rasumovsky Quartet and the Quintet in C.[5] We repeated them every day with growing pleasure, and every day we drank with enthusiasm to the health of the composer. What an immortal theme, that adagio.[6]

To hear it would give me solace even when dying! But alas, my friend, in Scotland we do not have a dozen persons (the professionals included) who could take a part in these quartets, and not one who could play *correctly* the first violin part in all of the three![7] What would my happiness have been, if fate had placed me in Vienna, where I would have been able to hear your quartets, sonatas and symphonies well played every day!

It is greatly to be wished that you compose some music in that grand and original style that is yours alone, but easier to play, such that it could be played by amateurs. Such works would be a true treasure to musicians. Simple and expressive music will always have great charm for all listeners, and music that is difficult to play will probably be neglected.

I have not yet published any of your airs; but upon the arrival of the 30, I shall soon have a volume of thirty completely ready, which I shall send you as soon as it is printed.

[Thomson's note to himself:]

The four airs sent in the preceding letter[8] were:

No. 1 Duet. Add a part for a 2ⁿᵈ voice

Andantᵉ poco Allegretto grazioso con moto

No. 2 For duet or trio, as Monsieur Beethoven pleases

Marcia maestoso e spiritoso

No. 3

Andante expressivo e teneramente

No. 4

Allegretto scherzando   [*sic*]

1. The date of the letter to which Thomson refers clearly reads "2. Février" in the copybook. Thomson may have meant Beethoven's receipt of February 27, 1813, which concerns the payment of 90 ducats for thirty airs (MacArdle & Misch No. 119) or Beethoven's letter of February 19, 1813 (Anderson No. 405). Beethoven's next letter is dated September 15, 1814 (Anderson No. 496; MacArdle & Misch No. 137).

2. Anderson No. 266.

3. These two letters seem not to have survived.

4. Beethoven seems not to have set any of these.

5. Op. 59, No. 1, and Op. 29.

6. The Adagio molto e mesto, the third movement of the String Quartet, Op. 59, No. 1.

7. The three Quartets, Op. 59.

8. The four Irish airs mentioned in paragraph 3 of the letter: WoO 157, No. 11 ("The Wandering Minstrel"); WoO 157, No. 6 ("The health to the brave"); WoO 158/II, No. 5 ("Erin! oh Erin!"); and WoO 157, No. 8 ("By the Side of the Shannon"), respectively. The third item was published posthumously (identified in Cooper, ed., *Compendium*, p. 271).

Incipit: Je vous prie de faire tenir. . . .

Sources: Summarized in MacArdle, "Beethoven and George Thomson," p. 38; and Hadden, *George Thomson,* pp. 327, 330 (with a quote of the two paragraphs concerning the string quartets). Copy in Thomson's copybook, British Library, Add. MS 35267, pp. 82r–84r.

177. August von Kotzebue[1] to Beethoven

Reval;[2] September 24, 1813

The bearer of this, Herr Hagen,[3] has been a music teacher in my house for three years, and because I have come to value him for his knowledge and his diligence, as well as for his moral character, I take the liberty to recommend him to you most highly in this regard as one of your staunchest admirers. Among these I also number myself and remain

Your most obedient,
Kotzebue

1. Born in Weimar, Kotzebue (1761–1819) studied law, entered the service of the Russian government and was assigned to a post in Estonia. Here he also exercised his talents as poet and playwright. In 1797, he moved to Vienna as manager of the Burgtheater, then back to Weimar (but could not get along with Goethe), then to Berlin. After 1806, he moved again to Russia, reentering government service in 1813. In 1811, he penned two occasional plays, *King Stephan* and *The Ruins of Athens,* for the opening of a new theater in Pesth, for which Beethoven composed incidental music. They premiered on February 10, 1812. Evidently, Beethoven was satisfied with Kotzebue's work and on January 28, 1812 (Anderson No. 344), wrote to the poet in Estonia, asking him to submit a potential opera libretto. Nothing came of the proposal, although Kotzebue wrote to Beethoven on April 20, 1812 (No. 161 above). Ultimately Kotzebue was assassinated in Mannheim in 1819 for his alleged conservative political opinions.

2. Reval (Tallinn), principal seaport and capital of Estonia.

3. Johann August Hagen (1786–1877) became vocal instructor of the Reval *Gymnasium* in 1815. He founded German and Estonian choruses in 1823, composed an oratorio, later published a hymnal in the Estonian language and became a major force in the city's musical life.

Incipit: Überbringer dieses, Herr Hagen. . . .

Sources: Thayer-Deiters-Riemann, III, 397; the original was then in the possession of Caroline van Beethoven, the widow of Beethoven's nephew Karl.

178. Beethoven to Anton Halm[1]

[Vienna; 1813 or 1814?][2]

I am sorry [not to have fulfilled?] your wishes in respect to the overture. . . . [No further text available.][3]

1. Halm (1789–1872) received his musical training in Graz, served in the army from 1809 to 1811, returned to Graz and then spent a period (1813–1814/1815) in the service of the Gyika de Désánfalva family in Hungary. In 1814 or 1815, he moved to Vienna, where he became acquainted with Beethoven and in April 1816 dedicated to the elder composer his Sonata in C Minor, Op. 15. See Frimmel, *Beethoven-Handbuch*, I, 192–196, for an account of their lukewarm friendship.

2. The note indicates neither place nor date of writing. Helms and Staehelin surmise the date as given above but do not indicate Halm's address at the time. In 1813–1814, he was living in Hungary and presumably had not yet made Beethoven's acquaintance. If Halm lived in Vienna when this letter was written, then it must surely date at least a year or two later than Helms and Staehelin believed.

3. The verb phrase is missing at the end of the German incipit, but the available text seems to indicate that Beethoven had disappointed Halm.

Incipit: Es thut mir leid, Ihren Wünschen in Ansehung der Overture. . . .

Sources: Helms and Staehelin, "Bewegungen . . . 1973–1979," p. 347. The letter came to light in the latter 1970s, long enough for its incipit to be recorded, and then disappeared into unknown ownership.

1814

179. Clemens Brentano to Beethoven

[Vienna; ca. January 3–6, 1814][1]

I quickly wrote down these songs[2] an hour before I went to your concert;[3] later, they will become better.[4] The last song is not complete, for David's harp[5] and Gideon's trumpet belong to you; you must heal the odious Saul. Excuse me, it is sincere love and I shall get better.

Your

Clemens Brentano

1. Because three of the four enclosed poems (probably celebrating Beethoven's concert of January 2, 1814) were published in Vienna's *Dramatischer Beobachter* on January 7, 1814, this letter must date from sometime between January 3 and 6.

2. The enclosed Romantic poems were *Vier Lieder von Beethoven an sich selbst* (Four songs of Beethoven to himself). The first contains various metaphors concerning the cosmos; the second is more earthy, with references to trials of hell and night. The third begins, "You have fought the battle, I set the battle to music," and concludes, "Wellington, Victoria! Beethoven! Gloria!" The fourth refers to Wellington, Vittoria, and the people's fight between the Pyrenees and Gibraltar, with allusions to classical and biblical characters. Kalischer's article/chapter provides the full text, along with variants as Brentano improved (or at least revised) his poetry.

3. Beethoven's concert of January 2, 1814, held in the Grosser Redoutensaal, consisted of *Wellington's Victory*, Nos. 6, 7 and 8 (i.e., those with patriotic content) from *The Ruins of Athens*, and the Symphony No. 7. Possibly Brentano refers to similar concerts held in the University Hall on December 8 and 12, 1813, but the publication of the poetry on January 7 makes a reference to the January 2 concert much more likely.

4. Brentano was slightly unbalanced and given to emotional flights of fancy; in its original form, the entire letter is a single long sentence. His letter to Beethoven of late summer 1813 (No. 175 above) also indicates that he may have become flustered in attempting to communicate with the revered composer.

5. Brentano's poems contain references to David, with whom one often associates a harp.

Incipit: Ich habe diese Lieder. . . .

Sources: Alfred Christlieb Kalischer, "Clemens Brentanos Beziehungen zu Beethoven," *Euphorion* 2 (1895), Ergänzungsheft No. 1, 55–59; included in his *Beethoven und seine Zeitgenossen,* vol. IV, *Beethoven und Wien* (Berlin: Schuster & Loeffler, 1909–1910), 236–241. Autograph in the Staatsbibliothek zu Berlin–Preussischer Kulturbesitz, Mus. ms. autogr. Beethoven 37, 28; listed in Kalischer, "Beethoven-Autographe," p. 65, and Bartlitz, p. 187.

180. Hungarian Poet (N——)[1] to Beethoven

Buda; February 1814[2]

Mein Herr!

I venture to place before you the draft for a universal German national anthem, a counterpart to the English "Rule Britannia," which every real Teuton, bearing the proud consciousness of Germany's dignity in his breast, has always envied the British. I do not regard my draft as complete—it belongs in spirit with Schiller's desire to capture in simple songs the essence of all the peoples of Germany[3]—but if your Godly art would give it fire and life, then my poor verse would soon be surpassed.

The effect of a majestic, solemn and—may I say—yet childlike-simple, and therefore surging melody will soon capture our better poets [to write verses to the melody].

And what time could be more appropriate than right now for our great and splendid Fatherland to have an all-inclusive national anthem? When would such a moment ever occur again?

I need not remind you what an effect that the power of the music in "La Marseillaise" once made upon the French people, and what pride "Rule Britannia" always awakens in the British. What are cold written words but mere words alone without music? But if these, the well-known words, thunder in our ears with the flame of emotion, arousing childlike appreciation for the German Fatherland and the proud awareness of our individuality, then the coldness of the written word dissolves into blissful ecstacy. The soaring pulse of your art induces the Teutonic peoples to rise above themselves!

Thus, only you can be the creator of the Teutonic national anthem! Give my meter, which (except for the chorus) is that of the English national anthem ("Rule Britannia"), a melody that enflames our exalted poets to produce their finest thoughts.

I deliberately chose the meter of "Rule Britannia" to assimilate us with this brother-folk; and by the same design the first verse is also translated word for word:

When Britannia first at Heav'n's command	Als Teuts Land einst des Schöpfers Hand,
Arose from out the azure Main!	Herforrief im azuren Port!
This was the charter, the charter of the land,	Diess war die Urkund, die Urkund unserm Land
And Guardian Angel sung this strain	Und Schutzgeist Engel sang diess Wort:
Chorus	Chor
Rule Britannia, etc.	Herrsche Teutonia, etc.

Otherwise it has nothing in common with "Rule Britannia" except that the second line and the underlined words[4] of the third line are to be sung twice.

The second and third verses[5] portray an old and new era, where Germany's language and customs are threatened with destruction.

The image of the fourth verse, I believe, is characteristic of us.

In historical fame, the fifth verse addresses the knights and citizens of Germany.

Our sense of world citizenship in the sixth, seventh and eighth.

The farmer, the forester (the science of forestry was exclusively born in northern Germany), merchant and industrialist in the ninth.

Our German wives and daughters in the tenth.

Our soldiers in the eleventh.

The last four verses are perhaps silent wishes, although not unattainable and impossible.

In your hands now lays my poor draft. If you honor my request, I would wish that the orthography of the song be retained, particularly the rejection of the letter V,[6] which forces the German tongue to such disgusting blunders. Merely for that would I wish to be recognized in later writings.

Accept my warmest esteem!

N——

1. Although living in Hungary, this poet, who signed himself "N——," obviously considered himself among the most German of Germans. Nevertheless, his handwriting is a curious combination of Latin and German Gothic characters.

2. Likewise prone to incomplete information in other matters, this *echt-teutsch* poet also omits the day of the month.

3. Indeed Beethoven achieved much the same end in his setting of Schiller's *An die Freude* in the Ninth Symphony, premiered in 1824.

4. This distinction is not present in the manuscript.

5. The full sixteen verses of doggerel that accompanied this letter will not be included here; the author's own summaries, no matter how unclear, provide sufficient evidence of their content.

6. To this end, the author replaces most *v*'s with *f*'s, resulting in such words as *Fersuch, Folkslied, follkommen* and *Ferstössen*. He uses *v* only in such words as *Verse* and *Versmass*, doubtless of foreign origin, and delights in such archaic German spellings as *Teutschland*, which allows him the direct linguistic parallel with *Teuton*.

Incipit: Ich wage es, den Fersuch eines allgemeinen teutschen Folksliedes. . . .

Sources: Ley, "Aus Briefen an Beethoven," pp. 154–155. Autograph in the Staatsbibliothek zu Berlin–Preussischer Kulturbesitz, Mus. ms. autogr. Beethoven 37, 52a/53; listed in Kalischer, "Beethoven-Autographe," p. 74, and Bartlitz, p. 190.

181. Anton Brunner[1] to Beethoven

[Vienna; February 27, 1814]

List of the Orchestra that supplied
services at Herr van Beethoven's
Akademie on Sunday, February 27, 1814,
together with rehearsals.[2]

Violin I[3]	Herr von Tekl.	5 florins X
	" Breyman	5
	" Schreiber	5
	" Otter	5
	" Zieglhauser	5 fl. X
	" Kail	5
	" Reussert	5
Violin II	" Fux	5

	"	Leitner	5	
	"	Krupka	5	
	"	Gebhard	5	
	"	Dalberg	5	
	"	Schweigl	5	
Viola	"	Altmietr	5	
	"	Stihay	5	
	"	Parton	5	
	"	Oster	5	
	"	Wischansky	5	
	"	Puschitzka	5	
Violoncello	"	Dont	5	
	"	Bachman	5	
	"	Huber	5 fl. X	
	"	Eichholzer	5	
	"	Hadler	5	
Contrabass	"	Melzer	7	Rehearsal on Friday
	"	Barta	5	
	"	Wohanka	5	
	"	Hadler	5	
	"	Grams	5	
	"	Förster	5	
	"	Leitner	5	
Winds				
Oboe[4]	"	Czerwenka	7	Rehearsal on Friday
	"	Eslair	5	
	"	Füttner	5	
	"	Hadler	5	
	"	Pritz	2	Rehearsal on Friday
Flute	"	Kail, Alois (Flauti)	5	
Clarinet	"	Friedlofsky	7	Rehearsal on Friday
	"	Rüttinger	7	Rehearsal on Friday
	"	Mösch	5	
	"	Dobihal	5	

Bassoon	"	Höllmeyer	7	Rehearsal on Friday
	"	Clement	5	
	"	Czeka	5	
Contrabassoon	"	Raab ⎫ large bassoon	5	
	"	Pollack ⎭	5	
Horn[5]	"	Kowslofsky	7	Rehearsal on Friday
	"	Hradetszky	7	Rehearsal on Friday
	"	Koch	7	Rehearsal on Friday
	"	Weidinger, Franz	7	Rehearsal on Friday
	"	Fischer	5	
[Trumpet]	"	Wegscheider	5	
	"	Trenka	5	
	"	Kail	5	
[Timpani]	"	Manker	5	
Trombone	"	Segner, Sr.	5	
	"	Segner, Jr.	5	
	"	Kaesmeyer	5	
[Percussion]	"	Höllmeyer (bass drum)	5	
	"	Rabel (cymbals)	5	
	"	Bittner (triangle)	5	
	"	Dreissig (snare drum)	5	

Brunner, for contacting everyone	10 fl.
Carriage for Mad. Milder at rehearsal	2 X
Servant for above	4 X
Same, at the performance	4 X
Porter for Grams's contrabass	1
[Sub-] Total	344 florins
[Deduction][6] [minus]	15
	329
[Deduction][7]	8
Total[8]	321

Witnessed: Received by:

Schuppanzigh[9]   Anton Brunner

1. As can be determined from the contents of this payroll list, Brunner acted as orchestra contractor for the professional musicians who played at Beethoven's concert at the Grosser Redoutensaal on February 27, 1814. Although he charged a 10-florin contracting fee, he is not listed among the performers. From the fees on the list, it seems that the musicians received 2 florins for a rehearsal and 3 for a performance. There must have been a rehearsal on Thursday, February 24, at which virtually all the professionals were present, and another on Friday, February 25, at which only 10 professionals joined the body of dilettantes and unpaid professionals who must have constituted about 50 percent of an approximately 123-member orchestra. See Beethoven's diary entry: "at my last concert in the Large Redoutensaal there were 18 first violins, 18 second violins, 14 violas, 12 violoncellos, 7 contrabasses, 2 contrabassoons" (Maynard Solomon, "Beethoven's Tagebuch," in *Beethoven Studies 3*, ed. Alan Tyson [Cambridge: Cambridge University Press, 1982], pp. 222–223; revised in his *Beethoven Essays* [Cambridge, Mass.: Harvard University Press, 1988], pp. 252–253).

2. This *Akademie* was the final in a series of four concerts begun on December 8, 1813. It included the Symphony No. 7, the trio *Tremate, empi, tremate,* Op. 116 (featuring soprano Anna Milder-Hauptmann), *Wellington's Victory,* Op. 91, and the premiere performance of the Symphony No. 8. None of these works is scored for contrabassoon, yet *two* contrabassoonists were present in the orchestra, probably playing a contrabass part.

3. Several directories allow at least a tentative identification of the musicians who played this concert: Franz Heinrich Böckh, *Merkwürdigkeiten der Haupt- und Residenz-Stadt Wien . . .* (Vienna, 1823), pp. 363–384 (reflecting data current in the first half of 1821); Anton Ziegler, *Addressen-Buch von Tonkünstlern . . .* (Vienna, 1823), reflecting information current in late 1822; *Hof- und Staats-Schematismus . . . Stadt Wien* (issues of 1800, 1801, 1803, 1804, 1805 and 1808); and the *Vollständiges Auskunftsbuch . . . in Wien . . . für Kaufleute, Fabrikanten, Künstler* (issues for 1804 and 1805). By using the sources noted above (and in spite of numerous variants in spelling), we may tentatively identify the following, including possibly their places of regular employment and their verified dates of activity, among the string section:

Violin I: Breymann (Breumann, Kärntnertor Theater, 1822); Schreiber (possibly a violist, Kärntnertor Theater, 1822); Joseph Otter (court theaters, 1822); Johann Nepomuk Ziegelhauser (Burgtheater and St. Stephan's Cathedral, 1822); and Carl Reissert (Burgtheater and St. Stephan's Cathedral, 1822). Kail might have been Joseph Khayll the elder, who, although known as an oboist, occasionally played violin.

Violin II: Peter Fuchs (Burgtheater, 1800–1822); Wenzel Krupka (court theaters, 1808); Johann Gebhard (court theaters, 1808); and Lorenz Schweigl (Burgtheater, 1808, 1822). Possibly Dalberg was related to the future piano virtuoso Sigismond

Thalberg (1812–1871), whose Viennese paternity remains shrouded in mystery, but whose surname was spelled by Böckh (p. 138) as Dalberg.

Violas: Mathias Altmutter (Matthias Altmütter or Altmüller, court theater violinist, 1800–1822); Joseph Stihay (or Stichey, court theaters, 1808; Kärntnertor Theater, 1822); Johann Barton (court theaters, 1808; Kärntnertor Theater, 1822); and Philipp Wschiansky (court theaters, 1804, 1805, 1808).

Violoncelli: Joseph Valentin Dont (possibly confused with Joseph Dönst, court theaters, 1808; Kärntnertor Theater, 1822) and Santi Hueber (Burgtheater and St. Stephan's Cathedral, 1822).

Contrabasses: Joseph Melzer (Mölzer, court theaters, 1808, 1821; Kärntnertor Theater, 1822); Joseph Barta (Partha, court theaters, 1808); Anton Grams (Kärntnertor Theater, 1822); Franz Förster (Theater an der Wien, 1821, 1822); and one Leitner (Kärntnertor Theater, 1822). Contrabassist Grams had played in the January 23, 1805, performance of the *Eroica* Symphony at the banker Würth's (see bill, January 28, 1805, No. 95 above) and probably on the reading rehearsals of the *Eroica* and the Triple Concerto in late May–early June 1804 at Prince Lobkowitz's palace (see bill, June 11, 1804, No. 81 above) and in the *Liebhaber Concerte* of 1807–1808 (see Beethoven to Collin [?], February or March 1808, No. 128 above). Although a member of the Kärntnertor Theater orchestra as late as 1822, he died in 1823 and therefore did not play in the first performance of Beethoven's Ninth Symphony in 1824. See also n.7, this letter.

4. On the basis of the sources listed in n.3, this letter, the following players may tentatively be identified among the woodwinds:

Oboist Joseph Czerwenka (court theaters, 1808, 1821, 1822); possibly oboist Emanuel Erler (Leopoldstadt Theater, 1822); and flutist Aloys Khayll (court theaters, 1821; Burgtheater, 1822).

Clarinets: Joseph Friedlowsky (Theater an der Wien, 1821, 1822; court theaters, 1822); Johann Rüttinger (Carl Rittinger, court theaters, 1808; Burgtheater, 1822); Conrad Mösch (Carl Mörsch, court theaters, 1808; Burgtheater, 1822); and Joseph Dobihal (Kärntnertor Theater, 1822).

Bassoons: Franz Höllmayr (court theaters, 1821, 1822; St. Stephan's Cathedral, 1822); Paul Clement (court theaters, 1808); and Valentin Czeka (Wenzel Soyka, Theater an der Wien, 1821, 1822). Contrabassoonist Raab may possibly be the contrabassist Ignaz Raab (Burgtheater, 1822). Although contrabass/contrabassoon is an unusual doubling, Böckh notes Joseph Melzer (in the contrabass section, above) as playing precisely this combination.

5. On the basis of the sources listed in n.3, this letter, the following players may tentatively be identified among the brass:

Hornists Joseph Kowalowsky (Josephstadt Theater, 1821; Theater an der Wien, 1822) and Friedrich Hradetzky (Hradetsky, court theaters, 1808, 1821; Kärntnertor

Theater, 1822). (Franz?) Joseph Weidinger was a court trumpeter but in 1821 was also listed as a "virtuoso on the Waldhorn" at the Josephstadt Theater. In this case, he probably played horn. Brunner neglected to provide a demarcation line between hornists and trumpeters. Based on the proportions of the works performed, Fischer (otherwise unidentified) may have been either, but the trumpet listings surely include Johann Wegscheider (court and field trumpeter, 1821); Clemens Trenka (Trnka, Theater an der Wien, 1822); and Anton Khayll (court theaters, 1821; Kärntnertor Theater, 1822).

Personnel lists for the *Liebhaber Concerte*, 1807–1808 (see n.3, this letter), confirm that Manker was a timpanist. Contractor Anton Brunner may also have been a timpanist, as an otherwise unidentified Brunner is listed in the 1804 and 1805 business directories (*Auskunftsbücher*) as a teacher of *Pauken*.

The first two trombonists are probably Leopold Segner (Theater an der Wien, 1821; Kärntnertor Theater, 1822) and Franz Segner (Theater an der Wien, 1822).

Among the percussionists, Höllmeyer is probably related to the bassoonist mentioned above, and Rabel may have been orchestra manager at the Theater an der Wien in 1822.

6. This deduction reflects the three presumable absences (Tekl, Zieglhauser, Huber) in the first violin and violoncello sections.

7. This deduction represents the carriage and servant fee for soprano Anna Milder-Hauptmann, which Brunner later took off, possibly on protest by Beethoven or Schuppanzigh.

Why contrabassist Grams charged cartage, while others did not, is uncertain. He had already charged cartage early in 1805 (see bill, January 28, 1805), and possibly in the spring of 1804 (see bill, June 11, 1804). In 1822, he lived in the building directly east of the Kärntnertor Theater, where he worked. Possibly Grams was partially disabled; in any case, all concerned must have agreed that the charge was justified.

8. The autograph covers three pages, with subtotals at the end of each page carried over to the top of the next. These have not been reflected in the transcription given here.

9. Ignaz Schuppanzigh (1776–1830) was concertmaster and, as a longtime friend of Beethoven's, evidently donated his services to this benefit concert for the composer. So too may have one of the violoncellists Kraft (see Beethoven to Zmeskall, April 22, 1813, No. 172 above).

Incipit: Verzeichniss des Orchester welches Sontag. . . .

Sources: Autograph in the Staatsbibliothek zu Berlin–Preussischer Kulturbesitz, Mus. ms. autogr. Beethoven 35, 82; listed in Kalischer, "Beethoven-Autographe," p. 53, and Bartlitz, p. 148.

182. *Wenzel Schlemmer*[1] *to Beethoven*

Vienna; February 28, 1814[2]

Bill

For copying, which I supplied for Herr v[an] Beethoven's
Grand *Akademie* on February 27, 1814:

Trio[3] . . . . 78 sheets

Symphony No. 8[4]
        Violin I (7 copies) . . . . 62 sheets
        Violin II (7 copies) .70   "
        Viola (5 copies) 48   "
        Basso[5] (8 copies) 86   "
        Winds . . . . .59½ "

Symphony in A [No. 7][6]
        Violin II, Viola, Bass (2 copies) . . . . .54½ "
                                               452 sheets

[452 sheets] at 12 kreuzer per sheet . . . . 90 florins, 24 kreuzer

Vienna; February 28, 1814

N.B. for ——[7]   Schlemmer

[Another sheet:]
   Received on this account   75 florins
   Sum previously received   15
                                     90 florins

       Duly received,

       W. Schlemmer

[In Beethoven's hand:]

N.B. Herr Schlemmer has already received 15 florins from me against his bill.

1. Wenzel Schlemmer (1760–1823) was possibly Beethoven's favorite copyist because of the care he took in deciphering the composer's often virtually illegible manuscripts. He began working for Beethoven as early as 1799.

2. For further information on the concert, see Brunner to Beethoven, February 27, 1814 (No. 181 above). A page of the Violin I part of the Symphony No. 7 (probably dating from December 1813) and the corrected final page of the Timpani part of the Symphony No. 8 (possibly dating from February 1814) are illustrated in Landon, *Beethoven: Documentary Study,* pp. 266, 309. The original performing materials of these two symphonies are in the Gesellschaft der Musikfreunde, Vienna.

3. *Tremate, empi, tremate,* Op. 116. The calculations for music copying were given in *Bogen* or folded sheets of four pages each.

4. The parts copied here for the Symphony No. 8 doubtless supplemented the set already available for the reading rehearsal at Archduke Rudolph's, probably on April 21, 1813. Together, they provide enough music for the orchestra that Beethoven had on stage for the February 27, 1814, *Akademie:* strings 18/18/14/12/8, with at least doubled winds (including perhaps 2 timpanists), and an extra contrabass part to be played by the 2 contrabassoonists. See Beethoven to Zmeskall, April 22, 1813 (No. 172 above), and Beethoven to Rudolph, undated (Anderson No. 330, probably April 20, 1813).

5. Basso meant violoncello and contrabass parts, here and in the note concerning the Seventh Symphony.

6. The parts for the Symphony No. 7 appearing on this bill may represent an enlargement of the orchestra for the February 27 *Akademie* over the three earlier concerts in this series or (more likely) replacements for parts lost in the ensuing period. The original set of parts must have been used at Archduke Rudolph's in April 1813 (see n.4, this letter), with the supplemental set copied by the December 8, 1813, concert.

7. This place in the manuscript is torn and wrinkled, and the writing is indistinct. *Incipit:* Über Copiatur welche ich. . . .

Sources: Autograph in the Staatsbibliothek zu Berlin–Preussischer Kulturbesitz, Mus. ms. autogr. Beethoven 35, 83; listed in Kalischer, "Beethoven-Autographe," p. 53, and Bartlitz, p. 148.

183. George Thomson to Beethoven

Edinburgh; April 23, 1814

Monsieur L. van Beethoven
Vienna

I received today the 30 Irish airs with your ritornellos and accompaniments, which were dispatched by way of Paris more than a year ago; it will not be necessary to send another.[1] I have had time to examine only a small number, but those seem to be extremely beautiful.

I do not know if you have received four airs that I sent last September to be harmonized by you. As you have perhaps not received these, I am sending a *duplicate* of them to you, with two airs more.[2] For these, I ask you to compose ritornellos and accompaniments in your delicate and cantabile style, and to deliver them to Messrs. Fries, who will pay you twenty ducats in cash for them.

You will receive with this letter the first volume of Irish airs with your ritornellos and accompaniments (the final air is harmonized by Haydn). The volume has just been printed, and will be published in a few days.[3]

I trust to your honor that you will not permit any of my songs, except those that are found in this volume, to appear on the Continent. As soon as I publish another volume, which will be next year, I shall send it to you.[4] But until you receive the volume printed by me, you will guard the manuscript in your hands as if it were *sacred,* and you shall not give it to anyone under any pretext whatsoever; for if you empowered any other person to print the work before me, you would deprive me of the same property that I have bought from you, and that has cost me so much.

If you have composed the ariettas for the *six* English songs [i.e., poetry] that I sent you recently,[5] Messrs. Fries, upon seeing this letter, will pay you twenty ducats in cash for these ariettas, the price that you originally requested, and if it is agreeable to you, I shall send you six more songs, which will be written expressly for you, as soon as I receive the aforementioned 6 ariettas or canzonettas.

Have you published any sonatas or quartets this past year? Do you intend to arrange the *Mount of Olives* for voices and piano with English words?[6]

It is with the greatest pleasure that I congratulate you upon the restoration of peace in Europe.

I have the honor to be, with great esteem, Monsieur,

Your friend and servant,

(signed) George Thomson

P.S. You will see that, because of the small amount of space, I have been obliged to omit the *prima volta* [first ending] in nearly all the airs. I am sending a Sonnet that has been addressed to you by an amateur of this city.[7]

1. Beethoven stated in his letter of February 19, 1813 (Anderson No. 405), that he had delivered the songs in triplicate to Fries; in his letter of September 1813, Thomson had asked Beethoven to have still another copy made and sent since the first three (supposedly sent by various routes to assure arrival in wartime conditions) had not arrived. Beethoven replied on September 15, 1814 (Anderson No. 496; MacArdle & Misch No. 137).

2. The materials sent previously were WoO 157, Nos. 6, 8 and 11, and WoO 158/II, No. 5. See September 1813 letter (No. 176 above) for details. The additional airs included with this letter were WoO 157, No. 2, and WoO 153, No. 6.

3. *A Select Collection of Original Irish Airs . . .* , vol. [1], fully described in Kinsky-Halm, pp. 634–635. The volume contained thirty airs: the entire WoO 152; Nos. 1–4 of WoO 153; and a single setting by Haydn to round out the collection.

4. Vol. 2 appeared in 1816 (see Kinsky-Halm, p. 644).

5. These are set forth in Thomson's letter of September 1813; Beethoven apparently never set them.

6. An English version of *Christ on the Mount of Olives,* Op. 85, with piano arrangement by Sir George Smart, was published by Chappell in London, ca. September 1814. The oratorio had been performed in London on February 25, 1814. For an account of this and similar events, see Thayer-Krehbiel, II, 309–312.

7. "Hark! from Germania's shore," by Thomson's friend, collaborator and correspondent George Farquhar Graham (1789–1867), first published in the *Scots Magazine and Edinburgh Literary Miscellany* 75 (October 1813), 776, and reprinted in every edition of Thayer: (1879) III, 301; Thayer-Deiters-Riemann, III, 444; Thayer-Krehbiel, II, 290; Thayer-Forbes, pp. 592–593. Only the last includes MacArdle's correct citation of the author and source.

Incipit: J'ai reçu aujourd'hui les 30 airs Irlandois. . . .

Sources: Summarized in MacArdle, "Beethoven and George Thomson," p. 39; and Hadden, *George Thomson,* pp. 330–331 (with a brief quote). Copy in Thomson's copybook, British Library, Add. MS 35267, pp. 96v–98r.

184. Beethoven and Georg Friedrich Treitschke[1] to [Baron Karl Wilhelm Adolph von Ende,] Intendant of the Grand-ducal Court Theater, Karlsruhe

Vienna; June 24, 1814[2]

To the Eminent Directorship
Grand-ducal Court Theater
Karlsruhe

The undersigned have the honor to offer to the Eminent Directorship herewith the libretto and score of their opera *Fidelio,* in [an] accurate and completely legitimate copy for a fee of 12 ducats in gold, to be used for their stage, without, however, any further rights to pass it on [to another company], or to allow the entire opera or parts of it to be copied.[3] This opera appeared several weeks ago at the I[mperial] R[oyal] Court Opera Theater here and had the good fortune to find more than the usual applause and always to attract full houses. The libretto and music are not to be confused with the opera of the same name performed several years ago at the I[mperial] R[oyal] Theater an der Wien, of whose score a few copies were stolen. The whole [opera] has been revised in accordance with altered conceptions that are more in keeping with theatrical effects, and over half of it is newly written.

All precautions have been taken for the protection of this property, and in any case the Eminent Directorship is requested not to place its trust in any other offers, but rather to be so kind as to notify the undersigned of any that are proposed.

The Eminent Directorship is requested to address its reply to the undersigned F. Treitschke.

With great respect, we sign ourselves,

Ludwig van Beethoven

Fr[iedrich] Treitschke
Imperial Royal Court Theater Poet[4]

1. Georg Friedrich Treitschke (1776–1842), poet, playwright and actor, had come to Vienna from Leipzig in 1802 and held various directorial and administrative positions in the city's theaters. He became assistant director of the Theater an der Wien in 1809 and made Beethoven's acquaintance in 1811. As court theater secretary, he assisted with the textual revisions of *Fidelio*, premiered in its final version on May 23, 1814.

2. This letter is essentially the same as Beethoven and Treitschke's letter to the National Theater in Stuttgart, June 24, 1814 (Anderson, III, 1447–1448, which also notes the existence of a virtually identical letter to the Royal Theater, Berlin, on June 23, given in earlier collected editions). While allowing in some passages for differences in translation method, the present version largely follows Anderson for the sake of consistency.

Treitschke may have written a dozen of these "form letters" to various opera houses in German-speaking (and even non-German-speaking) lands for his and Beethoven's signatures during the summer of 1814. Although Anderson includes one 1814 letter and refers to another, the Karlsruhe letter is given here in the name of completeness and (especially since Anderson's example is in an appendix) to indicate impetus in a proper chronological position for the Karlsruhe correspondence to follow, as well as other correspondence, both here and in Anderson, concerning the distribution of *Fidelio*.

In the Dessauer Sketchbook from 1814 (Nottebohm, *Zweite Beethoveniana*, pp. 299–300), Beethoven noted sums that he projected receiving from a scheme such as this:

Hamburg	15 ducats in gold
Frankfurt	15 ducats in gold
Carlsruhe	12 ducats in gold
Grätz	120 florins
Darmstadt	12 ducats in gold
Stuttgart	12 ducats in gold

Nottebohm commented that none of the cities in the above list witnessed a performance of *Fidelio* before 1831.

The figure for Karlsruhe is consistent with the present letter; that for Grätz may represent a fee that Beethoven hoped to get from Prince Carl Lichnowsky (died April 15, 1814) or his widow, Princess Maria Christiane (who did present Beethoven with a clock). The letter of offer to Berlin (Kastner-Kapp No. 437), dated June 23, is not reflected here.

As noted below, Von Ende (whose name Treitschke apparently did not know when blindly sending this solicitation letter) replied on August 16, 1814 (No. 185 below). Treitschke then replied on September 10, 1814 (No. 188 below).

In many ways, this method of distribution is the predecessor of the scheme to solicit sales of manuscript copies of the *Missa solemnis,* on which Beethoven and Anton Schindler embarked early in 1823.

3. The original reads, "jedoch ohne Mittheilungs- oder ganze und einzelne Bekanntmachungs-Rechte anzutragen."

4. On the autograph is a marginal note made in Karlsruhe, indicating that the letter was "presented on July 11, 1814." Von Ende's later marginal note concerning his August 16, 1814, reply is to be found in No. 185 below.

Incipit: Die Unterzeichneten geben sich die Ehre. . . .

Sources: Manfred Schuler, "Unveröffentlichte Briefe von Ludwig van Beethoven und Georg Friedrich Treitschke: Zur dritten Fassung des 'Fidelio,'" *Die Musikforschung* 35 (1982), 53–54, with extensive commentary. Autograph in the General-landesarchiv, Karlsruhe, 47/882.

185. Baron Karl Wilhelm Adolph von Ende to Georg Friedrich Treitschke and Beethoven

Karlsruhe; August 16, 1814[1]

We want to take the opera for the price,[2] on the condition that we can share it with the Court Theater in Mannheim.[3]

F[reiherr] v[on] E[nde]

1. On August 16, Von Ende, *Intendant* (director) of the Grand-ducal Court Theater, Karlsruhe, made this annotation of his reply on Beethoven and Treitschke's promotional letter of June 24, 1814 (No. 184 above); the actual letter of August 16 seems not to have survived. Treitschke, in turn, replied on September 10, 1814 (No. 188 below).

2. In a series of "form letters," including that sent to Karlsruhe, Treitschke and Beethoven had offered a manuscript copy of *Fidelio* for 12 ducats in gold.

3. The initial promotional letter had stipulated that the proffered opera not be passed on to another theater, but, as Treitschke's letter of September 10 indicates, composer and poet ultimately allowed Karlsrue to share its copy with Mannheim.

Incipit (this excerpt): Man wolle die Oper für den Preis nehmen. . . .

Sources: Manfred Schuler, "Unveröffentlichte Briefe von Ludwig van Beethoven und Georg Friedrich Treitschke: Zur dritten Fassung des 'Fidelio,'" *Die Musikforschung* 35 (1982), 53–54, with extensive commentary. Autograph in the Generallandesarchiv, Karlsruhe, 47/882.

186. George Thomson to Beethoven

Edinburgh; August 17, 1814[1]

Monsieur L. v. Beethoven
Vienna

I wrote you last April 23, letting you know that I finally received the 30 Irish airs that had been detained so long on their way, and I sent you, at the same time, a copy of the first printed volume, containing 30 airs with your ritornellos and accompaniments,[2] so that you could publish them on the Continent, if you approve of them.

I am sending you enclosed six Scottish airs[3] and a duplicate of six Irish airs that I already sent you; and for these airs, I ask you to be so kind as to compose ritornellos and accompaniments, as soon as you can without inconveniencing yourself. You have probably finished the last six airs, but I have not yet received them.

When you deliver the ritornellos and accompaniments to Messrs. Fries, they will pay you 3 Viennese ducats in cash for each air.[4]

I would like, after you have harmonized the airs in the ordinary manner, for you to harmonize three or four of the Scottish airs, choosing those that you prefer, as *trios* or *quartets* for voices, and, if possible, that you make the parts follow each other somewhat in the style of a *fugue* or of *imitation*. For each air thus harmonized I shall willingly pay you 3 ducats more.[5]

It will please me to have a reply to my last letter and all the news on the subject of music that you would like to tell me. I hope that you have recently published some new quartets and sonatas, and that we shall soon have the pleasure of seeing you in this country.

I am told that your *Mount of Olives* is going to be published soon in London.[6]

I have the honor to be, with great esteem, Monsieur,

Your friend and very humble servant,

George Thomson

[Thomson's note to himself:]

The two preceding letters [to Beethoven and Fries] sent to Mr. Broughton, August 17, 1814, with a request that he would forward the paquet by the first opportunity direct for Vienna.

1. This letter follows Thomson's letter of April 23, 1814 (No. 183 above); Beethoven replied to several Thomson epistles on September 15, 1814 (Anderson No. 496; MacArdle & Misch No. 137), although this letter of Thomson's seems to have crossed with Beethoven's reply in the mails. Beethoven's letter of October 1814 (Anderson No. 503; MacArdle & Misch No. 139) specifically mentions receipt of this, Thomson's August 17 letter.

2. *A Select Collection of Original Irish Airs . . .* , vol. [1]; see Thomson's letter of April 23 for details.

3. Barry Cooper has identified these as WoO 158/II, No. 6; WoO 155, No. 25; WoO 156, No. 6; and Op. 108, Nos. 24, 6 and 7.

4. In his accompanying letter to Fries, Thomson asks the banker to dun Beethoven into finishing the songs if he did not deliver them within a few weeks!

5. Beethoven did not comply with this request.

6. *Christ on the Mount of Olives,* Op. 85, in a piano arrangement by Sir George Smart, published by Chappell, London, ca. September 1814.

Incipit: Je vous écrivis le 23 Avril passé. . . .

Sources: Summarized in MacArdle, "Beethoven and George Thomson," p. 39. Copy in Thomson's copybook, British Library, Add. MS 35267, pp. 116v–117r.

187. Beethoven to Archduke Rudolph's Chief Cashier[1]

Vienna; September 1, 1814

Receipt

for 750 f[ull] w[eight], that is, seven hundred [*sic*] gulden f[ull] w[eight], the most kindly granted stipend that the undersigned has duly received unto himself from the Chief Cashier of His Imperial Highness, the Most

Illustrious Archduke Rudolph, namely from March 1, 1814, through the end of August, 1814[2]—hereby received.

Vienna, September 1, 1814

Ludwig van Beethoven

1. In conjunction with Prince Ferdinand Kinsky and Prince Franz Joseph von Lobkowitz, Rudolph had guaranteed Beethoven an annual stipend, beginning in 1809, providing that the composer remained in Vienna (for the contract, see March 1, 1809, No. 134 above). Of the three guarantors, only Rudolph seems to have paid his installments regularly and without Beethoven's resorting to occasional litigation or threats in order to collect the sums due him.

2. In the autograph, "March 1" replaces "September 1" (which is crossed out), and "August, 1814," replaces "February, 1815" (which is crossed out), a strange reversal of chronology. See also Beethoven's draft receipt reflecting the crossed-out dates and dated March 30, 1815 (No. 203 below).

Incipit: Quittung über 750 v.w. sage. . . .

Sources: Facsimilies in Gutiérrez-Denhoff, " 'o Unseeliges Dekret': Beethovens Rente," p. 138, and Bory, p. 135. The autograph is in the Beethoven-Haus, Bonn.

188. Georg Friedrich Treitschke to Baron Karl Wilhelm Adolph von Ende, Karlsruhe[1]

Vienna; September 10, 1814[2]

Herr Baron von Ende
Intendant, Grand-ducal Court Theater
Oberschenk, etc.
Karlsruhe[3]

Dear Sir!

The illness of my copyist, the only one to whom I could unhesitatingly entrust the difficult score of the opera *Fidelio,* prevented the early shipment that you wished for in your letter of August 16. For the exclusive use of

39

your theater and that at Mannheim, I delivered to the postal coach today one package in black oilcloth, marked "CT,"[4] and containing libretto and music of the above-named work. I hope that it arrives safely, and request most submissively that you settle the agreed-upon fee of 12 Rhenish ducats in gold, by means of a draft payable here, or in the absence of that, by a Frankfurt note of exchange.

Concerning the completeness [of the material], two musical pieces have been added, namely: No. 3½. Song, "Hat man nicht auch Gold," etc.; and No. 8. Aria, "Abscheulicher! Wo eilst Du," etc. The first song was in the earlier version and was added only at the request of the singer for several performances. In my opinion it impedes the flow of the plot and would better be left out. The Aria, No. 8, was written later for a special occasion; therefore it is equally practical to include or omit it.

Prepared to be of service to you on any occasion, I remain respectfully,

> Your most obedient servant,
> Fr[iedrich] Treitschke
> Imperial Royal Court Theater Poet

1. Von Ende was *Intendant* (director) of the Grand-ducal Court Theater, Karlsruhe.

2. Replies to von Ende's letter of August 16, 1814 (No. 185 above), which, in turn, responded to Beethoven and Treitschke's promotional "form letter" of June 24, 1814 (No. 184 above).

3. All correspondence spells the city's name as Carlsruhe, consistent with early nineteenth-century practice.

4. The abbreviation on the package probably indicates destination and sender: "Carlsruhe Treitschke." Note that a similar package that Treitschke sent to Berlin on September 15 (No. 189 below) bore the legend "BT."

Incipit: Die Krankheit meines Copisten. . . .

Sources: Manfred Schuler, "Unveröffentlichte Briefe von Ludwig van Beethoven und Georg Friedrich Treitschke: Zur dritten Fassung des 'Fidelio,'" *Die Musik-forschung* 35 (1982), 56–57, with extensive commentary. Autograph in the General-landesarchiv, Karlsruhe, 47/899.

189. Georg Friedrich Treitschke to August Wilhelm Iffland,[1] Berlin

Vienna; September 15, 1814[2]

To the post coach leaving today I delivered one package in black oilcloth,[3] marked "BT,"[4] containing a copy of the opera *Fidelio*,[5] which your worthy message of the 3d of this month requested. I hope that it arrives safely, and note only that:

[1] in respect to [the] singers [needed], this opera is easy to cast;

[2] it makes no [extraordinary] demands for costumes and scenery; but

[3] a good orchestra and chorus are especially required.

The arias, "Hat man nicht auch Gold," etc.[6] and "Abscheulicher, wo eilst du hin,"[7] in Act I were *inserted* — the former from the earlier version; the latter for the composer's benefit performance. I would add them to the score, [although] both of them — at least the former — *are better left out,* since they impede the flow of the plot.

The role of Rocco is a deep bass; Pizarro is a high bass; Jacquino and Florestan are tenors. Immediately upon receipt of your further instructions, I can send a score that has been inspected by the composer.[8]

1. August Wilhelm Iffland had been general director of the Royal National Theater, Berlin, since 1796. Iffland himself probably never read this letter; he was ill at the time and died on September 22, 1814.

2. Treitschke was replying to the Theater Direction's letter of September 3 (implied in text above), which in turn was a reply to Beethoven and Treitschke's letter of offer, dated June 23, 1814, given in pre-Anderson collected editions (see Kastner-Kapp No. 437). A similar June 24 letter to Stuttgart is translated in Anderson, III, 1447–1448. A June 24 letter to Karlsruhe appears as No. 184 above.

3. Literally, "waxed linen."

4. Possibly means "Berlin Treitschke," indicating destination and sender. See letter of September 10 (No. 188 above), describing a similar package marked "CT" (possibly "Carlsruhe Treitschke").

5. Treitschke used the term *Abschrift*, therefore indicating a handwritten copy; from his remarks at the end of this letter and the annotations made on it in Berlin

41

(see n.8, this letter), we may assume that the item sent was actually a libretto, rather than the score.

6. Rocco's gold aria was sung in the 1805 performance of the opera and reinserted by the singer Weinmüller only at a benefit performance for Beethoven on July 18, 1814, in spite of Treitschke's opposition.

7. The earlier versions of Leonore's scene and aria had been shorter.

8. The Theater Administration noted on Treitschke's letter: "On October 15, [1814,] the libretto *Fidelio* sent back since it is the opera *Leonore* that was given here." The latter reference was to Paër's *Leonore,* given in Berlin twice in 1810.

After Iffland died on September 22, 1814 (and during his illness beforehand), the Berlin Theater was administered by committee: the secretary, Esperstedt; the singer-actor Gern Sr.; the accountant Jacobi; the *Kapellmeister,* Bernhard Anselm Weber; and the privy war councillor, Schmuckler. Altmann believed that Gern was probably responsible for the return of the *Fidelio* libretto.

Count Carl Friedrich Moritz Paul von Brühl assumed the directorship of the theater on January 10, 1815, and produced Beethoven's *Fidelio* on October 11 of that year. See Bernhard Anselm Weber to Treitschke, April 8, 1815 (No. 204 below).

Incipit: Dem heute abgehenden Postwagen übergab ich. . . .

Sources: Altmann, "Zu Beethovens 'Fidelio,'" pp. 434–435. In 1904, the autograph was in the Registratur, General-Intendantur, Königliche Schauspiele, Berlin.

190. George Thomson to Beethoven

Edinburgh; October 15, 1814[1]

Monsieur L. van Beethoven

I have received your letter of September 15, with the corrections on the 30 airs, and where you say that I will have to pay you four zecchini in ducats for each of the 12 airs that I sent you last August. I consent to your request, and I have prefixed to this letter a note to Messrs. Fries to that effect.[2] I only ask that you compose the ritornellos and accompaniments in your simplest, most delicate and cantabile style.

In the list *of prices* that you have sent me, I notice that you ask 12 ducats for an *overture.* I would like to have one of them principally for the piano, a little in the character of national music, and in a style as gay or *scherzando* as you like. And if you approve of this, but not otherwise, it would please me for you to introduce the enclosed Scottish air, or any Scottish air that you prefer, at whatever place it should be in the overture. And if you enrich the overture, adding to it accompaniments for violin, a flute, a viola and a violoncello—ad libitum or instead obligati—I would be very content to pay you eighteen ducats for it, instead of twelve. But I shall be pleased to receive the overture, either for the piano alone, or with accompaniments, as it pleases you. As for the length of the overture, I need only say that I hope that it will not be shorter than the Overtures to *Don Giovanni* or *Die Zauberflöte* by Mozart.

When you send me the 12 airs and the overture, tell me whether it is agreeable to you to compose six or twelve *little hymns* or religious songs for voices in a simple and natural style for four ducats each; in which case, I shall send you the verses to which you will compose them. But unless you assure me that you will compose these pieces, I shall not take the trouble, or give you any either, by sending the verses.

The enclosed piece by Michael Haydn will give you an idea of the *type* that I want.[3]

If you have published some pieces of music like this for the church, or if there are some pieces of the same type by J[oseph] or M[ichael] Haydn, or Mozart or Winter, etc.,[4] I would be very obliged if you would send me some at the price of around three or four ducats. I am not speaking of great works such as the *Creation,* the *Seasons,* the *Requiem* or the Masses,[5] but I ask you to send me the vocal music by Haydn for *The Last Words of Jesus Christ.* If there are two editions, one adapted to German words and the other to Italian or Latin words, I prefer the latter.[6]

It gives me pleasure to know what occupies you now; it is a pity that you have not told me about those works. I have just received the London edition of your *Mount of Olives,*[7] a truly sublime work. Please note well that the copy of the 12 airs in manuscript, which I sent on August 17, is more correct.

Beyond the primary copy of the 12 airs in score, I ask you to have your copyist make another copy, written in a well-spaced style, for the voice and piano, with parts for the violin and violoncello written *separately* for the engraver, in the manner of the printed volume, and without *abbreviations.* I shall pay you extra for this copy, for it is very difficult to have music copied correctly here.

I have the honor to be, with great esteem, Monsieur, your friend and

Very humble servant,

(signed) George Thomson

[Thomson's note to himself:]

The hymn by Michael Haydn from Latrobe's first volume, "While conscious sinners," etc. was enclosed, and the following lines written over [in French]:

"Monsieur Thomson will be very obliged to Monsieur Beethoven for sending him a number of pieces of a character a little like this one, if he can find them, by the Haydns, Winter, Mozart, or some other great composer who may exist. If none of these things can be found in printed editions, Monsieur Beethoven will perhaps be so kind as to employ his copyist to collect and transcribe a dozen or twenty of them, indicating the author of each one."[8]

1. Replies to Beethoven's letter of September 15, 1814 (Anderson No. 496; MacArdle & Misch No. 137).

2. That note accompanies this letter in the copybook.

3. From Thomson's closing note, the work may be identified as "While Conscious Sinners," in the collection by Christian Ignatius Latrobe (1757–1836) *Selection of Sacred Music from the Works of the Most Eminent Composers of Germany and Italy*, 6 vols. (1806–1825). Latrobe was the secretary of the Unitas Fratrum (commonly called the "Moravians") in England, although his collection made a great number of Continental religious works known to a wide English-speaking audience. The contents of his collection are listed in William H. Husk, "Latrobe," *Grove* (1st ed.), II, 102–103; repeated in 2d ed. (1904), II, 650–651, but not in subsequent editions. "While Conscious Sinners" by Michael Haydn was listed as a *chorale* in the section "Service for Country Church."

4. In addition to the Haydn brothers and Mozart, Thomson cites the Mannheim-Munich composer Peter Winter (1754–1825). All four of these composers were ultimately represented in Latrobe's collection (see n.3, this letter).

5. The *Creation* and the *Seasons* by Haydn, the *Requiem* by Mozart, and Masses by either composer.

6. Haydn's *Seven Last Words of Christ* exists in the original version for orchestra, in an arrangement for string quartet, and in an arrangement with further modifications to include chorus with orchestra.

7. *Christ on the Mount of Olives*, Op. 85, in a piano arrangement by Sir George Smart, published by Chappell in London, ca. September 1814.

8. This is a somewhat different request from that made earlier in the letter. One wonders whether Thomson fancied himself a potential competitor to Latrobe.

Incipit: J'ai reçu votre lettre du 15 Septembre. . . .

Sources: Summarized in MacArdle, "Beethoven and George Thomson," p. 40, and Hadden, *George Thomson,* pp. 332–333 (with two paragraphs quoted). Copy in Thomson's copybook, British Library, Add. MS 35267, pp. 122v–124r.

191. Johann von Pasqualati[1] and Carl von Adlersburg[2] (Certificate on Beethoven's Behalf)

Vienna; October 20, 1814[3]

Certificate

We the undersigned certify in the interest of truth and can swear [under oath] if necessary that between Herr Louis van Beethoven and the Court Mechanic Maelzel,[4] both of Vienna, there took place several meetings at the house of the undersigned Dr. Carl v[on] Adlersburg, which concerned the musical composition by the first named, called *The Battle of Vittoria,*[5] and the journey to England. At these meetings, Herr Maelzel made several proposals to Herr van Beethoven, in order to obtain for himself the above-named work or at least the rights to its first performance. Since Herr Maelzel, however, was not present at the final scheduled meeting, nothing came of the matter, since the proposals he made to the former had not been accepted. Witnessed, according to our signatures.

Joh[ann] Freiherr v[on] Pasqualati
I.R. Patented Wholesaler

Carl Edler von Adlersburg
Court and Trial Attorney, and
I.R. Public Notary

1. Baron Johann Baptist von Pasqualati (1777–1830), owner of the Pasqualati Haus, Mölkerbastei No. 1239, where Beethoven lived for much of the period 1804–1815.

2. Dr. Carl von Adlersburg (1774–1855), Beethoven's legal adviser during this period.

3. For related correspondence, see Beethoven to Adlersburg, July 1814 (Anderson No. 485) and fall 1814 (Anderson No. 501), and Beethoven to Pasqualati, fall 1814 (Anderson No. 500).

4. Johann Nepomuk Maelzel (1772–1838), court mechanic and inventor of the improved metronome, among other musical-mechanical devices.

5. *Wellington's Victory,* Op. 91.

Incipit: Wir Endesgefertigte bezeugen zur Steuer. . . .

Sources: Schindler, *Beethoven in Paris,* pp. 152–153; Schindler (1860), pt. 2, pp. 345–346; Schindler-MacArdle, p. 489. Also Thayer, III (1879), 468; Thayer-Deiters-Riemann, III, 604–605; Thayer-Krehbiel, II, 274; Thayer-Forbes, p. 1096; with extensive commentary in all. Autograph in the Staatsbibliothek zu Berlin–Preussischer Kulturbesitz, Mus. ms. autogr. Beethoven 35, 12; listed in Bartlitz, p. 120.

192. George Thomson to Beethoven

Edinburgh; November 12, 1814[1]

Monsieur Louis van Beethoven
Vienna, Austria

My dear Monsieur,

I have just received your letter dated last month, where you tell me that you have composed a work on Wellington's triumph at the battle of Vittoria, in two parts, the battle and symphony; and where you ask me how much I will give you for this work.[2]

You do not speak of *voices,* and I conclude from this that the work is composed entirely for instruments. You do not speak of its length, and I am obliged to form an idea about this by guesswork. Permit me to tell you that you should have explained it more clearly, and you surely should have set the price yourself, something that the seller must do in any case.

You do not know, perhaps, that the score would not be of use to me in the least. In Great Britain we have such a small number of persons who play the violin well, that the sale of a symphony for large orchestra would not be enough to cover the expenses of engraving! This is so true that I assure you that I would not publish a symphony for large orchestra, even if you had made me a *present* of the score. The only form in which I would be able to publish the Battle, etc. would be as a Grand Sonata principally for the piano, with accompaniments for violins, etc. It is for you to say, then, what you will request for this work [arranged] as a sonata or concerto principally for the piano. Nonetheless, it is of much importance that if the score came into the possession of some music dealer, he could have it arranged, and published for the piano to his own advantage. This is a great difficulty unless the score were delivered directly to the person who bought the sonata.[3]

With regard to the *six canzonettas* with English words, permit me to remind you that, in your letter of February 19, 1813, which I have before my eyes at present, you requested twenty-five ducats for the six; I very much wish to give you this sum. I shall even give you thirty ducats, and if the canzonettas are appreciated by the public, I shall be very glad to take six more of them, at a greater price, [set] to words that I shall send you.

Here are the words that I have chosen for the first six songs:

[1.] "The Battle of Hohenlinden" — grand and sublime, beginning "On Linden when the sun was low."

[2.] "The farewells of a lover to his charming mistress" — full of tenderness, beginning "Once more, enchanting girl, adieu."

[3.] "The Happy Italian Shepherdess," singing the pleasures and beauties of the valley of her birth, beginning "Dear is my little native vale."

You will find these three songs in my letter of February 10, 1810.[4]

The three other songs for which I ask you to compose the music are as follows:[5]

1. "Song of Norman," a young warrior, who was obliged to tear himself from the arms of his beloved Marie at the moment of their marriage, having been ordered by Alpine, his commander, to march against his enemies. The song depicts the sorrow of his soul when, in lying down upon the hard earth on the eve of battle, he considers that the next day's combat will perhaps separate him forever from his beloved wife.

> The heath this night must be my bed,
> The bracken, curtain for my head, etc.
> Three stanzas.

2. "Song of a Soldier in Camp," full of fire and cheerfulness, reveling in his wine and in the company of his comrades, without anxiety about what might be his fate on the battlefield.

> Then soldier come fill high the wine,

> For we reck not of tomorrow, etc.
> Two stanzas.

Continuation of the preceding song, being a lamentation upon the unfortunate soldier by the wailing people who find him and the others, groaning and dying on the deserted field.

> Oh! thou hapless soldier,
> Left unseen to moulder, etc.
> One stanza.

This third part of the song (or 13 lines), the Lamentation, should be composed for three or four voices, of which two should be sopranos. And if it pleases Monsieur Beethoven, a little in the imitative style, in a simple form.

3. Song of an unhappy lover, deceived by his mistress, who has been unfaithful and married another—very moving and filled with profound sadness.

> Oh! had my fate been joined with thine,
> As once this pledge appeared a token etc.
> Two stanzas.

You will doubtless find it useful to avail yourself of the counsel of some of the English who are presently in Vienna, who will be able to give you an idea of the inflection of the English verses, and indicate for you the accent and the emphasis of the words.

I wrote to you on the 15th of last month,[6] granting you your request of four ducats for each national air, of which I sent you twelve enclosed. I am sending you enclosed here three more national airs, and I am returning one of those that you sent me, in the hope that you will be so kind as to redo it in a simpler and more cantabile style, because the ladies here would never want to play an accompaniment so chromatic.[7] In truth they would not be able to sing the air and, at the same time, play such a part in the left hand. In several of your accompaniments, you have included the melody of the air, or something very similar to it, in the piano part. This *arioso* type of accompaniment is the best adapted to our national taste; this is why I beg you to pay attention to this, in the accompaniments for all the airs now in your hands, at least in the piano part.

Messrs. Fries will pay you *thirty* ducats for the six canzonettas, *sixty* ducats for the fifteen airs, and *eighteen* ducats for the characteristic overture on Scottish music, when you show them this letter and deliver the manuscripts. They will also pay what the copyist charges for a duplicate of each work, written so that it is ready to be placed into the hands of the engraver, with each accompaniment *separate,* all of it very clear and without abbreviations.

Please write to me in French.

I have the honor, Monsieur, to be

Your friend and servant,

(signed) George Thomson

[Thomson's note to Beethoven,[8] enclosed with his concurrent letter to Fries:]

Three airs for which you will have the kindness to compose ritornellos and accompaniments.[9] In some of the airs, you have introduced *short* ritornellos of one or two bars, which I like very much. Continue to do so, please, everywhere that you find opportunity, for the ritornellos not only give respite to the voice, but they also embellish the song.

The song of the fishermen, while they row their boats. Monsieur Beethoven will have the kindness to arrange the second repetition of this air for three voices; and if he might write a bit of imitation in a very simple form, this would be quite agreeable. But if he does not think that the air may be treated in this manner, he may give short solos alternately to the voices, and then unite them in a simple harmony, or in whatever other manner that pleases him:

49

Song of the Fisherman

No. 3

Andante con moto

1. Answers Beethoven's letter of October 1814 (Anderson No. 503; MacArdle & Misch No. 139).

2. *Wellington's Victory,* Op. 91.

3. One of Beethoven's most popular works at the time, Op. 91 appeared in a piano arrangement by Beethoven, which was published by Birchall in London in ca. January 1816.

4. Beethoven seems not to have set these texts.

5. Beethoven did not set the "Song of Norman," but the first part of the soldier's song became WoO 157, No. 2, and the second part WoO 153, No. 10. The unhappy lover's song became Op. 108, No. 12.

6. See No. 190 above.

7. Barry Cooper suspects that Thomson is returning WoO 158/II, No. 1, but cannot confirm the identification, adding that Beethoven seems not to have redone any settings at this point.

8. Thomson noted to himself that the whole packet was sent to C. R. Broughton in London to be forwarded to Vienna.

9. "The sweetest lad was Jamie," Op. 108, No. 5; "Sympathy," Op. 108, No. 10; and "O Swiftly glides the bonny boat" (Song of the Fishermen), Op. 108, No. 19. The published versions differ slightly from the above excerpts given by Thomson.

Incipit: Je viens de recevoir votre lettre datée du mois dernier. . . .

Sources: Summarized in MacArdle, "Beethoven and Thomson," pp. 40–41, and Hadden, *George Thomson,* pp. 333–335 (with three paragraphs quoted). Copy in Thomson's copybook, British Library, Add. MS 35267, pp. 130r–132r.

193. *Beethoven to Wenzel Schlemmer (?)*

[Vienna; probably before November 29, 1814][1]

The duplicated parts must still be checked, since several mistakes have been found.[2]

N.B. In the Adagio, the 2d horn in G is missing.

1. This hastily written pencil note contains neither date, addressee nor signature. The proofreading of duplicated parts, including those for orchestra, occupied Beethoven many times, especially just before his public performances. This note's contents, however, indicates that the work in question contained both an Adagio section and a pair of horns in G. Number 4 in Beethoven's cantata *Der glorreiche Augenblick*, premiered on November 29, 1814, is scored for the requisite horns in G. The piece begins with an undesignated soprano recitative (with brief interjections in Andante and Presto), before finally settling into an *Adagio*, with the further designation Cavatina as the recitative ends. First sung by the soprano soloist, this Cavatina (presumably still in the basic Adagio tempo) is essentially repeated by the chorus; only now (with heavier orchestration to balance the chorus) do the horns enter. It would be easy enough for a copyist, working hurriedly, to miss this entry after so many measures of rest.

Beethoven's trusted copyist Wenzel Schlemmer (and his staff) did the copy work for *Der glorreiche Augenblick* (see Schlemmer's bill of ca. November 30, 1814, No. 194 below). This note, therefore, was probably directed at Schlemmer, unless Beethoven wrote it simply as a reminder to himself while proofreading.

2. The duplicated parts are specified in Schlemmer's bill of ca. November 30. The subject of this note is similar to Beethoven's letter to Haslinger of ca. April 24, 1824 (No. 360 below). Proofreading was obviously an onerous and time-consuming chore for Beethoven: around April 19 or 20, 1824, he jotted to himself in a conversation book, "Duplicated parts [*duplirte stimmen*], so that small [sectional?] rehearsals may be held" (Köhler et al., *Konversationshefte,* VI, 61). For a similar situation, when the Overture to *The Ruins of Athens* was being copied, see Schlemmer to Varena, March 24, 1812 (No. 159 above).

Incipit: Die duplirten Stimmen. . . .

Sources: Schwarz, "More Beethoveniana," p. 146; Klimovitsky, "Novoe o Beethovene," pp. 246–249 (facsimile on p. 247). Listed in Fishman's "Obschii obzor," p. 139, and his "Verzeichnis," p. 137. During the 1920s, the autograph was in the possession of the Leningrad Philharmonic Society (with no indication of its earlier provenance); at some point thereafter, it became part of the manuscript collection of the Institute of Theater, Music and Cinematography (now the Russian Institute of the History of the Arts), St. Petersburg, Fond 2, op. 2, No. 24 (formerly ed. chr. 18).

194. Wenzel Schlemmer to Beethoven

[Vienna; ca. November 30, 1814][1]

Bill[2] for copying the cantata *Der glorreiche Augenblick:*

	Sheets
Violin solo	4
Violin I (9 copies, at 15 sheets each)	135½ [*sic*]
Violin II (9 copies, at 15 sheets each)	135
Viola (6 copies, at 14½ sheets each)	87
Basso (9 copies, at 15½ sheets each)	136
No. 1 Winds	110½
No. 2 Winds	91
Score	68
ditto	69
Vocal [solo] parts	36
Soprano I (18, at 8 sheets each)	144
Soprano II (6, ditto)	48
Alto (12, ditto)	96
Tenor (18, ditto)	144
Bass (18, ditto)	144
[Preliminary] Total [number of] sheets	1,447
Choral director's score	21½
[Final total of sheets]	1,468½

For all of the above at 15 kreuzer per sheet: 367 fl.   7 kr.

1468 sheets at 12 kreuzer per sheet: [minus]   293 fl. 36 kr.

                                           73 fl. 21 kr.

Duly paid,

Schlemmer, Copyist[3]

1. Copyist Schlemmer did not date this bill, but the first performance of the cantata *Der glorreiche Augenblick* took place in the Grosser Redoutensaal on November 29, 1814. On the basis of the fact that Schlemmer presented his bill for the February 27, 1814, concert on the next day (see No. 182 above), the present document, reflecting November 29, was probably drafted on that day or the day after.

The concert consisted of the Symphony No. 7, the cantata and *Wellington's Victory*. See Thayer-Forbes, pp. 599–600, for details.

2. This heading is in the hand of Anton Schindler. Schlemmer's bill proper is expressed in *Bogen*, folded sheets of four pages each. While seemingly not correct in every detail, this bill comes to within a florin of charging Beethoven the correct amount and in fact errs in the composer's favor. The figure ½ at the end of the Violin I line does not belong there and may belong at the far right of the instrumental Basso line. The Basso line, however, is not computed correctly since $9 \times 15\frac{1}{2} = 139\frac{1}{2}$; thus, even if the figure ½ did belong at the end of this line, through arithmetical error Schlemmer undercharged Beethoven by three sheets.

The figures at the bottom are not clear, but it seems that Beethoven had paid Schlemmer for the entire copying job at the rate of 12 kreuzer per page when the correct charge, in fact, was 15 kreuzer. The net result is that Beethoven had to pay a remaining 73 florins, 31 kreuzer to settle this bill.

3. Beethoven jotted some computations, incomplete, on the reverse, indicating that he doubted some of the charges and wanted to double-check them, concluding: "more than 293 fl., 36 kr." He also wrote:

Total sum: 304 fl., 33 kr.;

Received: 200 fl.;

Remains: 104 fl., 33 kr.

This time he concluded: "Again, 10 fl. received for nothing."

Incipit: Rechnungsausweis über Copiatur der Cantate. . . .

Sources: Autograph in the Staatsbibliothek zu Berlin–Preussischer Kulturbesitz, Mus. ms. autogr. Beethoven 35, 84; listed in Kalischer, "Beethoven-Autographe," p. 53, and Bartlitz, p. 148. Facsimile (with little commentary) in Alan Tyson, "Notes on Five of Beethoven's Copyists," *Journal of the American Musicological Society* 23 (Fall 1970), 466–467.

1815

195. George Thomson to Beethoven

Edinburgh; January 2, 1815[1]

Monsieur Beethoven
Vienna

I wrote to you on November 12, sending you a "Song of a Soldier," beginning "Then soldiers come fill high the wine," etc.,[2] which I asked you to set to music. I now take the liberty to tell you that the author of this song very much wishes to replace it with the following song; and since it is very beautiful and worthy of your music, I join with the poet in begging you to have the kindness to compose a canzonetta on these words, instead of the "Song of a Soldier." If you have already composed this last, I ask you, nevertheless, to set the one that I am sending you now; and since I very much like this extra song, I shall gladly give you ten ducats to compose the music for it. Indeed the enclosed song was written expressly for you, and I do not know of any more beautiful in all of English poetry. The author is among the most zealous of your admirers, and I would be pleased to see his poetry honored by your music.[3]

With the original of the song I am sending you a translation in French *prose*,[4] so that, at the same time, you can see the general sentiment of the poetry and the meaning of the words, although I really feel that the translation gives only a very feeble idea of the exquisite beauties of the original. If you still need to be instructed concerning the pronunciation or the emphasis of the words, you can address yourself to some Englishman of taste, of whom I have no doubt that you could presently find several in Vienna.[5]

I shall be very pleased to receive the six or seven canzonettas, and the ritornellos and accompaniments to the 15 airs that are in your hands, and the overture on my national songs, as soon as you are able.

I have the honor to be, with great esteem, Monsieur,

Sincerely yours,

(signed) G. Thomson

[Thomson's note to himself:]

The above, with the original Cantata by Mr. [William] Smyth, and the following translation, sent to the care of Mr. Broughton, Secy. of State's Office, London, to be forwarded by him to Vienna.

[The incipits of the cantata were as follows:]

Recitative

Haste, haste, away, and quit the shade. . . .

Air

[Incipits of four stanzas:]

Again, my Lyre, yet once again! . . .

Ah, cease! . . . ye plaintive notes!

Around me airy forms appear. . . .

For still my Love may deign. . . .

1. Follows on Thomson's letter of November 12, 1814 (No. 192 above).

2. The song's first two parts are used for WoO 157, No. 2, and WoO 153, No. 10. Its poet was William Smyth.

3. Beethoven seems not to have set the recitative, but the air is used for Op. 108, No. 24.

4. The entire text will not be reproduced here. The incipit of the recitative (in its English original) is identified from Thomson's letter of March 20, 1815 (No. 201 below), the verses of the air from Op. 108, No. 24.

5. Representatives to and followers of the Congress of Vienna.

Incipit: Je vous écrivis le 12 Novembre. . . .

Sources: Summarized in MacArdle, "Beethoven and Thomson," p. 41. Copy in Thomson's copybook, British Library, Add. MS 35267, pp. 134r–135r.

196. Imperial Royal Landrecht to Beethoven and the Estate of Prince Ferdinand Kinsky[1]

Prague; January 18, 1815

Judgment

In accordance with the petition regarding this matter, submitted by Prince Kinsky's Trusteeship on January 6 of last year, the Chief Trusteeship's[2] consent will be granted: that the Princely Trusteeship pay to Ludwig v[an] Beethoven, in the name of the late Prince Ferdinand Kinsky, the maintenance stipend guaranteed him in writing in the month of March 1809 (nominally 1,800 florins)—a payment of 1,200 gulden, W.W.[3] from Prince Ferdinand Kinsky's estate of November 3, 1812, beginning under the following conditions: [conditions listed[4]], of which herewith the communication done by the I.R. Landrecht.

1. Prince Ferdinand Kinsky, one of Beethoven's three guarantors, died on November 3, 1812, after falling from his horse. Beethoven began the long process of receiving his stipend from the estate with extensive letters to Princess Karoline Kinsky on December 30, 1812, and February 12, 1813 (Anderson Nos. 393, 403 and 404).

2. The German terms are *Vormundschaft* and *Obervormundschaft*, respectively. The Chief Trusteeship was a panel appointed to deal with minors, wards and cases such as this one.

3. For an explanation of the two sums mentioned here, see Thayer-Krehbiel, II, 306, or Thayer-Forbes, p. 611.

4. Thayer does not reproduce this list of conditions.

Incipit: In Gemässheit des hierüber. . . .

Sources: Thayer-Deiters-Riemann, III, 489–490.

197. Beethoven to Baron Joseph von Pasqualati, Prague[1]

Vienna; [after January 18,] 1815[2]

Power of Attorney

It is hereby most kindly requested that Baron Josef von Pasqualati in Prague[3] present the claim due from the Prince Kinsky estate for me, and that he may do whatever is necessary in that regard.[4]

Vienna, on   1815[5]

Ludwig van Beethoven

1. Pasqualati was the younger brother of Beethoven's sometime landlord Baron Johann Baptist von Pasqualati.
2. This undated document derives from a period shortly after the Landrecht's judgment of January 18, 1815 (No. 196 above).
3. For a similar request, see Beethoven to Baron Johann von Pasqualati, spring 1813 (Anderson No. 412).
4. Nine months later, Pasqualati finally succeeded in securing Beethoven's stipend payment; see his receipt, dated October 31, 1815 (No. 212 above).
5. The date seems never to have been entered.
Incipit: Dass Herr Baron Josef von Pasqualati. . . .
Sources: Thayer, III (1879), 329; Thayer-Deiters-Riemann, III, 489–490.

198. Regierungsrat Sack[1] to Beethoven

Liegnitz, Silesia; January 29, 1815

Well-born Sir!
Highly-honored Herr Kapellmeister![2]

Among the many works of the hours that I have snatched away from business affairs and devoted to the Muses, there has lain in my desk for a considerable number of years an oratorio [libretto], which I, deeply moved, once assembled from my animated sentiments and put to paper. It has not been published, and has been shown only to a few close friends. When I picked it up again a short while ago, my soul became filled with the wish to discover if it was not appropriate for the Master of Exalted Music, whom I so often venerate at the piano and whose works provide me so much delight, to combine it with the flights of his tones. For your great, heart-stirring, deeply felt compositions, most highly honored Herr *Kapellmeister,* always lie before me, and to them I dedicate my Muses, which become consecrated to the Art of Tone![3]

I have now decided to carry out my intention, and send to you this oratorio, *Das Weltgericht* [The last judgment]. As far as I know, there are few appropriate oratorio [texts] on great, sublime subjects, and in a suitable and worthy style, that have not already been set to music. Perhaps Your Honor would not be displeased to have this text, and perhaps you will find substance therein and the enthusiasm to set it [to music]. If it is suitable to your spirit and taste, and if you deem it worthy of setting, then the subject would produce another work like Handel's *Messiah,* which in the past I heard in London and Berlin with devout rapture. Therefore, I hope, at least, that Your Honor will not wrongly interpret my boldness in submitting to you this text. I seek nothing more than to serve, and if it pleases you, to provide the occasion for a masterwork of music.[4]

Among the many reasons influencing my wish to visit Vienna once again is first and foremost that I wish to make your acquaintance personally, which I could not do when I traveled there (in Fall 1789),[5] and from there to Italy. Should destiny once again lead me there, it would give me the most exquisite joy to make the acquaintance of my favorite composer and bear witness to you of my high esteem.

If Your Honor would honor me with a reply, at the present time it would be most easily conveyed through my friend, the Royal Prussian State Councillor, Herr Jordan, who is now in Vienna, and who certainly would take care that it gets to me by the shortest route.

With greatest esteem I have the honor to sign myself Your Honor's

Most obedient servant,

Sack
Royal Prussian Privy Councillor

P.S. In case State Councillor Jordan is not immediately present, one of my other friends in the retinue of State Chancellor Prince von Harden-berg—either Court Councillors Barbe or Henn—can take care of getting the letter to me.[6]

1. Since Sack's first name seems not to be known—all printed references simply call the Prussian official "Regierungsrat Sack"—this edition has left his title, *privy councillor,* in German.

2. As a rule, this edition simplifies such formulaic salutations, but Sack's flowery phrases are retained as most consistent with his lofty intentions soon to be imparted.

3. *Tonkunst* (music).

4. The libretto calls for four Angels (soprano, alto, tenor and bass solos), two Earthly Voices (soprano and tenor solos), and a Chorus of Spirits and orchestra. Throughout the libretto (six printed pages in Virneisel, pp. 370–375), the poet provides his own outline concept of the vocal and instrumental setting, dynamics etc. but notes in a preface that these are not prescriptions for the composer, merely the poet's own feelings as he wrote the text.

During the action of the libretto, the angels in turn describe the approach and manifestation of the Last Judgment (various recitatives and arias) with commentary from the chorus. The earthly voices describe their own feelings about mortal dust and spirits rising to God, who (with choral exclamations) provides a new sun and bids the earthly voices "Be good, my children," before a final chorus of praise, honor and "Amen." Any resemblance between this and Handel's *Messiah* (a work that Beethoven particularly valued) is purely coincidental.

5. Presumably Sack was unaware that Beethoven himself did not move from Bonn to Vienna until November 1792.

6. The aforementioned Prussian officials were probably in Vienna for the congress.

Incipit: Unter vielen Arbeiten meiner. . . .

Sources: Virneisel, "Kleine Beethoveniana," pp. 368–375 (letter and libretto in full); letter excerpted in Ley, "Aus Briefen an Beethoven," pp. 149–150; mentioned in Thayer-Deiters-Riemann, III, 486. Autograph in the Staatsbibliothek zu Berlin–Preussischer Kulturbesitz, Mus. ms. autogr. Beethoven 35, 42; listed in Bartlitz, p. 130.

199. *Joseph Hammer*[1] *to Beethoven*

[Vienna;] Ash Wednesday, [February 8, 1815][2]

Immediately after the departure of the Pers[ian] ambassador, I intended to submit to the censor copies of my Persian *Singspiel* and Indian *Hirtenspiel* [shepherd play],[3] which were finished a few days before his arrival. Herr Zmeskall[4] informed me today, however, of your wish to set [to music] an Indian chorus of religious character,[5] and since my primary intention in the dramatically written poem was to portray the religious system of the Hindus as poetical and emotional, there might be something found in it that corresponds to your wish.

At the same time, sir, I also take the liberty of enclosing my Persian *Singspiel,* whose verses are more idealistic and musically written, and the oratorio *Die Sündflut* [The flood],[6] because the sublime subject of the latter, perhaps more than anything else that the Holy Scriptures provide us, could be mastered and victoriously dealt with by the loftiness of your spirit.

You might, perhaps fortunately, notice many mistakes in the execution of the text, but even if you should not find the whole [libretto] successful, I am still convinced that only through Beethoven's spirit does music have the power to bestir the seas and calm the floods.[7]

With my expressed esteem,

Your great admirer,

Hammer

1. Joseph (or Josef) Hammer (1774–1852), a noted orientalist, was appointed oriental adviser and interpreter to the imperial court in 1807. He hoped to make Eastern (Arabic, Persian and Turkish) literature better known in Europe and on January 6, 1809, published the first issue of his *Fundgruben des Orients*. In 1835, he was given the title Ritter von Hammer-Purgstall. Solomon provides considerable background information about this colorful character.

2. The letter, without specific place or date, indicates merely "Ash Wednesday." Beethoven answered it in an undated letter (Anderson No. 206). Kinsky believed the letter to date from 1823; Thayer placed it in 1809 (as did Anderson, following his example). Solomon proposed the year 1815, adopted here. In 1815, Ash Wednesday

fell on February 8. More recently, Sieghard Brandenburg has hypothesized the Beethoven-Hammer exchange as dating from 1819 (cited in Marie-Elisabeth Tellenbach, "Psychoanalysis and the Historiocritical Method: On Maynard Solomon's Image of Beethoven," *Beethoven Newsletter* [San Jose] 9, nos. 2–3 [Summer-Winter 1994], 122–127).

3. Probably *Anahib* and *Dewajani*, respectively, both reflecting Hammer's translation *Memnons Dreiklang.*

4. The name is abbreviated as "Zml."

5. During these years Beethoven became interested in a popularized form of oriental philosophy and religion and jotted quotations from the literature in his various notebooks, especially the famous *Tagebuch* (diary) of 1812–1818.

6. Or *The Deluge,* as Shedlock translated it. Thayer-Deiters-Riemann, III, 66, notes a German oratorio of this title, text by Dobenz, music by Ferdinand Kauer, produced at the Leopoldstadt Theater, Vienna, on December 24, 1809. This does not, however, seem identical with Hammer's version.

7. An allusion to the title and subject of his libretto.

Incipit: Ich wollte soeben nach der Abreise. . . .

Sources: Thayer-Deiters-Riemann, III, viii (giving the year as 1809); Kalischer (German), I, 208; Kalischer-Shedlock, I, 134 (giving the year as 1808); Kastner (1910), pp. 152–153 (giving the year as 1809, per Thayer). Solomon, "A Beethoven Acquaintance," pp. 13–15, adopts Shedlock's translation with minor changes and revises the year to 1815. Autograph in the Staatsbibliothek zu Berlin–Preussischer Kulturbesitz, Mus. ms. autogr. Beethoven 35, 41; listed in Kalischer, "Beethoven-Autographe," p. 49 (giving no year), and Bartlitz, p. 129 (giving the year as 1808).

200. Carl Amenda[1] to Beethoven

Talsen; March 20, 1815[2]

My Beethoven![3]

After a long silence, for which I take the blame,[4] I approach with an offering to your splendid muse, so that it reconciles you with me and that you again think about your almost estranged Amenda. Oh, those unforgettable days! when I was so close to your heart, when that loving heart and the magic of your great talent bound me inextricably to you! — they always remain as a most beautiful image in my soul. Among my innermost feelings they are a jewel that no amount of time can rob from me.

From your own lips, I sometimes used to perceive how much you wished for a worthy subject for a grand opera. I believe that you have not yet found one. Well, see: I offer it to you now! I am sending you herewith an opera whose like, I boldly venture to assert, has not yet existed. That you and no other should compose it is also the wish of the poet, a sincere friend of mine.[5] This copy is in his own delicate handwriting—how otherwise would it have been possible to get an entire opera in a letter envelope? If you will make yourself acquainted with the small characters [of the handwriting] and especially the spirit of the whole, you will soon [be able to] read it fluently. Also you can quickly have a larger copy of it made; but then, my friend, get to work soon, and show the world, even here, what Beethoven is capable of doing when he works con amore.

You will be pleased to note how this text is arranged entirely in consideration for the music, how insightfully the scenes and all the arias are ordered. Only one thing, perhaps, will seem awkward to you: the considerable length of the piece, which will probably necessitate your composing a few numbers straight through, without musical repeats. On the other hand, I already anticipate gladly how, with so many fine [dramatic] situations, you will overflow with your own type of delicacy or power; how you will give the different characters their individual style; and finally how you will summon the complete fullness of harmony[6] (which is completely available only at *your* command) in the great ensemble scenes and in the various murder spectacles. Oh, if I and my loyal Berge,[7] who likewise pays homage with wonderment to your great muse, could be with you even some of the time during this work, and at that moment of its origins feel so much with you and enjoy it with you! I was formerly one of these fortunate ones;[8] you surely do not lack such admirers even now! I know the longing of your unconstrained heart; it is the perfection of [your] art. Now then, deliver to the world the first of your operas![9] I am still fortunate enough that in it you will think of me, and I shall be able to delight in the rapture with which the world will unfailingly receive the masterwork of my two sincerest friends.

Now write to me very soon, so I know if you received this letter with its enclosure, surely of importance to you. But especially write to me, even if only a few words, about how you are. Indeed I have not been entirely without reports of you up to now. Newspapers and travelers have told me of you; your splendid compositions have often spoken of you to my heart; and yet all this has only increased my longing for news from you yourself.

Your hearing suffers? My poor friend! How very sorry I feel for you![10] Are you otherwise well, though? You must be: the fame that you most recently shared with Wellington[11] indicates it.

Is our good Zmeskall still living? I doubt it.[12] Greet our mutual friends when you see them, especially the Streichers.[13]

As always, I am still living the simple life of a country pastor in a pleasant country seat, with my good Jeanette at my side, and in most brotherly company with my sincerest friend Berge, surrounded by a small world of children, of which five dear children are my own.[14] Although not entirely free from cares, still (Thank God!) we are fairly happy and looking forward to a better future.

I very seldom have musical pleasures, although I occasionally travel to our capital, Mitau, where a superb girl, Marianne von Berner, is incontestably distinguished as a violinist of the first magnitude. I also heard Baillot from Paris there once. Oh, what a powerful instrument the violin is when Baillot's soul speaks through it! After I heard you play on our last evening at Zmeskall's, I have never again been so powerfully moved by any mortal as I was by Baillot. He had at that time been in Vienna and spoke enthusiastically of you, preferred nothing above playing your pieces, and confessed that he had played before you only once, but in great embarrassment.[15]

Dear Beethoven, bless us violin players again soon with quartets![16]

I close, in order to leave our friend Berge space enough to add a few lines, which he wants to write you about your [*sic*] *Bacchus*. God's best blessing on you, my eternally dear Beethoven. My address is: Herr Pastor Amenda, Talsen in Curland.

Friend Berge needs more space and will write on his own sheet,[17] so this little spot still belongs to me. I shall use it to ask the question: my Beethoven, won't you make a musical tour sometime? You have long been known and praised throughout the world for your works, but people long above all to meet you in person. Golden peace finally blesses the world again[18] and especially encourages the muses. You would be able to earn great profits from [your] tours; they would be [convenient] for your use of the spas and conducive to your health; and as was once the case with Haydn, the good Viennese would come to value you even more after your return from abroad.[19] And finally, if you were also to visit the North and came on a tour to St. Petersburg through Mitau and Riga, how you would be received! Then I would hurry to embrace you, and in a few days would lead you here. Oh, I would be most happy to entertain my most affectionately beloved Beethoven in my home! Think about it, my friend!

Again, farewell.

1. The Latvian Carl (Karl) Amenda (1771–1836) had spent 1798–1799 in Vienna, where he became tutor to the families of Prince Lobkowitz and Constanze Mozart. As a competent violinist, Amenda soon entered Beethoven's circle of friends, and the two remained intermittently in touch through letters and mutual acquaintances after Amenda's departure for the north in the summer of 1799. Back in Latvia, Amenda was appointed Lutheran pastor in Talsen in 1802 and, in 1820, provost of the Kaudau (Kandava) diocese. See Thayer, III (1879), 503–505.

2. Talsen (Talsi) is roughly 60 miles northwest of Riga and Mitau (Jelgava) in Courland/Curland (Latvia). Beethoven had not yet received this letter when he wrote to Amenda on April 12, 1815 (Anderson No. 541).

3. In addition to this affectionate salutation ("Mein Beethoven!"), Amenda uses the familiar *Du* throughout his letter, as the composer likewise did in his letters to Amenda.

4. Beethoven's earlier surviving letters to Amenda date from about the time of his return to Courland in the summer of 1799 (Anderson Nos. 32 and 36) and from the summer of 1801 (Anderson Nos. 52 and 53). Amenda replied to Beethoven's earliest letters in late 1799 or early 1800 (No. 31 above).

5. The libretto that Amenda sent was *Bacchus,* a "grand lyric opera" in three acts by Rudolph vom Berge. Beethoven briefly considered the subject of a Greek opera in late 1815 or early 1816: the Scheide Sketchbook, pp. 52–53, contains a reference to the god Pan (see Nottebohm, *Zweite Beethoveniana,* pp. 329–330; and Johnson-Tyson-Winter, p. 245). As late as the second half of 1818, he also briefly considered a scenario for a symphony (ultimately the Ninth) using a text reflecting Greek mythology in an Adagio and a "Feier des Bacchus" as the (final?) Allegro (see Nottebohm, *Zweite Beethoveniana,* p. 163).

6. *Harmonie,* which could also indicate a full wind section.

7. The librettist.

8. Amenda, therefore, must have witnessed the progress made on various Beethoven compositions during their 1798–1799 acquaintance and, surely, the first version of String Quartet, Op. 18, No. 1, which he took home with him in the summer of 1799.

9. Amenda seems not to have been aware of *Leonore/Fidelio.*

10. In Beethoven's letter of July 1, 1801 (Anderson No. 53), Amenda had been one of the first to learn of the composer's hearing problems.

11. It is not clear whether Amenda is referring to Beethoven's composition *Wellington's Victory* or whether he simply meant that Beethoven's music and Wellington's

military triumphs over Napoleon had both received thorough coverage by the press.

12. Born in 1759, the government official and amateur violoncellist Nikolaus Zmeskall von Domanowecz was destined to live (albeit plagued by gout) until 1833.

13. Piano makers Johann Andreas Streicher (1761–1833) and his wife, Nannette (1769–1833), married since 1794, from whom Amenda bought a piano through the mail in the summer of 1801.

14. As a Lutheran pastor, Amenda may also have been the town's schoolteacher. He had been tutor in the house of Prince Lobkowitz during his stay in Vienna, worth mentioning that a noble in the Catholic Hapsburg capital would have a Protestant tutor in his household. The same holds true for Constanze Mozart.

15. Pierre Baillot (1771–1842), renowned violinist, composer and pedagogue, left France in August 1805 for a three-year tour of Russia, stopping in Vienna on his way there. He attempted to call on Beethoven at his apartment but finally met him in the convivial atmosphere of a suburban inn. See René Baillot, "Baillot a Vienne," *Ménestrel* 31 (October 2, 1864), 349–350; and Pierre Baillot, *The Art of the Violin*, trans. and ed. Louise Goldberg (Evanston: Northwestern University Press, 1991), xv–xix, 499 and passim.

16. Composed in 1810, Beethoven's String Quartet, Op. 95, was published by Steiner, Vienna, in September 1816, with a dedication to the above-mentioned Zmeskall.

17. The letter from Berge seems not to have survived.

18. That is, after the Napoleonic wars. It seems that Amenda was not yet aware of Napoleon's escape from exile on Elba and his arrival on the Continent on March 1.

19. A reference to Haydn's two highly successful journeys to London, 1790–1792 and 1794–1795.

Incipit: Nach langem, schuldvollen Schweigen. . . .

Sources: Thayer-Deiters-Riemann, III, 501–503, provides the full text of the letter and a list of characters from Berge's libretto. Summary only in Thayer, III (1879), 341; Thayer-Krehbiel, II, 314–315; and Thayer-Forbes, pp. 617–618. Autograph in the Staatsbibliothek zu Berlin–Preussischer Kulturbesitz, Mus. ms. autogr. Beethoven 35, 40; listed in Kalischer, "Beethoven-Autographe," pp. 48–49, and Bartlitz, p. 129. Vom Berge's libretto (six leaves, twelve pages) is also in the Staatsbibliothek zu Berlin–Preussischer Kulturbesitz, Mus. ms. autogr. Beethoven 37, 3; listed in Bartlitz, p. 185.

201. George Thomson to Beethoven

Edinburgh; March 20, 1815

Monsieur Louis v[an] Beethoven

I have received your letter of last February ———.[1] You at first asked me for 12 ducats for an overture, and you now ask me for four times that sum! Two years ago you asked me for 25 ducats for six original airs, and you presently ask nearly three times this price! Unfortunately, I am not in the position to give such a fee, neither for the one work, nor for the other. I have abandoned [the prospect of] the overture.

For the *six airs,* concerning the poetry for which I have taken infinite trouble, I shall give you thirty-five ducats; and I do this solely to please my own taste, for it is very uncertain that the sales of these airs, when they are printed, will ever repay me that sum, with the cost of engraving or printing, of the paper, etc. If you do not wish to accept 35 ducats, I ask you to be so kind as to put into the fire all the verses that I have sent you. If you wish to accept that sum, the airs must be composed specifically for the following songs:[2]

[1.]   "The Battle of Hohenlinden," beginning "On Linden when the sun was low."

[2.]   "The farewells of a lover to his charming mistress," beginning "Once more, enchanting girl, adieu."

[3.]   "The Happy Italian Shepherdess," singing the pleasures and the beauties of the valley of her birth, beginning "Dear is my little native vale."

[4.]   The song beginning with the recitative, "Haste, haste away, and quit the shade."

If you write me that you accept this offer, I shall send you the two other songs (which are of ordinary length), and while waiting you can compose the four mentioned above. The two that I shall send are upon charming subjects that I like very much.

Be so kind as to send the ritornellos and accompaniments of the 15 airs, as soon as they are ready, for which Messrs. Fries will pay you the fee that you have asked. I hope that you have arranged some for three voices, that is to say, those that you believe best suited to such.

I am told that your *Battle* has been performed by a large orchestra in London, to great applause.[3] There is also a Mass of your composition that [will be] performed, and that, they say, is a very sublime work.[4]

Do not call me a "Merchant of Music."[5] I am an *Amateur;* and I sell only my national airs, which I do *wholesale.*

I have the honor, Monsieur, to be, with much esteem,

Your friend and very humble servant,

(signed) G. Thomson

1. Thomson leaves a blank where the day would be designated in the copy in his copybook. The reply is to Anderson No. 529: Thayer (1879), III, 452, gave the date of Beethoven's letter as February 7; Anderson did likewise; MacArdle, however, examining the same document in the British Library (Add. MS 35264, p. 192), noted, "day of the month not filled in."

2. Beethoven did not provide arrangements of the first three and in the fourth, first proposed on January 2, 1815 (No. 195 above), arranged only the air ("Again, my Lyre," Op. 108, No. 24), and not the opening recitative.

3. *Wellington's Victory* was performed at the Drury Lane Theatre, under Sir George Smart, on February 10, 1815.

4. The Mass in C, Op. 86. According to Thayer's interviews with Smart, only portions of the Mass were performed in 1816 and 1817 and the complete work not until later (Thayer-Krehbiel, II, 310).

5. Beethoven's letter, in English, had addressed the Scot as "Mr George Thomson, merchant in the musical line." Anderson does not give the address, but all editions of Thayer (notably Thayer-Krehbiel, II, 308) do so.

Incipit: J'ai reçu votre lettre du —— Fevrier passé. . . .

Sources: Summarized in MacArdle, "Beethoven and Thomson," p. 41; and Hadden, *George Thomson,* pp. 329–330. Copy in Thomson's copybook, British Library, Add. MS 35267, pp. 142r–143r.

202. *Johann Kanka*[1] *to Prince Rudolph Kinsky's Cashier*

Prague; March 26, 1815[2]

[Declaration]

Instead of the maintenance contribution of the nominal 1,800 florins, assured in writing by the late Prince Ferdinand Kinsky in the month of May 1809,[3] and reduced to 726 florins in *Wiener Währung*, Ludwig van Beethoven, on the strength of the I.R. Landrecht's communication, dated Prague, January 18, 1815, is granted to be paid annually, beginning with November 3, 1812, [the sum of] 1,200 florins in *Wiener Währung* from Prince Ferdinand Kinsky's estate.

From this maintenance contribution at 1,200 florins
[annually], there is due Herr Ludwig van Beethoven, for
the period from November 3, 1812, until the end of
March, 1815 (2 years, 4 months, 27 days) an amount of . . . . . 2,890 florins
Because, however, he [Beethoven] received, following
the aforementioned I.R. Landrecht's communication, 60
I.R. ducats from the late Prince Ferdinand Kinsky, charged
against the account of this maintenance contribution, and
this according to the exchange rate of 6 fl. 51 in effect at
the time of receipt in the month of October 1812, the
following sum is to be deducted from the above amount . . . . . <u>411 florins</u>
and there remains the outstanding maintenance
contribution for the aforementioned time to be paid to
Herr Ludwig van Beethoven . . . . 2,479 florins

These two thousand four hundred seventy-nine gulden in *Wiener Währung* of outstanding maintenance contribution are today, duly and in cash, to be received in full authority and in hand by the aforementioned Ludwig van Beethoven from the chief cashier for Prince Rudolph Kinsky's trust. Confirmed by the undersigned with his own signature.

Johann Kanka, J.D.   Joseph B. von Pasqualati[4]

Wenzl Wezowsky, as Witness

1. Johann Kanka (1772–1865), Bohemian lawyer, pianist and composer, who served as the executor of the estates of Princes Kinsky and Lobkowitz. Beethoven met Kanka in Prague in 1796 and again in 1811 at the Bohemian spas; thus the attorney/musician acted honorably to secure Beethoven the stipend owed him.

2. See the Imperial Royal Landrecht's judgment, January 18, 1815, and Beethoven's power of attorney to Pasqualati, after January 18, 1815 (Nos. 196 and 197 above).

3. Beethoven's stipend, guaranteed by Prince Kinsky, Prince Franz Joseph Lobkowitz and Archduke Rudolph. Kinsky had died on November 3, 1812 — thus the significance of the date as repeated in this document.

4. As can be seen in Beethoven's power of attorney, originating after January 18, 1815, the composer empowered the Viennese lawyer Pasqualati to present his claim to the Kinsky estate.

Incipit: Dem Ludwig van Beethoven sind statt. . . .

Sources: Thayer-Deiters-Riemann, III, 490–491, from a copy of the document then in the Prince Kinsky Registry Office, Prague.

203. Beethoven to Archduke Rudolph's Chief Cashier

Vienna; March 30, 1815[1]

Receipt

for 750 f[ull] w[eight], that is, seven hundred fifty gulden f[ull] w[eight], the most kindly granted *stipend*, which the undersigned has *duly received* unto himself from the *Chief Cashier* of His Imperial Highness, the most Illustrious Archduke *Rudolph, namely, from September 1, 1814, through the end of February, 1815* — hereby received.

Vienna, March 30, 1815[2]

1. Frimmel noted that this document, on a very irregularly torn sheet of paper, appeared to be either the remainder of a receipt or a draft of a statement of receipt. He transcribed roughly twenty words and numbers that were clear, without indicating (other than by ellipses) whether other (presumably indistinct) words were present. In German, the words and numbers and their order are virtually identical with those in Beethoven's receipt to Rudolph's cashier, dated September 1, 1814 (No. 187 above). The English reconstruction/translation here is patterned after that document, with the words corresponding to the German text given by Frimmel rendered in italics.

If this document was a receipt rather than a draft, then Beethoven's signature and seal may have been torn from the lower portion of the sheet.

2. Written on the exterior: "Dekre[t] u. Quitt[ung]" (Decree and Receipt) in ink; "2 fl. Stemp[el] Bogen" (2 florins stamp [per?] sheet) below it in pencil.

Incipit: [Quittung über 750 v.w. sage. . . .]

Sources: Frimmel, "Neue Beethovenstudien" (1895), p. 18. At that time, the autograph was in the collection of wholesale merchant Franz Trau, Vienna.

204. Bernhard Anselm Weber[1] to Georg Friedrich Treitschke[2]

Berlin; April 8, 1815[3]

Honorable Friend!

In December we received very definite reports that our King would meet with the Russian Czar in Berlin at the end of January.[4] People were already making plans for the festivities. Since I was busy with the completion of [incidental music for] *Epimenides Erwachen* by Herr von Goethe,[5] I could begin no other work that would have been suitable for a concert for the reception of the monarchs. Therefore, out of anxiety, I had recourse to you, my honored friend! I absolutely cannot blame Herr van Beethoven, to whom I send heartiest greetings, if he does not wish to distribute his works before he publishes them. As I already said, it was an idea of the moment, born of anxiety.[6] For that reason, I would like to ask Herr van Beethoven again: when he sends his works that are composed for musical *Akademies* [i.e., concerts] to be published, if he would kindly have a copy[7] sent to me immediately, so I am the first person who can have them performed in Berlin.

I have suggested to our new director, General-Intendant Count Brühl, to obtain Herr van Beethoven's opera *Fidelio* for our stage. He has given me the mandate to write to you, my honored friend, and to obtain the score from you, as you offered us for 15 ducats. Therefore, be so kind as to send a good, and especially a correctly copied score of the opera *Fidelio*, together with the libretto, here to my attention. Really take care, my honored friend, that it is not as error ridden as most scores copied in Vienna. Truly, we have already received such scores from there, and I have had to sit over them for days and weeks in order to correct the errors. Please, please!

Epimenides Erwachen, a festival play [*Festspiel*] by Herr von Goethe, to which I composed incidental music, was given with great success and applause on the 30th and 31st [of March] in the great Opera Theater to celebrate the entry into Paris.[8] It is in one act, but lasts exactly two and a half hours. It was a risky undertaking. However, in spite of the unfavorable circumstances of time, it turned out well. The day is very noteworthy for me in my artistic life. If an opera displeases, one can, with God's help, compose another, but this day, eternally noteworthy for Prussia and the entire world, could never be repeated.

I am most sincerely interested in the success that your wife earned in London.[9] Although I have never had the honor to meet her in person, I have heard many glorious things about her, and these always gave me joy.

Farewell! Remain most sincerely, as I am likewise

Most sincerely yours,

B. A. Weber

[P.S.] Pass my greetings on to *Kapellmeister* Weigl.[10]

1. Born in Mannheim, Weber (1764–1821) had held lesser posts in Berlin before his formal appointment as music director of the Royal Theater in 1796.

2. Theatrical official in Vienna, who in 1814 revised the libretto of *Fidelio*.

3. Beethoven and Treitschke wrote to the Royal Theater in Berlin on June 23, 1814 (see June 24, 1814, No. 184 above, for a similar letter to Karlsruhe, and September 15, 1814, No. 189 above, to August Wilhelm Iffland, for developments in Berlin prior to the present letter).

4. Friedrich Wilhelm III and Alexander I met in Berlin in January 1815, during a period of crisis in the Congress of Vienna, to discuss the proposed partition of Saxony.

5. *Des Epimenides Erwachen* by Johann Wolfgang von Goethe (1749–1832) played in Berlin and Weimar without lasting success.

6. Weber must have written to Beethoven sometime after the interim Theater Direction rejected *Fidelio* on October 15, 1814 (see Treitschke to Iffland, September 15, 1814), probably early in 1815, asking him to send works appropriate to a concert. This letter seems not to have survived. In late 1823 and early 1824, Beethoven seriously considered Berlin as the location for the premiere of his Symphony No. 9.

7. Weber uses the word *Exemplar* rather than *Abschrift*, indicating that he means a printed copy.

8. The Allies' entry into Paris after the Napoleonic Wars.

9. Treitschke's wife was a noted dancer.

10. In 1793, Weber had gone to Vienna (among other cities) to engage singers for Berlin. Here he met Antonio Salieri (1750–1825), who encouraged his composition of stage works, and probably became acquainted with Joseph Weigl (1766–1846), composer and conductor at the Court Theater, Vienna. Weigl had studied with and been championed by Salieri as early as 1785.

Incipit: Wir haben im Dezember. . . .

Sources: Schwarz, "Beethoven und Berlin," pp. 89–90. In 1912, the autograph was in the possession of the art dealers Gilhofer & Ranschburg, Vienna.

205. Beethoven to Sigmund Anton Steiner[1]

[Vienna; ca. May 16, 1815][2]

My sincerest thanks, my worthy L[ieutenant] G[eneral], for your intercession with the landlord once more, although I am sorry that you have wasted a single word, since I really am *too kind* for the likes of these house owners, where the landlord plays the leading character.[3] I need, for inspection, the written parts of the Overture in C and the Violin Sonata in G[4] for a few days, and ask you for them, with the assurance that you will receive both works back as soon as possible. In haste,

Your best
Generalissimus,

Ludwig van Beethoven

[Steiner's annotation:][5]
May 16, 1815
Given out,
on the condition of return:
1 Sonata with violin accompaniment
1 Overture in C.

[Haslinger's annotation:]
On May 20, 1815,
the aforementioned two works
have been returned.[6]

[Exterior:]
For Herr von Steiner

1. Steiner (1773–1838) was a prominent Viennese publisher whose business was located in the Paternostergasse. Beethoven enjoyed a friendly but checkered relationship with the firm and termed Steiner the "Lieutenant General," his partner Tobias Haslinger the "Adjutant" or "General Adjutant," proofreader Anton Diabelli as "Diabolus," and himself as "Generalissimus."

2. Steiner's annotation, "May 16, 1815," seems to indicate that Beethoven wrote this letter on that date or very shortly before.

3. Beethoven seems to have enlisted Steiner's aid more than once during this period in his squabbles with landlords. This quarrel could have been with Anton von Rachowin, owner of the Bartenstein Haus, Mölkerbastei No. 94, which Beethoven occupied from February 1814 until the fall of 1815, or Count Lamberti, proprietor of Seilerstätte No. 1055/1056, where he may have moved as early as the spring of 1815 and remained until April 1817.

4. The *Namensfeier* Overture, Op. 115, and the Violin Sonata, Op. 96.

5. Steiner's and Tobias Haslinger's annotations are written below, and at a right angle to, Beethoven's text.

6. This does not quite agree with Beethoven's letter of May 20 (Anderson No. 542), which asks for the loan of three more works, with the promise of having all of them (including the two noted here) back to Steiner the following Monday. See also No. 206 below for further possible details.

Incipit: Meinen herzlichen Dank, mein werther G.L. . . .

Sources: Transcribed and edited by Sieghard Brandenburg in Staehelin, "Unbekannte . . . Schriftstücke," pp. 44–49, with facsimile and extensive commentary. Autograph in the Beethoven-Haus, Bonn, NE 125.

206. Beethoven to Nikolaus Zmeskall von Domanovecz[1]

[Vienna; possibly May 20, 1815][2]

Dear Z!

I request you to send me the Quartet by about 4 o'clock this afternoon at the latest, because I need it urgently. In case your servant finds no one home, he should merely give it to the building superintendent below.[3]

Entirely your
Beethoven

1. Earlier readings indicate that the letter was addressed to "S." The salutation on its facsimile, however, clearly reads "lieber Z!" (as Beethoven often greeted his friend Zmeskall). None of the above hypothesized a date.

2. Beethoven signed this letter using German (as opposed to Latin) script. Max Unger believed that he discontinued this practice around 1820, while Alan Tyson placed the transition to Latin signatures about 1817.

An amateur violoncellist, Zmeskall received the dedication to Beethoven's String Quartet, Op. 95, when Steiner & Co. published it seemingly in September 1816. It was not advertised in the *Wiener Zeitung* until December 21, however, nor did Beethoven send a dedicatory copy of the printed music to Zmeskall until December 16 (Anderson No. 681). Sometime thereafter (Anderson No. 682), Beethoven sent Zmeskall a correction for the first violin part, but this would not have necessitated his requesting the quartet in such pressing language as this brief letter exhibits.

More likely, this letter dates from May 20, 1815, when Beethoven also wrote to Steiner, "I still need . . . the Symphony in A, the String Quartet in F minor. . . . Some foreigners have turned up here, and I can't refuse to let them see some of my recent compositions. . . . At about three o'clock this afternoon I will send for the scores . . ." (Anderson No. 542). It is possible that the composer had given Steiner a score to the quartet, while Zmeskall still had a manuscript set of parts, and that he wanted to ensure the presence of at least one copy for his late afternoon meeting. The foreign visitors probably included Charles Neate, who ultimately took the Quartet, Op. 95, home with him to London in February 1816, with the hopes of achieving simultaneous publication there on Beethoven's behalf.

3. From roughly February 1814 until the fall of 1815, Beethoven lived on the second floor (American designation) of the Bartenstein Haus No. 94, on the Mölkerbastei, adjacent to the Pasqualati Haus (Klein, *Beethovenstätten*, p. 78). The building superintendent as designated in the letter, was a woman (*Hausmeisterin*).

Incipit: Ich bitte Sie mir das Quartett. . . .

Sources: Drouot Rive Gauche (Pierre Berès), *Autographes Musicaux,* auction catalog (Paris, June 20, 1977), item 11. Quoted briefly in Helms and Staehelin, "Bewegungen . . . 1973–1979," p. 357. In 1983, the autograph was in a private collection in France. On May 10, 1995, it was auctioned again: Laurin-Guilloux-Buffetaud-Tailleur, Drouot Richelieu, *Auction Catalogue* (Paris, May 10, 1995), item 133 (with facsimile of the recto).

207. Chief Steward Sperl (on Behalf of Countess Marie Erdödy)[1] to Beethoven

[Jedlesee, near Vienna;] July 20, 1815[2]

I've come from Jedlersee as messenger[3]
To him who next to God is the greatest composer.
The graciousness of Countess von Erdödy
Invites you to take punch
And whatever else the country has to offer.
The two-horsed carriage stands at the ready
To drive you there with me;
Until half past one I'll wait for you.

Sperl

Chief Steward

1. Countess Anna Marie Erdödy (1779–1837). Married to Count Peter Erdödy since 1796, she had been acquainted with Beethoven since 1803. For a period before March 1809, Beethoven had lived in their house, but a quarrel sent him seeking new lodgings. By 1815, the friendship was renewed. The family had an estate in Jedlesee (or Jedlersee), ten miles north of Vienna, across the Danube from Heiligenstadt and Nussdorf. Although spelled Jedlersee in Sperl's message, the village was called Jedlesee at least as early as 1683 (Klein, *Beethovenstätten,* p. 82). Sperl's title in German is *Oberamtmann.* On October 19, 1815 (Anderson No. 563), Beethoven humorously referred to Sperl as the "sober justice in his *high office.*"

2. Answered by Anderson No. 549, which (on p. 519, n.1) also provides a looser but poetically rendered version of the present invitation. To some extent the poem implies that it had been written in Vienna itself, but the argument is academic.

3. The original poem is eight lines of rhymed couplets.

Incipit: Ich kam von Jedlersee als Both. . . .

Sources: Thayer, III (1879), 344; Thayer-Deiters-Riemann, III, 509; Anderson No. 549. Autograph in the Staatsbibliothek zu Berlin–Preussischer Kulturbesitz, Mus. ms. autogr. Beethoven 38, 16; listed in Kalischer, "Beethoven-Autographe," p. 76, and Bartlitz, p. 193.

208. Countess Marie Erdödy to Beethoven

[Jedlesee, near Vienna; Summer 1815][1]

To the laurel-crowned Majesty
    of exalted Music
Ludwig v[an] Beethoven,[2]
an Ardent Entreaty from the Muses
    of Jedlersee,
that their beloved Apollo
might yet spend
the present day in their midst.

    Fiat

Apollo's first son!
Thou greatest of the great spirits,
Supreme master of music,
Whom all Europe now knows,
Whom Apollo himself indulges
And, from the throne of the Muses,
Rewards with his crown:
Hear our prayer,
Remain today in our midst.
The great man Beethoven
Gives *Fiat* to our hopes.

        Marie the Elder[3]
        Marie the Younger
        Fritzi the Unique
        August *ditto*
        Magister ipse[4]
        Violoncello the Damned[5]
        Old Baron of the Empire
        Officious Steward[6]

1. This humorous poem, in the countess's hand, possibly dates from sometime close to the poetic message of July 20, 1815 (No. 207 above).

2. The initial *v* here (as in so many other references to Beethoven) may indicate an intentional confusion of the German nobility particle for the Flemish original.

3. Countess Marie, with humorous references to her children Marie (Mimi), Friederike (Fritzi) and August (Gusti), with her household following.

4. The family tutor, Johann Xaver Brauchle (according to Anderson). Haupt, p. 71, calls him Joseph Xaver Brauchle.

5. Joseph Linke, the violoncellist, who had come into the Erdödys' employ after the breakup of the Rasumovsky Quartet.

6. *Ober-Mann-Amt,* a pun on Chief Steward Sperl's title, *Oberamtmann.*

Incipit(s): (*a*) An die lorbeerkrönte Majestät. . . . (*b*) Apollo's erster Sohn! . . .

Sources: Thayer, III (1879), 346; Thayer-Deiters-Riemann, III, 510; Kalischer (German), II, 284–285; Kalischer-Shedlock, I, 368–369. For a copy of this letter, along with a potentially sordid account of Countess Erdödy's and Brauchle's actions during this period, see Günther Haupt, "Gräfin Eródy und J. X. Brauchle," *Der Bär* (1927), 70–99.

209. *George Thomson to Beethoven*

Edinburgh; August 20, 1815[1]

My dear Monsieur,

I have received the 15 airs with your ritornellos and accompaniments that are full of splendorous beauty, and I have had the greatest pleasure in listening to them.

In the slightest way, No. 7 is not adapted to the taste of our young ladies: it is too complicated and too difficult for them to play correctly. The air in question[2] begins thus:

It is impossible for the accompaniments of these simple airs to be too easy, either for the eye or for the hands.

Enclosed I am sending you two more favorite airs. Be so kind as to compose ritornellos and accompaniments for them, and also a second voice for *soprano* (or for tenor, if more appropriate) and also a voice for bass. You will compose these voice parts, either in simple counterpoint or with a little *imitation,* where you find such imitations proper, as you have done successfully in No. 15 of the last group.

Be so kind, as soon as it suits you, to give the two airs to Messrs. Fries, who will pay you eight ducats in cash. I shall have the pleasure to send you 15 or 20 airs more, as soon as I receive the two enclosed.

I have the honor, Monsieur, to be with great esteem, your friend and

Your very humble servant,

(signed) G. Thomson

[Thomson's annotation:]

The three airs sent[3] begin thus:

No. 1 Allegretto grazioso

No. 2 Andante amoroso con moto e con molto espressione

No. 3

Allegretto risoluto

1. Responding to the shipment represented in Beethoven's receipt to Fries, June 10, 1815 (MacArdle & Misch No. 158).

2. WoO 158/II, No. 6, "O Mary ye's be Clad in Silk."

3. Barry Cooper has identified these airs as, respectively, WoO 153, No. 13, "'Tis sunshine at last" (set for soprano and tenor, but Thomson suppressed the tenor);

WoO 157, No. 7, "Robin Adair" (set for soprano, tenor and bass as requested); and Op. 108, No. 11, "Oh! Thou art the lad of my heart," transposed (set for soprano).

Incipit: J'ai reçu les 15 Airs. . . .

Sources: Summarized in MacArdle, "Beethoven and Thomson," p. 42. Copy in Thomson's copybook, British Library, Add. MS 35267, pp. 155v–156r.

210. Beethoven to Prince Franz Joseph Lobkowitz's Chief Cashier[1]

Vienna; August 30, 1815

Receipt

for one thousand gulden (f[ull] w[eight]), 20 kreuzer (as three back payments)[2] from Prince Lobkowitz's Chief Cashier, duly received.

Vienna, August 30, 1815

Ludwig van Beethoven

[At an angle:] That is, 1,000 fl., f[ull] w[eight], 20 kr.

N.B. This payment concerns the years:

1814	825 f 20 k
1815 (1st quarter) . . .	175 f ——
Total	1,000 f 20 k

The above payment duly received.[3]

Ludwig van Beethoven

1. Along with Archduke Rudolph and Prince Ferdinand Kinsky, Lobkowitz had guaranteed Beethoven an annual stipend, beginning in 1809 (see the contract of March 1, 1809, No. 134 above).

2. Beethoven's terminology is confusing here, thus the more detailed figures in the *nota bene* below. Ultimately, Beethoven did receive all the payments, even though he often had to employ intermediaries and legal counsel to assist him in securing them. Gutiérrez-Denhoff, pp. 143–145, presents a list of all Beethoven's stipend receipts from Prince Lobkowitz and, after 1816, his estate.

Incipit: Quittung über Ein Tausend Gulden [v.w.] 20 x. . . .

Sources: Gutiérrez-Denhoff, " 'o Unseeliges Dekret': Beethovens Rente," pp. 136 (facsimile), 143. Autograph in the Státni oblastní v Litoměřcích, pobočka Žitenice. Plevka, "Vztah Beethoven," pp. 331–339, contains a substantial list of Beethoven's receipts for Lobkowitz's stipend.

211. Herberstein, Imperial Royal
Treasury Office, to Carl van Beethoven

Vienna; October 23, 1815

To the Imperial Royal Cashier of the Chief Treasury Office, Carl von [*sic*] Beethoven.

Neither from the most mediocre request for a leave of absence, dated March 8 of this year; nor the hitherto submitted certificate from Joseph Pelar, Chief Surgeon in the Allgemeines Krankenhaus [General Hospital]; nor from the review document handed down from the Lower Austrian Administration, is the cashier Carl von [*sic*] Beethoven to be seen as suffering from an incurable disease,[1] and consequently totally unfit for further service. Rather, one has much more sufficient reason to come to the last-named conclusion on the basis of his inappropriate employment, constantly interrupted for three years; on his specific and punishable disinclination for his duties; and on his customary negligence.

Out of goodwill for his past service, however, Cashier Carl von Beethoven will, without fail, be ordered on November 2 of this year to begin his cashier's position at the Chief Treasury Office; to work regularly and without interruption; and to perform with diligence and zeal the duties of that office, which, in the healthful and easy situation at the Chief Treasury Office, require only moderate exertion. If he fails to do so, one would be compelled to view this as an unseemly example to all the other treasury officials, and to treat it severely according to the existing regulations. It is the wish of the Treasury Service, however, that, for the benefit of the Treasury Service itself, he be transferred as quickly as possible to an easier Chancery staff position or a Commissioner's position. That this might be achieved, influence will be used with the Imperial Royal Court Treasury as well as with the Imperial

Royal United Redemption and Repayment Commission, and cashier Carl von Beethoven will hereafter be informed of their declaration, and in the event of a vacant position, will immediately present his wishes for a suitable staff position to the appropriate authority.[2]

Herberstein

1. Intermittently ill for over a decade, Carl van Beethoven died of consumption on November 15, 1815.

2. Beethoven was greatly angered by this letter to his brother and later wrote the following note on it: "This miserable bureaucratic product caused the death of my brother, since he really was so sick that he could not perform his duties without hastening his death.—A fine monument to these uncouth high officials. L. van Beeth."

Incipit: Weder aus dem mittelst Urlaubsgesuch. . . .

Sources: Ludwig Schiedermair, "Neue Schriftstücke zu Beethovens Vormundschaft . . . ," *Neues Beethoven-Jahrbuch* 8 (1938), 59–60, with considerable commentary. Autograph in the Beethoven-Haus, Bonn.

212. *Baron Joseph B. Pasqualati*[1] *(on Beethoven's Behalf) to Prince Rudolph Kinsky's Chief Cashier*

Prague; October 31, 1815

Receipt

for 600 fl[orins], i.e., six hundred gulden f[ull] w[eight], which, in power of attorney for Herr Ludwig Beethoven, I have duly received according to the I[mperial] R[oyal] Landrecht's decree, dated Prague, January 18, 1815, from the annual stipend of 1,200 fl[orins] granted by Prince Ferdinand Kinsky's estate:[2] maintenance stipend, as the semiannual legacy, from April 1 until the end of September, t[his] y[ear], and from Prince Rudolph Kinsky's Pupillary Chief Cashier in Prague, duly received today, and hereby certified.

Prague, October 31, 1815

[At an angle:]
That is, 600 fl[orins], 1815   Jos. B. Pasqualati
                                                as Power of Attorney

[He] is still alive.[3]
Vienna, November 11, 1815
E. S. [illegible], Dr. of Surgery
Ignaz Baumann, Building Superintendent
Ludwig van Beethoven

1. Joseph B. Pasqualati was the younger brother of Beethoven's friend and some-time landlord on the Mölkerbastei Johann Baptist Pasqualati. Beethoven had assigned to Joseph Pasqualati the power of attorney for the present purpose sometime after January 18, 1815 (see No. 197 above).

2. Prince Ferdinand had died on November 2, 1812, from a riding accident. This payment was part of the stipend agreed on on March 1, 1809 (contract in Thayer-Forbes, p. 457). Gutiérrez-Denhoff provides a history of Kinsky's payments and a list of receipts (pp. 140–143); MacArdle & Misch (pp. 72–73) provide an English-language summary history and list of receipts.

3. In the case of annuities, some reliable witness (often a priest) had to attest that the designated recipient was, in fact, still alive on the date of payment.

Incipit: Quittung über 600 fr., d.i. sechs hundert gulden v.w. . . . .

Sources: Gutiérrez-Denhoff, " 'o Unseeliges Dekret': Beethovens Rente," pp. 139 (facsimile), 141. Autograph in the Beethoven-Haus, Bonn.

213. Carl van Beethoven, Will and Codicil

Vienna; November 14, 1815

Certain that all men must die and feeling myself near this goal,[1] I am, however, in full possession of my faculties, and freely and voluntarily deem it good to make the following, my last dispositions.

1. I commend my soul to the mercy of God, but my body to the earth from which it came and desire that it be committed to the earth in the simplest manner in accordance with the rites of Christian Catholicism.

2. Immediately after my death, four holy Masses are to be said, for which I designate 4 gulden.

3. My universal heirs are commanded to pay the pious legacies according to law.

4. Since my wife, at our marriage, duly brought and paid me 2,000 florins in B. bonds, for which, however, I gave no receipt, I acknowledge receipt of

these 2,000 florins in B. bonds and thus desire that these 2,000 florins in B. bonds, as well as the deposit, be rectified in accordance with the existing marriage contract.

5. I appoint my brother Ludwig van Beethoven guardian.[2] Inasmuch as he, my deeply beloved brother, has often aided me with truly brotherly love in the most magnanimous and noblest manner, I expect, with full confidence and with full trust in his noble heart, that he shall bestow his love and friendship that he often showed me, also upon my son Karl, and do all that is possible to promote the intellectual training and further welfare of my son. I know that he will not deny me this, my request.

6. Since I am convinced of the uprightness of Dr. Schönauer, Court and Appellate Advocate, I appoint him Trustee for probate, as well as for my son Karl with the understanding that he be consulted in all matters concerning the property of my son.

7. Since the appointment of heirs is the essential matter in a will, I designate my beloved wife Johanna, née Reiss, and my son Karl as universal heirs to all my property after the deduction of my existing debts and the above bequests, and that my entire estate shall be divided between them in equal portions.

8. I must further note that the wagon,[3] horse, goat, peacocks and the plants growing in the vessels in the garden are the property of my wife, since these objects were all purchased with money from the legacy received from her grandfather.

In true witness whereof, I have not only signed this, the declaration of my last will with my own hand, but to aid in its execution have also expressly requested three witnesses.

Thus done, Vienna, November 14, 1815.

Carl van Beethoven,

m.p.

Carl Gaber, m.p.
  House owner, Breitenfeld, No. 9.
Benedikt Gaber, m.p.
  House owner, Breitenfeld No. 25
Johann Naumann, m.p.
  House No. 5, Breitenfeld

[Annotation:] "This will was delivered under seal to the I.R. Lower Austrian

Landrecht by the Karl Scheffer solicitor Dr. Schönauer on November 17, 1815," etc.

Codicil to My Will

Since I have observed that my brother, Herr Ludwig van Beethoven, desires after my eventual death to take wholly to himself my son Karl, and wholly to withdraw him from the supervision and training of his mother, and further, since the best of harmony does not exist between my brother and my wife, I have found it necessary to add to my will that I by no means desire that my son Karl be taken away from his mother, but that he shall always and as long as his future destiny permits remain with his mother, to which end she as well as my brother shall direct the guardianship over my son Karl. Only through harmony can the purpose that I had in appointing my brother guardian of my son be attained; therefore, for the welfare of my child, I recommend *compliance* to my wife and more *moderation* to my brother.

God permit the two of them to be harmonious for the welfare of my child. This is the last wish of the dying husband and brother.

Vienna, November 14, 1815.

Carl van Beethoven,

m.p.

We, the undersigned, certify in accordance with the truth that Herr Carl van Beethoven declared in our presence that he had read the statement on the opposite page[4] and that the same is in accordance with his will; finally we certify that he signed it with his own hand in our presence and requested us to witness it.

Thus done, November 14, 1815.

Carl Gaber, m.p.

Benedikt Gaber, m.p.

Johann Neumann, m.p.

[Annotation:] "This codicil was delivered under seal to the I.R. Lower Austrian Landrecht by the Karl Scheffer solicitor Dr. Schönauer on November 17, 1815," etc.

1. Beethoven's brother Carl died on November 15, 1815.

2. This sentence originally read: "Along with my wife I appoint my brother Ludwig van Beethoven co-guardian." The phrase "Along with my wife" and the "co-" were crossed out. A fragment written by the composer and preserved in the Beethoven-Haus, Bonn, explains the reason for the change: "I knew nothing about the fact that a testament had been made; however, I came upon it by chance. If what I had seen was really to be the *original text,* then passages had to be stricken out. This I had my brother bring about, since I did not want to be bound up with such a bad woman in the matter of such importance as the education of the child" (Thayer-Forbes, pp. 624–625, quoting Beethoven, *Entwurf einer Denkschrift,* ed. Dagmar Weise [Bonn: Beethoven-Haus, 1953], p. 13).

3. *Wagen,* either a wagon or a carriage.

4. The witnesses' attestation was obviously on the page opposite the codicil proper. The discrepancy between Naumann and Neumann as the name of the third witness originated in Thayer (1879).

Incipit(s): (a) In der gewissheit. . . . (*b*) Da ich bemerkt habe. . . .

Sources: Thayer, III (1879), 355–357; Thayer-Deiters-Riemann, III, 517–519; Thayer-Krehbiel, II, 320–321; Thayer-Forbes, pp. 623–625. Clause 5 with clause 6 summarized in Schindler, 3d ed. (1860), pt. 1, p. 253, and Schindler-MacArdle, pp. 217–218. Copy in the Staatsbibliothek zu Berlin–Preussischer Kulturbesitz, Mus. ms. autogr. Beethoven 35, 16; listed in Bartlitz, p. 121.

214. City of Vienna to Beethoven

Vienna; November 16, 1815[1]

By the Magistrat of the I[mperial] R[oyal] Capital and Residence City of Vienna, Herr Ludwig van Beethoven—upon action of the Public Hospital's Management Commission, and in consideration that in the past years he not only made available the performance of his musical instrumental compositions free of charge for the benefit of the men, women and children in the St. Marx Hospital, but also, with unpretentious willingness, personally took over their leadership, and through this humanitarian endeavor procured for the Public Hospital's Poor Fund such rich proceeds that through it the poor men, women and children, humbled by old age and infirmity, could be provided comfort and alleviation of their destinies—will be granted tax free the *civil rights*[2] of this Capital and Residence City as proof of the acknowledgment of his merit and of the esteem for these good sentiments.

Stephan Edler von Wohlleben,
I[mperial] R[oyal] Lower Austrian
Administrative Councillor
and Mayor;
Jos[eph] Karl Gruber,
Magistrat Councillor;
Johann Hofstätter,
Secretary.

1. On the exterior: "To Herr Ludwig von [*sic*] Beethoven" and a note, signed by one Köstler, indicating that the letter had been sent on November 28, 1815.

2. *Bürgerrecht,* an honor conferring "freedom of the city," rather than actually designating the composer an "honorary citizen of the city of Vienna" (*Ehrenbürger der Stadt Wien*). See Breuning, *Memories of Beethoven,* pp. 79–80 and 134, n.133.

Incipit: Von dem Magistrate der. . . .

Sources: Thayer, III (1879), 362–363; Thayer-Deiters-Riemann, III, 524 (mention only in Thayer-Krehbiel, II, 325, and Thayer-Forbes, p. 628); Kastner (1910), pp. 371–372 (seemingly copied from Thayer-Deiters-Riemann); most recently (with corrections to Thayer-Deiters-Riemann's transcription and copious surrounding material) in Jäger-Sunstenau, "Beethoven als Bürger der Stadt Wien," pp. 140–141. Facsimile in Bory, p. 183. Autograph in the Archiv der Stadt Wien.

1816

215. *George Thomson to Beethoven*

Edinburgh; January 1, 1816

Monsieur Louis van Beethoven
Vienna

Monsieur Beethoven

I have received the three airs that you sent me last month,[1] of which I found the ritornellos and accompaniments to be very excellent. More so than previous times, you have set them in the simple and cantabile style that is so pleasing to the lovers of national music. At the same time, you never lack those original ideas that produce the great charm of the composition in all the fine arts, and that are always produced only by true genius.

I am sending you, enclosed, six more airs, and it will give me great pleasure to see you, in composing ritornellos and accompaniments, continue to write in the same simple and easy style.

I would very much like to obtain some samples of the vocal music of the various nations of Europe: from

Germany
Poland
Russia
The Tyrol
Venice, and
Spain,

that is to say, *two* or three airs from each of these countries. I am not speaking about the compositions of living cultivated authors, but about purely national melodies, stamped with the character of the music of each country, and which are cherished by the people, as are the Scottish and Irish airs that I have sent you. I would like these airs to be in a pleasing style, and regular enough to be united with the poetry.

In a city like Vienna, where there are musicians from all countries, I believe that you could find the airs of which I speak without trouble, or at least a portion of these airs. And if you are willing to do me this favor, and then compose for these airs ritornellos and accompaniments in a style appropriate to each one, you will give me great pleasure, and Messrs. Fries will pay you four ducats in gold for each one.[2]

But I ask you to observe that these airs would not be of any value to me unless the ritornellos and accompaniments were of your own composition. Perhaps you know some national airs different from those of which I have spoken, [and] that are beautiful. In this case, you will very much oblige me by sending me some of these airs, with ritornellos and accompaniments composed by you. I would like you to choose airs that do not have a great range for the voice, those that do not descend below C, and that do not climb above E, for example:

or perhaps

If you have the kindness to send me these national airs, I ask you to indicate, by two or three words under each song, what the style is, or the subject of the words to which it is set, and from which country it comes.

Be so kind as to dispatch two copies of them, of which one should be written in a *spacious* manner.

I have the honor, Monsieur, to be your friend and

Your very humble servant,

(signed) George Thomson

P.S. We are very impatient to see some new quartets, trios, etc., for violins, etc., of your composition.

1. Responding to the shipment represented in Beethoven's receipt to Fries, November 4, 1815 (MacArdle & Misch No. 162). The three airs were WoO 153, No. 13, WoO 157, No. 7, and Op. 108, No. 11 (see Thomson's letter of August 20, 1815, No. 209 above).

2. Barry Cooper has identified the six airs as Op. 108, Nos. 15, 16, 12, 8 and 14, and WoO 158/II, No. 16 (Cossack air).

3. The genesis of a set of eighteen songs: WoO 158/I, Nos. 2–6, 9–15, 18–21 and 23, and WoO 157, No. 12.

Incipit: J'ai recu les trois airs. . . .

Sources: Summarized in MacArdle, "Beethoven and Thomson," p. 42, and Hadden, *George Thomson,* p. 335. Copy in Thomson's copybook, British Library, Add. MS 35267, pp. 169r–170r.

216. The Imperial Royal Lower Austrian Landrecht to Beethoven

Vienna; January 9, 1816[1]

This notice and its supplements, concerning the reopened transactions of Karl v[an] Beethoven,[2] are executed by the Magistrat of this place, on the basis of the request on his behalf, the elucidated criminal acts,[3] the ensuing clarifications, and the decreed appointment of the petitioner to the exclusive guardianship of his nephew, the minor Karl v[an] Beethoven.

The decree will be drawn up, insofar as it concerns this exclusive appointment, which abolishes the decree of co-guardianship (ad n.e. 25 622), dated November 22, 1815.[4] The mother Johanna van Beethoven and the Estate Trustee Dr. Schönauer are to be informed of this.

From the I.R. Lower Austrian Landrecht

1. This decision is the result of Beethoven's petition to the Landrecht, December 20, 1815 (Anderson, III, 1362–1364). It was not sent until January 17, 1816. The original indicates the year as 1815, an understandable slip of the pen so early in the year.

2. It is not clear at this point whether the Landrecht means the settlement of Carl's will and codicil (see November 14/17, 1815, No. 213 above) or the welfare of Carl's son, Karl; Beethoven had referred to both in his petition.

3. Beethoven's petition had strongly alluded to Johanna van Beethoven's criminal background.

4. See Thayer-Forbes, pp. 634–635, for a summary of these events and documents.

Incipit: Diese Anzeige samt Beilagen. . . .

Sources: Schiedermair, "Neue Schriftstücke zu Beethovens Vormundschaft . . . ," *Neues Beethoven-Jahrbuch* 8 (1938), 64. Autograph presumably in the Beethoven-Haus, Bonn.

217. Beethoven to Nikolaus Zmeskall von Domanovecz

[Vienna; January 21, 1816][1]

What's going on, my dear Z, with this *white brook?*[2] Wherein many people who believe me *black* want me to be washed *white?* I do not understand it.—

If it is possible for me, I shall appear at your place today, and of course with my nephew, whose guardian I was appointed the day before yesterday in the full Council meeting at the Landrecht and shook the president's hand.[3]

I shall therefore now ask all my friends and foes to seek to create, in this, my dear nephew, something better than I myself.

Farewell from your
L. v. Beethoven

[Exterior;]
For Herr von Zmeskall

1. Zmeskall noted that he received this undated letter on January 21, 1816; presumably Beethoven wrote it the same day.

2. The wording here, "mit diesem weissen Bach," is a pun on the name of Salzburg physician and poet Alois Weissenbach, a mutual friend (see Weissenbach to Beethoven, November 15, 1819, No. 264 below). The "black" and "white" elements in this paragraph represent corresponding wordplay in the German original. Presumably Beethoven was commenting on some passages about him in Weissenbach's book, *Meine Reise zum Congress* (1816).

3. On the exterior of the copy of Beethoven's "vows for the performance of his duties," dated January 19, 1816, is written: "Today appeared Ludwig van Beethoven as the legally appointed guardian of his nephew Karl and vowed with solemn handgrasp before the assembled council to perform his duties" (Thayer-Forbes, p. 634).

Incipit: Was solls mein lieber Z mit diesem weissen Bach?

Sources: Stargardt, *Autographen aus allen Gebieten: Katalog 602* (Marburg, November 27–28, 1973), p. 157, item 157, with a facsimile of Beethoven's signature. Quoted briefly in Schmidt, "Addenda . . . Beethovenhandschriften," pp. 219–220; Helms and Staehelin, "Bewegungen . . . 1973–1979," p. 348. Autograph in the Beethoven-Haus, Bonn, NE 93, since 1973. Full transcription kindly supplied by Sieghard Brandenburg.

218. *Beethoven to Charles Neate*[1]

[Vienna; probably late January or early February 1816][2]

I shall come to you tomorrow morning. I have much to do on behalf of my poor nephew, but by today everything will almost be taken care of. Good health, my dear friend.

Your,

Beethoven

[Exterior:]
    For Mr. Neate[3]

1. Charles Neate (1784–1877), British pianist, violoncellist and composer, who came to Vienna in May 1815 and remained until ca. February 7, 1816. He became one of Beethoven's strongest champions in England and corresponded with the composer off and on for the next decade.

2. The tone of this French-language note is similar to other undated items that Beethoven presumably sent Neate in January and early February 1816 (Anderson Nos. 599, 606 and 606a). Beethoven's reference here to his "poor nephew" finds echo in his letter to Antonie Brentano, February 6, 1816 (Anderson No. 607), sent with the departing Neate, which refers to Karl as "a poor, unhappy child."

As seen in the Landrecht's decree of January 9, 1816 (No. 216 above), Beethoven was awarded sole guardianship on that date, although the decree was not sent until January 16. The activities on Karl's behalf to which Beethoven alludes could be any number of details concerning the guardianship and, especially, getting the youngster situated in a school during this period, up to Neate's departure from Vienna on ca. February 7.

3. Beethoven spells his name "Niete."

Incipit: Je viendrai chez vous demain. . . .

Sources: Transcribed and edited by Rudolf Elvers in Staehelin, "Unbekannte . . . Schriftstücke," pp. 49–50. Autograph in the Staatsbibliothek zu Berlin–Preussischer Kulturbesitz, Musikabteilung N. Mus. ep. 907.

219. Ferdinand Ries to Robert Birchall, London[1]

38 Foley Place, London; Thursday, [February 7, 1816][2]

Mr. Ries's compliments[3] to Mr. Birchall—and [he] has just received a letter from his friend Beethoven, dated the 20th of January,[4] in which he mentions that the Symphony in A[5] must not come out before the month of June, as the music-seller in Vienna cannot have it printed before. The Sonata with Violin[6] as well as the Trio[7] are to arrive with the next post. The Sonata is to appear in the month of May; Beethoven himself will fix the time for the Trio.[8]

1. Robert Birchall (ca. 1760–1819), prominent British publisher and music dealer. For roughly two years Birchall's health had prevented him from participating fully in business affairs, and he often worked through his associate (and ultimate successor) Christopher Lonsdale (see Lonsdale's letter of November 8, 1816, No. 235 below). Beethoven, likewise, was represented in London by his friend and former pupil Ferdinand Ries.

2. Chrysander notes that the postmark reads "7 o'clock, Feb. 8 1816"; since February 8 was a Friday, Thursday (as written by Ries) was February 7.

3. Without changing the essence of the text, I have filled in abbreviations ("Compt^s" here) and corrected minor errors or oddities in spelling, capitalization, punctuation etc. Those wishing to cite the text in its original quaintness (Ries, of course, was not a native English speaker or writer) need only consult Chrysander. Much the same editorial policy has been followed in the letters penned by Lonsdale on behalf of Birchall during this period.

4. Beethoven's letter of January 20, 1816 (Anderson No. 596).

5. Symphony No. 7, Op. 92, published by Steiner in Vienna. The version sent to Birchall was a piano arrangement.

6. Violin Sonata, Op. 96.

7. Piano Trio, Op. 97 (*Archduke*).

8. On the sheet is also an annotation in Lonsdale's hand:

Beethoven's Battle Symphony printed in London Jan. 15, 1816, in Vienna, April 1816.

Sonata Op. 96	Oct. 3, 1816,	Jan. 1817.
Trio Op. 97	Dec. 5, 1816,	Jan. 1817.
Symphony in A Op. 98 [*sic*]	Jan. 6, 1817,	Dec. 1818.

Beethoven himself seems to have supplied this erroneous opus number to Birchall; see his letter to Birchall, October 1, 1816 (Anderson No. 662). Lonsdale's information about the Viennese publication dates erred by as much as thirteen months. Compare it with information given under the respective entries in Kinsky-Halm.

Incipit: Mr. Ries Compt⁵ to Mr. Birchall. . . .

Sources: Chrysander, "Beethoven's Verbindung," p. 431; Hill, *Ries: Briefe,* p. 99. In 1863, the autograph was in the possession of Robert Lonsdale, London.

220. Cajetan Giannatasio del Rio[1] to Beethoven

[Vienna; February 11, 1816][2]

Dear Sir!

At the interview of the mother and your charming nephew today, I have to insist that you, as guardian, show me formal authority in[3] a few lines, by which power I can, without further ado, refuse to allow her to take the son with her. If it is demonstrated that the child will be ruined in her company, this could, indeed, effect a very severe privation for a loving mother; nevertheless, this is most necessary for the good education of the child and for the undisturbed order of my institution. It also will not do for her to visit the child too much, for he always mourns her departure and, for that reason, will be disturbed in his present new path of life. Such tensions also generally place an educator in a difficult position. But out of great esteem for you, and in full sympathy for your truly fatherly love of the little fellow, [I] undertook the very difficult task of educating him under such circumstances. I therefore request you once again for power from the mediation of a legal authority, by which I can forcefully offer resistance to the presumptions of the mother, and protect myself against cases of conflict, failing which, her access [to the child] may be predicted.

I have the honor, with all esteem, to be

Your most devoted servant and friend,

Giannatasio del Rio

1. Giannatasio del Rio (1764–1828) had owned a boarding school in Vienna by 1798. After preliminary interviews, Beethoven placed nephew Karl in the school on

February 2, 1816, hoping to keep the youngster away from the allegedly evil influences of Johanna van Beethoven.

2. The date is supplied in various editions of Thayer (see the source note to this letter).

3. Thayer transcribes this word as "in"; Jäger-Sunstenau reads it as "und" (and). *Incipit:* Auf der heutigen Entrevue. . . .

Sources: Hanns Jäger-Sunstenau, "Beethoven-Akten im Wiener Landesarchiv," in *Beethoven-Studien: Festgabe der Österreichischen Akademie der Wissenschaften, zum 200. Geburtstag von Ludwig van Beethoven,* ed. Erich Schenk (Vienna: Hermann Böhlaus Nachf[olger], 1970), 15. The document is quoted briefly in Thayer-Deiters-Riemann, III, 540; Thayer-Krehbiel, II, 332; Thayer-Forbes, p. 635. Autograph in the Landesarchiv, Vienna, H.-A.-Akten Persönlichk. 2/2 fol. 12.

221. Ferdinand Ries to Beethoven

London; March 19, 1816[1]

Monsieur L. van Beethoven

Pasqualati Haus, Mölkerbastei, Vienna

My dear Beethoven,

I received your last letter and went immediately to Birchall,[2] who at first wanted absolutely nothing to do with it, in that he had to pay a monstrous postal charge here—but I finally succeeded, and you will probably have received already the sum of 10 ducats transmitted to Messrs. Fries & Co. It gives me limitless pleasure to be able to carry out this matter according to your wishes. Write me to which Empress of Russia the arrangement of the Symphony is to be dedicated. There are two of them, the old widowed one and the wife of the present Czar.[3]

Should the Trio and the Sonata not be dedicated to someone? At least you should adorn a friend with immortality by the dedication, if it cannot otherwise be used on your behalf.[4]

When shall these pieces appear? Neate[5] has been here for 14 days, and we have received your Overtures,[6] one of which will be performed on the next Concert.[7] I was extraordinarily curious to see the score of the Symphony in A, and I cannot tell you what enjoyment it provided me. Through the contemptible actions of several members of our Philharmonic Society, we are in a somewhat disagreeable situation, and we have already considered how we will best arrange it, to receive these manuscripts, e.g. Symphony[8] and Cantata,[9] as [our] property, and to provide for you an ordinary *small English fee*—only it is not yet entirely agreed upon.[10] Five members of the Society have been chosen to arrange the matter, which, however, the Society must approve before it can be carried out. Neate is one of them; I am, too, and so are two good acquaintances of mine. And I hope that we succeed in persuading the whole Society to give a public concert on which nothing but your new and older compositions will be performed. It would create an extraordinary sensation here, since all the finest artists belong to it [i.e., the society], and it would thus be our rightful tribute, that we all with joyous hearts offer to our Beethoven (I need not say more). The profit should be brought to a round sum and, I hope, be presented to you as a small indication of our gratitude for the many happy moments that you, through your divine moods, have so often provided us. *But this must still remain between us.*

My wife is terribly proud to have received your greeting and returns it sincerely. She knows how much you did for me, and thanks you sincerely for it.[11] Send me as a remembrance a new portrait of you,[12] *but write a few words under it,* and give me an opportunity to prove my love and gratitude. From the heart of

Your

Ferd. Ries

1. Answers Beethoven's letter of January 20, 1816 (Anderson No. 596), which arrived in London on February 7, and possibly his letters of February 10 and 28 (Anderson Nos. 609 and 615). Beethoven replied on May 8, 1816 (Anderson No. 632). As can be seen, Ries sent this letter to Beethoven's old Mölkerbastei address; Lonsdale/Birchall must have used this address as well since Beethoven corrected him, giving the current Seilerstätte address, on October 1, 1816 (Anderson No. 662).

2. See Ries's letter to Birchall, February 7, 1816 (No. 219 above).

3. In his letter of May 8, 1816 (Anderson No. 632), Beethoven delayed telling Ries the identity of the dedicatee, but he did tell Birchall on October 1 (Anderson No. 662): Elisabeth Alexieva, the wife of Czar Alexander (see also Kinsky-Halm, p. 260).

4. Evidently the Trio, Op. 97, and the Violin Sonata, Op. 96, received no further dedications beyond those to Archduke Rudolph. According to Birchall's note, Op. 96 was published in London on October 30, 1816, and Op. 97 on December 5. (See

the letter of February 7, 1816.) Ries may have been hinting that Beethoven dedicate one of these items to him; Beethoven must have thought so and teased Ries about it in his May 8 letter.

5. Charles Neate (1784–1877), London pianist, violoncellist and composer, spent from May 1815 to ca. February 7, 1816, in Vienna.

6. The overtures to *The Ruins of Athens*, Op. 113, and *King Stephan*, Op. 117, and the *Namensfeier* Overture, Op. 115.

7. It remains uncertain which of these works was performed by the Philharmonic Society. In any case, the British were unhappy with the quality of the overtures.

8. Symphony No. 7 in A.

9. Other references to a cantata may be found in Beethoven's letters to Neate, May 18, 1816 (Anderson No. 636), and to Sir George Smart, ca. October 11, 1816 (Anderson No. 664). The composer's description in the latter indicates that he meant *Der glorreiche Augenblick*, Op. 136.

10. For more details on this debate, see Neate's letter to Beethoven, October 29, 1816 (No. 234 below).

11. Harriet Mangeon, an Englishwoman whom Ries had married in 1814.

12. Ries doubtless wanted a copy of the 1814 engraving by Blasius Höfel (after Louis Letronne); Beethoven had probably given Neate a copy on his departure from Vienna in early February.

Incipit: Ich erhielt Ihren letzten Brief. . . .

Sources: Ida Marie Lipsius (La Mara), *Musikerbriefe aus fünf Jahrhunderten, nach den Urhandschriften . . . ,* 2 vols. (Leipzig: Breitkopf & Härtel, 1886), II, 73–75; Hill, *Ries-Briefe,* pp. 102–103. Offered for sale in International Autographs, *Autograph Letters, Manuscripts and Documents,* [Catalog] no. 18 (New York, 1967), item 6, p. 4.

222. Beethoven to Fries and Co.

[Vienna; possibly late March or April 1816][1]

[Front of card:]
Are there no letters here from Thomson in Scotland?

[Reverse of card:]
Beethoven
Seilerstätte 1055 & 1056
Third floor[2]

1. The banking firm of Fries & Co. handled Beethoven's correspondence with and payments from the amateur folk song collector and publisher George Thomson

in Edinburgh. This note is on a small card, with the inquiry on one side and Beethoven's address on the other. Staehelin believes that the completeness of the address indicates that Beethoven may have moved there only recently and wanted to avoid confusion. Staehelin followed Kurt Smolle's speculation (*Wohnstätten,* pp. 50–51) that Beethoven moved to the Seilerstätte address shortly after March 21, 1815 (and essentially lived there until April 24, 1817), and places this card sometime between March 21 and late April 1815, written in anticipation of the arrival of Thomson's letter of March 20 (No. 201 above).

Rudolf Klein (*Beethovenstätten,* pp. 89–91), however, believes that Beethoven did not move to Seilerstätte until the fall of 1815, which would contradict Staehelin's dating. Beethoven surely did not wait impatiently for new commissions or corrections from Thomson; he probably *did* keep a watch for payments from the Scottish publisher, however, and one such payment was made to him on May 2, 1816 (MacArdle & Misch No. 182).

2. American fourth floor.

Incipit: Ob keine Briefe aus Schottland. . . .

Sources: Transcribed and edited by Martin Stahelin in Staehelin, "Unbekannte . . . Schriftstücke," pp. 42–44, with extensive commentary. Autograph in the Herzog August Bibliothek, Wolfenbüttel, Briefsammlung Vieweg No. 77.

223. Beethoven to Anton Pachler[1]

Vienna; April 22, 1816

My dear P.

You can do me a great kindness *today* if you will accompany me this *afternoon* to the Alstergasse, where the estimate of the house's value will be determined.[2] Thus, kindly let me know *in writing, where* I can get ahold of you around 3 o'clock this afternoon. I am still not very well, otherwise I would have come to see you long ago. In haste,

Your Friend,

Beethoven

[Exterior:]
For Herr Pachler

1. The jurist Dr. Anton Pachler was the brother of Graz attorney Dr. Carl Pachler, who would marry the amateur pianist Marie Leopoldine Koschak on May 12, 1816.

2. The evaluation (for estate purposes) of brother Carl's house, Alstervorstadt No. 121, next to the Hernalserlinie. Beethoven therefore wished to have an experienced legal/business representative at hand when the assessment was being made. The house was valued at 16,400 florins. For the physical description of the building, which seemingly accompanied the assessment, see the inventory, late April 1816 (No. 224 below), n.3.

Incipit: Sie können mir *heute.* . . .

Sources: Transcribed and edited by Robert Münster in Staehelin, "Unbekannte . . . Schriftstücke," pp. 50–54, with facsimile and extensive commentary. Autograph in an unspecified private collection in 1983.

224. *Inventory of Carl van Beethoven's Estate*[1]

[Vienna; probably late April 1816][2]

Inventory
Taken of the Estate of the Late
C. v. Beethoven

[Assets]

Cash . . . . none
Outstanding payments . . . . none
Capital . . . . none
Real Estate: The building [*Haus*], which
        according to the Inventory-Estimate[3]
        is valued at 16,400 florins; therefore,
        to each of the two universal heirs,
        Johanna and Karl v. B., falls a share
        at 8,200 florins.
Precious items, a silver clock . . . . 25 florins
Clothing and linens . . . . 100 florins
Books . . . . <u>70 florins</u>
                                       195 florins
        The aforementioned effects are, according to
        the Marriage Letter, property of the wife.

[Liabilities]
Employment Security of the Deceased . . . . 2,200 florins
   in 2½% bonds.
Liabilities on the building:
   Heissmann for . . . . 5,000 florins
   Outstanding interest . . . . 107 florins, 38 kreuzer
[etc.][4]

According to the evidence provided by the widow, there are shown:
   Liabilities of . . . . 8,534 florins
   Exceeding the assets of . . . . 8,395 florins
Therefore the dowry of the widow is to be entered in response *without credit.*

   1. Thayer calls this an extract from the inventory, communicated to him by Dr. August Schmidt.

   2. Beethoven's brother Carl died on November 15, 1815 (see his will and codicil of November 14/17, 1815, No. 213 above). While some sort of inventory may have been made shortly thereafter, the present document seems not to have originated until at least April 22, 1816, when the inventory-estimate was made (see n.3, this letter, and Beethoven's letter to Anton Pachler of April 22, 1816, No. 223 above).

   3. The inventory-estimate of "the house belonging to Carl v. Beethoven, No. 121 in the Alservorstadt, next to the Hernalserlinie" describes the building in this manner:

> A small walled and vaulted cellar; a garden of average size, with various fruit trees, and a small greenhouse; an average courtyard; two apartments on the ground floor, backwards facing the Adlergasse, consisting of two kitchens and two rooms; the other apartments in the front of the building facing the Adlergasse [Hauptstrasse?], consisting of nine rooms, four chambers, seven kitchens. There are three staircases to the first floor [American second floor] — two of wood, and one of stone.
>
> On the first floor, a hallway, five rooms, five chambers, three kitchens, one stone stairway to the attic, and 2 attic rooms.

Thayer comments: "It was thus one of those humble, but spacious houses, which were earlier so common in the Viennese suburbs, which could be divided into the greatest number of apartments possible (in this case twelve), to earn income from the rent." Thayer also provides considerable discussion about the building's location and so forth. Both editions of Thayer give the date of the inventory-estimate as April 22, *1815,* possibly a typographical error: Beethoven's letter to Pachler (April 22, 1816, No. 223 above) indicates that the report was to be prepared on that afternoon;

moreover, it seems improbable that Carl's property would have been evaluated for estate purposes *prior* to his death on November 15, 1815.

4. The copy, as printed in Thayer, does not detail the other roughly 1,225 florins in liabilities.

Incipit: Inventar, aufgenommen über die Hinterlassenschaft. . . .

Sources: Thayer, III (1879), 506–507; Thayer-Deiters-Riemann, III, 633–634.

225. Franz Xaver Embel[1] to Beethoven

[Vienna; probably Spring (before June 3) 1816][2]

The Civil Artillery Corps[3] of the I[mperial] R[oyal] Capital and Residence City of Vienna requests the honor of possessing a march for Turkish music[4] from the pen of Herr Louis van Beethoven. This cannon[5] introduces the Artillery Corps and truly the petitioner, who shall give this request to the proper authority.[6]

Franz Xaver Embel
Magistrat Councillor and
Municipal High Treasurer
Lieutenant Colonel of the
Civil Artillery

1. In 1815, Embel was municipal high treasurer (*Stadtoberkämmerer*) in the Political-Economic Senate and lived in the Rabengasse No. 519.

2. Schindler's note on this letter says that it originated in "1815 or 1816." Since the march mentioned is probably WoO 24, whose autograph is dated June 3, 1816, this letter predates that time. According to Johnson-Tyson-Winter, sketches that "do not come very close to the final version" appear on pp. 108–112 of the Scheide Sketchbook. An examination of the pattern of the projects sketched here after the Canons, WoO 168, dated January 24, 1816 (on p. 55), leads to the conjecture that this letter probably dates from March or April 1816, if Beethoven did not tarry long in fulfilling the request.

3. A civilian militia, rather than a professional army unit.

4. *Marsch zur grossen Wachtparade,* No. 4, in D, WoO 24, Beethoven's most extensive military march in form, harmonic boldness and instrumentation. In his letter to publisher C. F. Peters on March 20, 1823 (Anderson No. 1158), Beethoven did allow that several regimental bands might combine their forces for the performance of this "grand march."

5. An illustration of a cannon, the corps' logo, occupied most of the sheet on which this letter was written (see illustrations).

6. Beethoven's swift reply to this request may have been an effort to promote political favor during his battle for the custody of his nephew Karl.

Incipit: Das bürgerliche Artillerie Corps. . . .

Sources: Thayer-Deiters-Riemann, IV, 475–476; Nohl, *Beethoven's Leben*, III, 831; Nottebohm, *Zweite Beethoveniana*, p. 347. An important source is Georg Schüne-mann, "Beethovens 'Kanone,'" *Die Musik* 32, pt. 2 (August 1940), 377 and the plate opposite (facsimile). Sketches discussed in Johnson-Tyson-Winter, pp. 244–245. Autograph in the Staatsbibliothek zu Berlin–Preussischer Kulturbesitz, Mus. ms. autogr. Beethoven 35, 86; listed in Kalischer, "Beethoven-Autographe," p. 57, and Bartlitz, p. 149.

226. George Thomson to Beethoven

Edinburgh; July 8, 1816

Monsieur Louis van Beethoven

My dear Monsieur,

I have received your last package, containing the 6 airs that I had sent you, and 18 of various nations chosen by you yourself, with which I am very content.[1] I find your ritornellos and accompaniments entirely charming; there are some that one may never admire enough. I would like very much to be able to impress upon our public their great beauty, but alas, it will take time for this. If you will be in England for one or two seasons, occupied by performing your superb pieces in public, the people would doubtless soon lose their taste for the confusion of poor and contemptible music with which they are now infatuated, and come to love that which is truly original and beautiful.

In order to finish the volume with which I am occupied at the moment, I still need some foreign airs for the voice. Would you be willing to be so kind as to procure for me some samples of the airs mentioned below,[2] of a pleasing and gracious character, and add to them ritornellos and accompaniments, as before:

> 1 Swedish air
> 1 Danish air

1 Sicilian air

1 Calabrian air

If it is possible for you to procure these for me, you would give me great pleasure; but if you cannot find Danish or Calabrian airs, send me, in their place, another Sicilian air and a Tyrolean air. I am delighted with the airs from the Tyrol that you have sent me; they are absolutely full of character and beauty. Tell me, I beg of you, are there more just as fine?

I ask you, also, to compose ritornellos and accompaniments for the seven airs enclosed,[3] and to add two parts for the voice to those portions of the airs that are marked "Coro per tre voci."

I beg you to make all the ritornellos and accompaniments simple and easy to play, for otherwise it will be in vain for me to publish them.

When you deliver the eleven[4] airs to Messrs. Fries, and show them this letter, they will pay you forty-four ducats in cash; and they will be so kind as to draw upon me for the amount, as usual.

One copy in score will be enough for me, with a separate copy of the accompaniments of the violin and of the violoncello; but please tell your copyist that the lines must not be crowded in so little space.

I have arranged for you to be sent a copy of my second volume, which has just been printed,[5] and I would like to know that you have received it.

If you have not already harmonized the air that I sent you alone last time,[6] do not set it at all.

I have the honor to be, etc.

(signed) G. Thomson

1. Responds to the shipment represented in Beethoven's receipt to Fries, May 2, 1816 (MacArdle & Misch No. 182). All but one of the eighteen and one of the six are in WoO 158/I (see January 1, 1816, No. 215 above).

2. Barry Cooper has identified the four Continental songs that Beethoven sent as WoO 158/I, Nos. 17 (Swedish), 7 (Tyrolean), 22 (Hungarian) and 8 (Tyrolean).

3. Barry Cooper has identified the seven airs enclosed as WoO 158/III, No. 1; WoO 156, No. 5; Op. 108, No. 25 (the foregoing from *The Beggar's Opera*); WoO 158/III, No. 2 (from Rousseau's *Le devin du village*); Hess 168; WoO 157, No. 1; and Op. 108, No. 22.

4. The number in the copybook reads "Dix" (ten); possibly Thomson miscounted.

5. *A Select Collection of Original Irish Airs . . .* , vol. [2], including items in WoO 153, 154 and 157. The preface is dated May 1816.

6. Thomson's letter of January 1, 1816, does not indicate any single air as having been sent separately from the six enclosed with it.

Incipit: J'ai reçu votre dernier paquet. . . .

Sources: Summarized in MacArdle, "Beethoven and Thomson," p. 43, and Hadden, *George Thomson,* pp. 336–337. Copy in Thomson's copybook, British Library, Add. MS 35267, pp. 172v–173v.

227. *Archduke Rudolph to Beethoven*

Baden; July 16, 1816[1]

Dear Beethoven,

I thank you for the Sonata that you sent me, and accept your dedication with much pleasure.[2] I am doing my utmost to practice it, in order to reflect the art of the composer (to whom the publisher, through the truly beautiful printing, [also] pays his deserved tribute) as well as that of the player.[3]

Just strive to restore your health, so I may soon play it in your presence, and upon that occasion tell you again how much I am

Your most devoted,

Rudolph, Archduke

1. Answering Beethoven's letter of July 11, 1816 (Anderson No. 640).

2. The Violin Sonata, Op. 96, dedicated to Rudolph, had just been published by Steiner in July.

3. Rudolph was an accomplished pianist. The violin part had been written for the famous French violinist Pierre Rode, with whom Rudolph first performed it on December 29, 1812, at the residence of Prince Lobkowitz. (See also Rudolph's letter to Beethoven, January 5, 1813, No. 168 above.)

Incipit: Ich danke Ihnen für die mir. . . .

Sources: Thayer, III (1879), 395; Thayer-Deiters-Riemann, III, 560, taken from a copy made by Otto Jahn.

228. Beethoven to Dr. Carl von Bursy[1]

[Vienna; July 24, 1816][2]

Although I know from everyone that you complain about me and impute that I have not received you well, I am still prepared—since you appear to place value in such things—to inscribe something for you in your *Stammbuch*.[3]

Yours truly,

L. van Beethoven

[Exterior:]
To Herr C. Bursy

1. Born in 1791, Bursy was a medical doctor and later, like Beethoven's friend Alois Weissenbach, became a surgeon in Salzburg. Like another of Beethoven's friends, Carl Amenda (see March 20, 1815, No. 200 above), Bursy was a Courlander, and he came bearing an introduction from Amenda, then living in Talsen. Bursy first visited Beethoven on June 1, 1816, and his visits can be documented at least through July 29 of that year. His diary entries, June 1–July 27, are published in Kerst, *Erinnerungen*, I, 197–204, with an abbreviated version of the June 1 entry in Thayer-Forbes, pp. 644–645.

2. Fishman describes this item as an "entry in an *Album* of C. v. Bursy," a single sheet 12 x 19 cm. The autograph note itself is undated; the dating here follows Fishman.

3. This clause implies that Bursy must have handed Beethoven a *Stammbuch* (autograph book); thus the present note must have been written in addition to that entry. Moreover, Beethoven also inscribed Bursy's copy of *Fidelio* with a slightly altered excerpt from Leonore's aria (Kerst, *Erinnerungen*, I, 203):

"Komm' Hoffnung, lass den letzten Stern des Müden nicht erbleichen,
O komm,' erhell' sein Ziel, sei's noch so fern!
           Ludwig van Beethoven
           July 29, 1816"

Incipit: Obschon ich von alle dem. . . .

Sources: Fishman's "Obschii . . . avtografov Beethovena," p. 137, and his "Verzeichnis . . . Beethoven-Autographe," p. 134. Autograph in the Latvian State Archive of History (Latvijas Valsts Vēstures Archīvs), Riga (F.5759, op. 2, delo 415, 1. 103a).

229. Christopher Lonsdale[1] (for Robert Birchall) to Beethoven

[London;] August 14, 1816[2]

Sir,

Mr. Birchall received yours of the 22nd of last month and was surprised to hear [that] you have not yet received the additional £5.0.0. to defray your expenses of copying, etc. He assures you [that] the above sum was paid to Messrs. Coutts & Co. [on] March 15th last, to be transmitted to Messrs. Fries & Co. of Vienna for you, which he supposed you would receive as safe as the previous sum. In consequence of your last letter, inquiry has again been made at Messrs. Coutts & Co. respecting it, and they have referred to their books and find that Messrs. Fries & Co. were written to on the 13th of May, and in that letter the following extract concerning you was contained:

"London, May 13, 1816.

To Messrs. Fries & Co. — We have received from Mr. Birchall a further sum of Five Pounds on your account, for the use of Mr. Beethoven; you will therefore please account to that gentleman for the same, and include the amount in your next bill upon us. — Coutts & Co."

If Mr. Beethoven will call on Messrs. Fries & Co. and get them to refer to that letter, no doubt it will immediately be paid, as there is a balance in their favor at Messrs. Coutts & Co. of £5.0.0., which was not included in their last bill on London.

Mr. Birchall is sorry [that] you have not received it as soon as you ought, but he hopes you will be convinced [that] the fault does not lie[3] with him, as the money was paid to the bankers [on] the day after Mr. Ries spoke about it.[4]

Mr. Birchall wishes particularly to have the Declaration returned to him as soon as possible, and likewise wishes you to favor him with the dedications and operas [i.e., opus numbers] which are to be put to the Trio, the Sonata and the Grand Symphony in A.[5] The publication of the Sonata has been delayed a long time in consequence of that, but he hopes [that] you will not delay forwarding *all upon receipt of this*. When you write again, Mr. Birchall will be glad to know your sentiments respecting writing Variations to the most favorite English, Scotch or Irish Airs, for the pianoforte with an accompaniment either for the violin or violoncello,[6] as you find best—about the same length as Mozart's airs "La dove prende" and "Colomba o tortorella," and Handel's "See the conquering Hero comes" with your Variations.[7] Be so good, when you oblige him with your terms, etc., to say whether the Airs need [to] be sent [to] you; if you have many, perhaps mentioning the names will be sufficient. In fixing the price, Mr. Birchall wishes you to mention a sum that will include copying and postage.

For R. Birchall,

C. Lonsdale

1. Lonsdale (1795?–1877) seems to have been publisher Robert Birchall's agent at this time, but he became a partner in the firm on Birchall's death in 1819 (see articles under "Birchall" in *Grove 5* and *New Grove*).

2. Answers Beethoven's letter of July 22, 1816 (Anderson No. 643); answered by his letter of October 1, 1816 (Anderson No. 662).

3. The original reads "lay."

4. Beethoven's friend and former pupil Ferdinand Ries, who partially served as intermediary between Beethoven and Birchall. See Beethoven's letters to Ries, May 8 and June 11, 1816 (Anderson Nos. 632 and 639). On August 3, 1816, Beethoven signed a receipt acknowledging that he had received £5 from the Viennese banking firm of Fries as payment from the London firm of Thomas Coutts, who was forwarding the payment for Robert Birchall (Ira Brilliant, "Beethoven Auction Report," *Beethoven Newsletter* [San Jose] 9, nos. 2–3 [Summer-Winter 1994], 145–146).

5. Piano Trio, Op. 97; Violin Sonata, Op. 96; and a piano arrangement of the Symphony No. 7, Op. 92 (which Beethoven mistakenly identified as Op. 98 in his October 1, 1816, letter).

6. Beethoven replied to this point in his October 1 letter. Lonsdale and Birchall may have been aware that Beethoven was engaged in similar activities for George Thomson in Edinburgh.

7. Beethoven's Variations (for piano and violoncello) on "Bei Männern, welche Liebe fühlen" (WoO 46) and "Ein Mädchen oder Weibchen" (Op. 66) from Mozart's *Zauberflöte* and on the properly identified chorus from Handel's *Judas Maccabaeus* (WoO 45), respectively.

Incipit: Mr. Birchall received yours of the 22nd. . . .

Sources: The original English version in Chrysander, "Beethoven's Verbindung . . . ," pp. 432–433. German translation in Thayer, III (1879), 405–406, and Thayer-Deiters-Riemann, III, 569–570; possibly from the copy in the Staatsbibliothek zu Berlin–Preussischer Kulturbesitz, Mus. ms. autogr. Beethoven 38, 8; listed in Bartlitz, p. 192. The letter was restored to English in Thayer-Krehbiel, II, 345–346, and Thayer-Forbes, pp. 649–650. In 1863, the original (or, more probably, a copybook copy) was in the possession of Robert Lonsdale, London.

230. Anton Diabelli[1] to Beethoven, Baden

Vienna; August 22, 1816

Herr v[an] Beethoven,

In my opinion, Hoffmeister's conditions are absolutely not acceptable.[2] I think that you should stick to the demands that you have already made, namely, *3,000 florins C.M.* for the public authorization to issue your piano works and to edit them at the same time; and an average of 40 ducats apiece for the new sonatas, of which there will be one for each volume. The payment is to take place in the following manner: the publisher shall pay 2,000 florins C.M. immediately after the receipt of your authorization for the edition, [and] the remaining 1,000 florins upon the delivery of the last volume of the piano works. Concerning the additional fee for the new sonatas, the 40 ducats are to be paid each time after the receipt of a new sonata.

Furthermore, you should be free to deliver the volumes one after another; even if they were not engraved immediately, at least your part of the transaction would be finished within a few months. Thus, in a short time you would have a tidy little sum at hand and then could begin to compose greater works unhindered, frankly without having to delay because of money. Then, with new works you could also begin entirely new ventures that perhaps would give you security for the future and protect you from cares. Nothing at all is gained by payment according to a certain number of ducats per page, and I absolutely advise you against it. According to his reckoning, the publisher will surely bring in 4,000 florins, although perhaps after ten or more years.

If you lend a hand to such an undertaking (which can only be done once, for all time), then [either] you have to get something fabulous out of it, or the works can remain in their old editions for now. What do you care whether the publisher sells 500 copies or even more, and why should your payment depend upon the purchase of copies?

I hope very confidently that the publisher will agree to your demands, if you will let them be known to him as your final and specific wishes. Consider now which way seems the best and most advantageous to you; I believe, at least, that it could result in a very good business deal.

Your most obliging,

Diabelli

[P.S.] I hope to be able to send you an answer from your nephew tomorrow.[3]

1. Born near Salzburg, Diabelli (1781–1858) came to Vienna in 1803 as a young composer and later entered the firm of publisher S. A. Steiner as a proofreader and editor. In 1818, Diabelli went into the publishing business for himself, in partnership with Pietro Cappi. In humorous correspondence, Beethoven often referred to him as "Diabolus" or "Provost Marshal." As Sieghard Brandenburg, Beethoven-Archiv, Bonn, notes, the family name was originally Demon or Damon, which Diabelli's father Italianized in 1778. Although often called Antonio in the English-language literature, Diabelli was baptized Anton.

2. The Leipzig publishing firm of Hoffmeister & Kühnel had been bought by Carl Friedrich Peters (1779–1827) in 1814.

3. Beethoven had been staying in Count Ossolinsky's house in Baden (with frequent trips into Vienna) since July 29. His nephew Karl was at that time in Cajetan Giannatasio del Rio's boarding school.

Incipit: Die Bedingungen des Hoffmeisters. . . .

Sources: Excerpts in Schindler (1860), pt. 2, pp. 38–39, and Schindler-MacArdle, p. 255. Autograph in the Staatsbibliothek zu Berlin–Preussischer Kulturbesitz, Mus. ms. autogr. Beethoven 35, 44a; listed in Kalischer, "Beethoven-Autographe," p. 49, and Bartlitz, p. 130.

231. *Beethoven to Artaria & Co.*[1]

Baden; September 10, 1816

Artaria & Company

I ask you to be so kind, in case letters come [addressed] to me, as to send them directly to me here, because confusion would arise otherwise; as soon as I come to the city, I shall let you know or visit you myself. I thank you for your troubles on my behalf up to now, and, as reluctant as I am [to be] troublesome to anyone, I cannot change it at this moment, and must take unfair advantage of your kindness.

Your most devoted servant,

L. v. Beethoven

1. Beethoven probably dealt with the firm, located in Vienna's Kohlmarkt, through Domenico Artaria (1775–1842).

Incipit: Ich bitte Sie, die Gefälligkeit zu haben. . . .

Sources: J. A. Stargardt, *Autographen aus drei alten Schweizer Sammlungen, Auktion [No.] 66/652* (Basel, September 19, 1992), item 430, p. 220 (facsimile, p. 221); summarized in Ira Brilliant, "Music Auction Report," *Beethoven Newsletter* (San Jose) 8, no. 1 (Spring 1993), 26.

232. *Peter Joseph Simrock*[1] *(for Nikolaus Simrock) to Beethoven*

Vienna; September 28, 1816[2]

The undersigned attests hereby that he has received from Herr Ludwig van Beethoven two Sonatas with Violoncello accompaniment[3] for the fee of 70 Dutch ducats, which Herr van Beethoven cedes to him for the whole Continent, with the stipulation that such shall not appear until Herr van Beethoven gives notice to do so, to which I hereby bind myself.

Pet. Jos. Simrock
for my father N. Simrock

Ludwig van Beethoven

1. Peter Joseph Simrock (1796–1870), second son of and later successor to the Bonn publisher Nikolaus Simrock, visited Vienna in September 1816 and took back with him Beethoven's letters of September 29 to Antonie Brentano (Anderson No. 660) and Franz Gerhard Wegeler (Anderson No. 661). Further background in Frimmel, *Beethoven-Handbuch,* II, 181.

2. On a simple quarto sheet, this document was in Simrock's hand but was also signed by Beethoven.

3. The Violoncello Sonatas, Op. 102, published by Simrock in Bonn and Cologne in March 1817 (in time for the Easter Fair). The Viennese edition of 1819 bore the dedication to Countess Marie Erdödy; the sonatas had been written in the summer of 1815 for the violoncellist Joseph Lincke, then in her employ.

Incipit: Unterzeichneter bescheinigt hierdurch. . . .

Sources: Schmidt, *Beethoven-Briefe,* app. 1, no. 2; Erich H. Müller, "Beethoven und Simrock," *Simrock-Jahrbuch* 2 (1929), 39. Autograph presumably in the Simrock archives, destroyed in World War II.

233. George Thomson to Beethoven

Edinburgh; October 20, 1816[1]

Monsieur Beethoven,

It is with a great deal of regret that I find myself obliged to tell you that, after having taken extreme trouble in trying to have English verses written for the 19 airs of various nations that you sent me, I have been forced to abandon my plan to make them into songs because the meter and the singular style of these airs do not agree with either the *form,* or the *character* of English poetry. It has therefore been in vain that our poets have attempted to unite them with verses.[2]

It is, therefore, a question of knowing what I ought to do with these airs and your beautiful accompaniments.

Since I find it impossible to make them into songs, I have conceived the idea that you would be able to revise them in the form of *potpourri overtures* for the piano, and that I could publish them successfully in this form. I would therefore like you to be so kind as to arrange the 19 Russian, Tyrolean, Venetian airs, etc., into six overtures—introducing the airs into each overture in the manner that seems best to you, and interspersing them with ideas or pieces of your own composition, according to the suggestions of your inimitable genius. Indeed, the more you place of yourself in these overtures, the more I shall be delighted by them. In the price list that you sent me last winter, you asked 12 ducats for a completely original overture. Now I hope that you will not ask more than half this price for arranging the national airs into overtures. Even at such a price, they will cost very dearly, because I have already paid you 76 ducats for the 19 airs. I therefore hope that you will consider 36 ducats to be a liberal fee for arranging them.

You can arrange them for piano alone, or, it might be desirable for you to keep the violin and violoncello accompaniments that you have already supplied.

It would perhaps have a nice effect if you gave each overture the character of a single nation, placing in it only the airs proper to that nation; that is to say, that you could make *a Spanish overture* containing all the Spanish airs. This really cannot be done in all cases, but you might be able to approximate it by classifying together the airs of the various nations that have the greatest affinity; for example, you might be able to place the Venetian and Portuguese airs in the same overture, the Russian and Polish airs in another, and the German and Swiss airs in a third. But it is for you to judge whether this idea is good.

Permit me also to suggest to you that each overture might begin with an introduction and end with a finale of your composition. The waltz is very popular in our country, and you might perhaps write some of those finales on themes in that style. But although I have taken the liberty of offering you these ideas, I ask you to follow them only as far as you approve of them.

When you consider the difficulty in which I find myself concerning these 19 airs and the loss that I have suffered, I hope that you will very willingly take a little trouble to render them useful to me. [Text in copybook ends here.]

1. Follows on Thomson's letter of July 8, 1816 (No. 226 above).

2. Barry Cooper has identified these as the eighteen items from WoO 158/I, and WoO 157, No. 12 (detailed in the notes to Thomson's letter of January 1, 1816, No. 215 above), as well as WoO 158/I, No. 16 (Cossack air).

Incipit: C'est avec beaucoup de chagrin. . . .

Sources: Summarized in MacArdle, "Beethoven and Thomson," p. 43, and Hadden, *George Thomson*, pp. 337–338. Copy in Thomson's copybook, British Library, Add. MS 35267, pp. 178r–179v.

234. *Charles Neate*[1] *to Beethoven*

London; October 29, 1816[2]

My dear Beethoven,

Nothing has ever given me more pain than your letter to Sir George Smart. I confess that I deserve your censure, that I am greatly at fault; but must say also that I think you have judged too hastily and too harshly of my conduct. The letter I sent you some time since, was written at a moment when I was in *such* a state of mind and spirits that I am sure, had you seen me or known my sufferings, you would have excused every unsatisfactory passage in it. Thank God! it is now all over, and I was just on the point of writing to you, when Sir George called with your letter. I do not know how to begin to answer it; I have never been called upon to justify myself, because it is the first time that I ever stood accused of dishonor; and what makes it the more painful is "that I stand accused by the man who, of all the world, I most admire and esteem, and one also whom I have never ceased to think of, and wish for his welfare, since I made his acquaintance." But as the appearance of my conduct has been so unfavorable in your eyes, I must tell you again of the situation I was in previous to my marriage.

Until the question upon which my whole happiness depended was decided, whether I should be permitted by the family to marry my wife, which I did on October 2nd, I was not able to appear as an artist. Now I remain a musician. Also I did not want someone else to negotiate for you from the fear that it would not happen as it should. I am notified that I have not kept my word with you, which is untrue; but I have neglected everyone, everything including myself.[3]

All your music remained in my drawer unseen and unheard. I, however, did make a very considerable attempt with the Philharmonic to acquire for you what I thought you fully entitled to.[4] I offered all your music to them upon condition that they made you a very handsome present; this they said they could not afford, but proposed to see and hear your music, and then offer a price for it; I objected and replied, "that I should be ashamed that your music should be put up by auction and bid for! — that your name and reputation were too dear to me"; and I quitted the meeting with a determination to give a concert and take all the trouble myself, rather than that your feelings should be wounded by the chance of their disapproval of your works. I was the more apprehensive of this, from the unfortunate circumstances of your Overtures[5] not being well received; they said they had no more to hope for, from your other works. I was not a Director last season, but I am for the next, and then I shall have a voice which I shall take care to exert. I have offered your Sonatas[6] to several publishers, but they thought them too difficult, and said they would not be saleable, and consequently made offers such as I could not accept, but when I shall have played them to a few professors, their reputation will naturally be increased by their merits, and I hope to have better offers. [Money is very tight here, and the times are unusually wretched.[7]] The Symphony you read of in *The Morning Chronicle* I believe to be the one in C minor; it certainly was not the one in A, for it has not been played at a concert. I shall insist upon its being played next season, and most probably the first night.[8] I am exceedingly glad that you have chosen Sir George Smart to make your complaints of me to, as he is a man of honor, and very much your friend; had it been anyone else, your complaint might have been listened to, and I injured all the rest of my life. But I trust I am too respectable to be thought unfavorably of by those who know me. I am, however, quite willing to give up every sheet I have of yours, if you again desire it. Sir George will write by the next post, and will confirm this. I am sorry you say that I did not even *acknowledge* my obligation to you, because I talked of nothing else at Vienna, as every one there who knows me can testify. I even offered my purse, which you generously always declined.

[I have taken great trouble about the dedication of your Trio,[9] and only found one lady who offered ten guineas in return. If you are satisfied with this, please let me know. Sir G.S. will give you his opinion with regard to a concert for your benefit. He understands such matters better than I do. I hope, however, that the Philharmonic will organize a concert for you—free of expense. I again assure you that you have no two better friends than Sir G.S. and myself. Whatever is done in London to your advantage and honor will take place through us. I now hope that you will think better of me. I am once again, as formerly, a free man.

Write to me in French or German with Latin letters. I shall write by next post to Häring.[10]][11]

Pray, my dear Friend, believe me to remain,

Ever yours, most sincerely,
C. Neate

[My address:
Charles Neate, Esq.
No. 10, High Row
Knightsbridge, London][12]

1. Charles Neate (1784–1877), English pianist, who had departed Vienna on ca. February 7, 1816, after spending eight months there and becoming closely acquainted with Beethoven.

2. Answers Beethoven's letter to Smart, ca. October 11, 1816 (Anderson No. 664); answered by Beethoven's letter to Neate, December 18, 1816 (Anderson No. 683).

3. The preceding paragraph was omitted from the Moscheles version. In restoring it, Thayer-Deiters-Riemann created a redundancy with a paragraph whose flattering tone originated, seemingly, in the Moscheles version: "I remain in my profession, and with no abatement for my love of Beethoven! During this period I could not myself do anything publicly, consequently all your music. . . ."

4. This statement and Neate's story following are consistent with the circumstances described in Ries's letter to Beethoven, March 19, 1816 (No. 221 above).

5. *The Ruins of Athens,* Op. 113; *King Stephan,* Op. 117; *Namensfeier,* Op. 115.

6. Violoncello Sonatas, Op. 102 (see Anderson No. 664).

7. This sentence is found in the Berlin manuscript but not in the Moscheles version.

8. The Symphony No. 5 in C Minor was first performed in London on April 15, 1816; the Symphony No. 7 in A was possibly first heard there on June 9, 1817 (Kenneth M. Craig Jr., "The Beethoven Symphonies in London: Initial Decades," *College Music Symposium* 25 [1985], 80–81, although the author wonders whether the Symphony No. 7 might not be among several unidentified works performed earlier).

9. Trio, Op. 97; see Beethoven to Birchall, October 1, 1816 (Anderson No. 662).

10. Johann Baptist Häring, Viennese businessman and accomplished amateur violinist.

11. These two bracketed paragraphs are found in Berlin but not in Moscheles.

12. The address is present in Berlin but not in Moscheles.

Incipit: Nothing has ever given me more pain. . . .

Sources: The original English text for this letter seems not to have survived; all existing versions seem to be based on two sources. The first is an abbreviated, slightly altered version in English that appeared in Moscheles's edition of Schindler's 1840 biography (pp. 238–240) but was not in the author's German original. Moscheles probably received his copy from Neate himself, possibly from an 1816 copybook entry. The second source is a manuscript abbreviation and translation into German, housed in the Staatsbibliothek zu Berlin–Preussischer Kulturbesitz. In it the first paragraph (as given in Moscheles) is summarized in a sentence or two, with seemingly full translation beginning thereafter.

Nohl, *Neue Briefe* (1867), pp. 116–118, is a translation of the Moscheles source, with a postscript (about the trio) derived from the Berlin copy, and he duly acknowledges both sources. Thayer, III (1879), 408–410, and Thayer-Deiters-Riemann, III, 571–573, print what is seemingly a translation of Moscheles with an inserted second paragraph from Berlin, without realizing that the insertion duplicated some information already in Moscheles. Thayer-Krehbiel, II, 347–348, provides Moscheles's version without the insert, while Thayer-Forbes, pp. 651–652, translates the document with the insertion as it appeared in Thayer-Deiters-Riemann, without catching the redundancy extant there. Both Kalischer, (German) III, 96–99, and Kalischer-Shedlock, I, 428–430, present the Berlin material in their respective languages, while only Kalischer-Shedlock, I, 411–412, also gives the Moscheles version in its entirety in English.

The present text, admittedly a composite from the two sources, takes Moscheles as its basis since it most closely represents Neate's English original (for consistency, however, I have Americanized spellings). To this I have added passages from Berlin where they seemingly would have existed in Neate's original, while also eliminating the redundancy created by Thayer-Deiters-Riemann, and have noted these changes above. Moscheles and Berlin differ somewhat on the elements related concerning Neate's discussions with the Philharmonic Society and their order of presentation in the text. While the present edition follows Moscheles, with exceptions noted, the reader to whom such variants could be critical might wish to consult the Kalischer or Kalischer-Shedlock collections.

The Berlin manuscript (Mus. ms. autogr. Beethoven 35, 43a) is listed in Kalischer, "Beethoven-Autographe," p. 49, and Bartlitz, p. 130.

235. Christopher Lonsdale (for Robert Birchall) to Beethoven

London; November 8, 1816[1]

Sir:

In answer to yours of the 1st [of] October, I am desired by Mr. Birchall to inform you [that] he is glad to find [that] you are now satisfied respecting his promise of paying you £5 in addition to what you received before according to agreement; but he did not think [that] you would have delayed sending the receipt signed after receiving the 130 ducats merely because you had not received the £5, which latter sum was not included in the receipt. Till it arrives, Mr. Birchall cannot, at any rate, enter into any fresh arrangement, as his first care will be to secure those pieces [that] he has already paid you for, and see how they answer his purpose as a Music Seller, and without the receipt he cannot prevent any other Music Seller from publishing them. In regard to the airs with variations,[2] the price of £30, which is supposed you mean *for each,* is considerably more than he could afford to give, ever to have any hopes of seeing them repay him. If that should be your lowest price, Mr. Birchall will give up his idea of them altogether.[3] The Symphony in A will be quite ready for publication in a week; Mr. Ries (who has kindly undertaken the inspection of your works)[4] has it now [and is] looking [it] over—but it will not come out *till the day comes* [that] you may appoint.[5]

Mr. Birchall fears the Sonata in G and the Trio in B♭ [6] have been published in Vienna before his; he will be obliged to you [if you] inform him, when you write, of the day that they were published. I am sorry to say that Mr. Birchall's health has been very bad for two or three years back, which prevents him from attending to business; and as there are, I fear, but little hopes of his being much better, he is less anxious respecting making *any* additions to his catalogue than he otherwise would have been. He is much obliged to you for the offer of the Sonata and the Trio,[7] but he begs to decline it for the reasons mentioned before.

Hoping to hear soon respecting the paper sent for your signature,

> I am, Sir, for Mr. Birchall, etc.
> C. Lonsdale

P.S. The Sonata in G is published and the Trio will be in a few days.[8] Is Mr. Beethoven's opera of *Fidelio* published? Where and by whom?[9]

1. Answers Beethoven's letter of October 1, 1816 (Anderson No. 662); answered by Beethoven's letter of December 14, 1816 (Anderson No. 680). Sotheby's gives Birchall's address as New Bond Street.

2. In his letter of August 14, 1816 (No. 229 above), Lonsdale had asked Beethoven for a quote concerning English, Scottish or Irish airs with variations, to which Beethoven replied on October 1 (Anderson No. 662).

3. Sotheby's description of the draft indicates: "In a deleted section, the writer makes the point that they could not countenance buying a piece for more than ten or twelve pounds, inclusive of Beethoven's expenses, and gives reasons for this."

4. Ferdinand Ries, Beethoven's friend and former pupil, then living in London.

5. According to Lonsdale's note on Ries's letter of February 7, 1816 (No. 219 above), Birchall published the piano arrangement of the Symphony No. 7 on January 6, 1817.

6. Both Op. 96 and Op. 97 were advertised by Steiner in Vienna on July 29, 1816. Lonsdale's note (see n.5, this letter) indicates that they were published in Vienna in January 1817.

7. In his October 1 letter, Beethoven had offered generic items that Anderson (No. 662) identified as the Piano Sonata, Op. 101, and an unfinished piano trio in F minor.

8. The same pieces mentioned in connection with n.6, this letter: the Violin Sonata, Op. 96, appeared in London on October 30, 1816, and the Piano Trio, Op. 97, was issued on December 5 (according to Lonsdale's note; see n.5, this letter).

9. Beethoven also replied to this question on December 14, 1816.

Incipit: In answer to yours' of the 1ˢᵗ. October. . . .

Sources: Original English version (from the autograph or a copybook copy, owned in 1863 by Robert Lonsdale, London) in Chrysander, "Beethoven's Verbindung," pp. 435–436; Thayer-Krehbiel, II, 350; Thayer-Forbes, p. 653. German translation in Thayer, III (1879), 412–413; Thayer-Deiters-Riemann, III, 574–575. A surviving draft is described and briefly quoted, with partial facsimile, in Sotheby & Co., *Music, Continental Manuscripts and Printed Books,* auction catalog (London, May 9–10, 1985), item 6.

236. George Thomson to Beethoven

Edinburgh; December 20, 1816

Monsieur L. van Beethoven

I hope that you will have received my letter of last October 20,[1] and that your package in reply will not be long in arriving. Among other things, I asked you in it to write a *Scottish* Overture in a playful, lively and scherzoso style. Now I find, that instead of placing this overture at the beginning of a little opera entitled *The Jolly Beggars,*[2] it would be more fitting and more to my advantage to place it at the front of a volume of Scottish melodies[3] for which you and Monsieur Haydn have written the accompaniments, which contains a variety of tender, passionate, gay and cheery airs. You will perceive that the overture must have a character conforming to this variety. It is why you will yield to my entreaties to begin it with a tender and touching Adagio; following this might come light and joyous movements.

Of the seven airs that were sent to you last July, I have notified you to harmonize only the two that begin with these notes:[4]

By sending me these two as soon as possible, you will oblige me infinitely.[5]

Permit me to urge your particular attention to everything that has been mentioned above.

I await with great impatience your reply to the proposal that I have you arrange the nineteen foreign airs in the form of six overtures, *in whatever manner pleases you.*

I have the honor, Monsieur, to be, with great esteem,

Your friend and very humble servant,

(signed) G. Thomson

1. See above. Answered by Beethoven's letter of January 18, 1817 (Anderson No. 736).

2. Robert Burns's *The Jolly Beggars* was set as a cantata for Thomson by Henry R. Bishop (1786–1855).

3. Presumably the planned vol. 5 of Scottish airs.

4. The music example is lacking in Thomson's copybook.

5. Thomson says virtually the same thing in his letter of January 24, 1817 (No. 238 below), but the second time he does provide the musical examples.

Incipit: Je me flatte que vous aurez reçu ma lettre du 20 Octobre. . . .

Sources: Summarized in MacArdle, "Beethoven and Thomson," pp. 43–44, and Hadden, *George Thomson,* pp. 339–340. Copy in Thomson's copybook, British Library, Add. MS 35267, pp. 183r–184r.

237. Beethoven to Herr (Joseph?) Dollinger[1]

[Vienna; 1816/1817?][2]

You will forgive the late arrival of the book,[3] but for a considerable time my health has been in an almost critical state; this is the reason for the delay.[4]

With regards,

Yours sincerely,

Ludwig van Beethoven

[Exterior:]

To Herr von Dollinger

1. The exterior address, to "H. von Dollinger," was earlier misread as "Gustav Dollinger." Among several individuals with this surname in Vienna during this period, the most likely recipient is Joseph Dollinger, an amateur violinist in the Gesellschaft der Musikfreunde and a member of the society's board of directors by 1822 (see Böckh, *Merkwürdigkeiten*, p. 355; Ziegler, *Addressen-Buch*, pp. 114, 135).

2. Beethoven signed his name here using German (as opposed to Latin) script. Max Unger believed that he discontinued this practice around 1820, while Alan Tyson placed the transition to Latin signatures about 1817. If the unidentified book mentioned in the text was Alois Weissenbach's *Meine Reise zum Kongress* (1816), a copy of which was circulating among Zmeskall, Beethoven and their friends in 1816–1817 (see Anderson Nos. 625 and 756), that would confirm the period for this letter's genesis as speculated by Helms.

3. Earlier transcriptions gave this word as *Brief* instead of *Buch*. The possible identity of this book is discussed in n.2, this letter.

4. Beethoven's health was in a precarious condition during the first months of 1816, as several letters in Anderson and the present collection attest.

Incipit: Sie verzeihen die späte Ankunft. . . .

Sources: Excerpt previously published as MacArdle & Misch No. 376 and Anderson No. 1249. Complete text, with corrected transcription, edited by Marianne Helms in Staehelin, "Unbekannte . . . Schriftstücke," pp. 54–57. Autograph in a private collection, Göttingen, in 1983.

1817

238. George Thomson to Beethoven

Edinburgh; January 24, 1817[1]

Monsieur van Beethoven,

I hope that you will have received my letters of last December 20 and October 20. I shall be pleased to have your reply and all the news on the subject of music that you are willing to tell me.

I am sending you, enclosed, 10 Scottish airs,[2] and for these airs I ask you to be so kind as to compose ritornellos and accompaniments in your delicate and cantabile style, *as soon as you can.*

Of the airs that were sent to you last July, I have notified you to harmonize only the two that begin with these notes:[3]

One of our Scottish Lords—named Fife—conveyed to me the other day a message that you had confided to him several years ago, since which time he has been principally in Spain. He says that you asked him to tell me that I was neglectful or tardy in not sending you melodies. If I have been tardy, I ask you earnestly not to follow suit, but to be so kind as to send these 12 melodies with all possible dispatch. In doing this you will oblige me particularly, and Messrs. Fries will give you fifty ducats in cash when you deliver the manuscript of the 12 into their hands.

I await your reply to the proposal that I have you arrange the nineteen foreign airs in the form of six overtures, in whatever manner pleases you.

I have the honor, etc.

1. Follows Thomson's letter of December 20, 1816 (No. 236 above); crossed in the mails with Beethoven's letter to Thomson, January 18, 1817 (Anderson No. 736; MacArdle & Misch No. 207).

2. Barry Cooper has identified these as Op. 108, Nos. 1, 3, 4, 9, 13, 17 and 21; WoO 157, No. 10; and WoO 158/II, Nos. 3 and 4.

3. This was already said in the December 20, 1816, letter, as was later material in this letter. Among the themes quoted, "The Highland Watch," Op. 108, No. 22, is in a different key; the second theme quoted was not among the seven sent. It seems never to have been sent or set; in any event, Barry Cooper has not been able to locate it.

Incipit: Je me flatte que vous aurez reçu mes lettres du 20 Decembre et. . . .

Sources: Summarized in MacArdle, "Beethoven and Thomson," p. 44, and Hadden, *George Thomson,* p. 340. Copy in Thomson's copybook, British Library, Add. MS 35267, pp. 184r–185r.

239. Ferdinand Ries to Beethoven

London; June 9, 1817[1]

My dearest Beethoven!

Again I have been entirely forgotten by you for a long time,[2] although I can hardly think of any reason other than your too numerous activities and, as I must unfortunately hear from other people, a serious illness as well.[3] Truly, dear Beethoven, the gratitude that I owe you, *which I must eternally owe you,* is unalterable—and I believe that I may say with a sincere heart that I have *never* forgotten it, although I have many times been described to you by my enemies as ungrateful and envious; thus I have had the most ardent desire to prove it to you in more than words. This fond desire has now finally (I hope) been fulfilled, and I hope to find again in my old teacher, *my old and affectionate friend.* The Philharmonic Society, of which our friend Neate[4] is now also a director, and at whose concerts your compositions are preferred to all others, wishes to give you evidence of its great esteem and its gratitude for the many beautiful moments that we have so often enjoyed in your extraordinarily ingenious works; and I feel it really a most flattering compliment to have been empowered with Neate to write to you first on the subject. In short, my dear Beethoven, we would very much like to have you among us here in London next winter.[5] Friends will receive you with open arms; and to give you at least one proof of this I have been commissioned in the name of the Directorship of the Philharmonic Society to offer you 300 guineas on the following conditions:

1st. You are to be here in London next winter.

2d. You are to write two grand symphonies for the Philharmonic Society, which are to remain its property.

3d. You must bind yourself not to deliver any composition for grand orchestra for any concert in London, or direct any concert *before* or *during* our eight concerts, which begin at the end of February and end in the middle of the month of June (without the consent of the Philharmonic Society), which certainly will not be difficult.

Do not understand by this that we want to tie your hands; it is only in case opposition concerts, which we have already put down once, should rise again, since these gentlemen might plan to have you [for themselves] *against us* instead of for us. At the same time it could call up a great many enemies, asking you to decline something yourself, when the responsibility for such an action would rest entirely with us directors, and we do not want to have to deal with such a matter. We are all sincerely disposed in your favor, and I believe that every opportunity to be helpful to you in your plans would sooner give us pleasure than any desire to restrict you in the least.

4th. You are not to appear publicly in the orchestra at any concert until our first two concerts are over, unless you want to give a concert yourself, in which case you can give as many as you please.

5th. You are to be here before the 8th of January 1818, and when the concerts are over, you are under *absolutely no* obligation to the Society except to give us preference in *the future* in case we offer you *the same conditions* that *others* do.

6th. In case you accept the engagement and perhaps need money for the journey, you may have 100 guineas in advance. This is the offer that I am authorized to make to you by the Society.

All negotiations with publishers are left *open* to you, as well as those with Sir G[eorge] Smart, who has offered you 100 guineas for an oratorio in one act, and who has specially commissioned me to *remind* you *concerning a reply,* since he would like to have the work for next winter.[6] The *Intendant* of the Grand Italian Opera, G. Ayrton,[7] is a particular friend of ours. He does not want to commit himself definitely, but he gave his promise that he wants to commission you for an opera.

Your own concert, or perhaps *concerts,* may bring you a fine sum of money as well as other engagements in the country. Neate and I rejoice like children at the prospect of seeing you here, and I need not say that I will do all in my power to make your sojourn profitable and pleasant. I know England, too, and do not doubt your success for a moment.

Moreover, we need someone here who will put life into things again and bring the gentlemen of the orchestra into accord.[8]

Yesterday evening was our last concert, and your beautiful Symphony in A[9] was given with extraordinary applause. It frightens one (just think of us symphony writers) when he sees and hears such a work. Write me a definite answer very soon, and give me hope to see you yourself here very soon.

I remain always

Your thankful, sincere friend,

Ferd. Ries

[P.S.] My sincere greetings to Herr von Zmeskall,[10] Zizius,[11] Krumpholz[12] and other friends.

1. Answered by Beethoven's two letters of July 9, 1817 (Anderson Nos. 786 and 787), with preliminary background in his letter to Zmeskall, July 7, 1817 (Anderson No. 784).

2. Beethoven's most recent surviving letter to Ries is dated June 11, 1816 (Anderson No. 639). In the meantime he had penned a total of at least seven letters to Robert Birchall, Sir George Smart and Charles Neate, although most of them date from 1816.

3. Beethoven fell ill in October 1816 and remained weak into the spring of 1817. For a running account of his health, see his letters to Zmeskall, November 3, 1816 (Anderson No. 669), to Archduke Rudolph, ca. November 12, 1816 (Anderson No. 671), to Peter Joseph Simrock, February 15, 1817 (Anderson No. 759), and to Countess Marie Erdödy, June 19, 1817 (Anderson No. 783).

4. Charles Neate, who had spent from May 1815 to ca. February 7, 1816, in Vienna.

5. None of Beethoven's projected journeys to London took place, despite his optimistic projections.

6. The London-born Smart (1776–1867) had been knighted in 1811 for conducting successful concerts in Dublin. From 1813 to 1844, he conducted forty-nine concerts of the Philharmonic Society. He came to Vienna and met Beethoven in September 1825.

7. Despite the initial G., this seems to be a reference to William Ayrton (1777–1858), composer, operatic manager and writer on music. From 1823 to 1833, he edited the *Harmonicon* (London).

8. Considering the further deterioration in his hearing at about this time (as noted by Fanny Giannatasio del Rio), Beethoven may have been shy at the prospect of conducting an unfamiliar orchestra in public. Maelzel's letter to Beethoven, April 19, 1818 (No. 248 below), refers to a hearing device for conducting, which he had constructed in anticipation of their projected tour together.

9. Previous correspondence (including Beethoven's letter to Neate, December 18, 1816, Anderson No. 683) indicates clearly that the symphony in question was No. 7 in A, Op. 92. Ries's manuscript, however, seemingly indicated the key "A," followed by an apparent doubled-cross symbol, resembling a sharp, probably similar to that following the inscription "Missa solemnis in D," illustrated in Stieler's often-reproduced 1819 portrait of Beethoven. In both cases, otherwise serious scholars have proffered silly transcriptions of these keys as A♯ (or even B♭!) and D♯, respectively. Whether a simple flourish, a natural sign, or a sign to indicate a major key, this symbol may not be interpreted as a "sharp" in this context.

10. Beethoven's letter to Zmeskall, July 7, 1817 (Anderson No. 784), confirms that the composer passed along Ries's greetings and then enlisted Zmeskall's aid in mailing his reply, two letters written on July 9, 1817 (Anderson Nos. 786 and 787).

11. Johann Nepomuk Zizius (1772–1824), prominent Viennese attorney, professor at the University of Vienna and a founder of the Gesellschaft der Musikfreunde.

12. Wenzel Krumpholz (ca. 1750–1817), violinist and mandolinist, acquainted with Beethoven since his arrival in Vienna in around 1795. On May 2, 1817, he had died suddenly of apoplexy while walking on the Glacis (which, having lost its original strategic value as an open area, was converted into a pleasant parkway around the city walls). The next day, Beethoven set "Rasch tritt der Tod," WoO 104, the song of the monks from Schiller's *Wilhelm Tell*, in Krumpholz's memory.

Incipit: Sehr lange bin ich wieder ganz. . . .

Sources: Thayer-Deiters-Riemann, IV, 30–31 (taken from a copy made by Otto Jahn, in turn taken from the Fischhof manuscript); partial translation in Thayer-Krehbiel, II, 369–371; full translation in Thayer-Forbes, pp. 674–675. Also in Kalischer (German), III, 179–181; Kalischer-Shedlock, II, 52–53. The text with discussion of variant sources in Hill, *Ries—Briefe*, pp. 114–116, and Brenneis, "Fischhof-Manuskripte," pp. 63–65. The present translation reflects the fullest text in the Fischhof Manuscript, Staatsbibliothek zu Berlin–Preussischer Kulturbesitz (from Thayer-Deiters-Riemann and Brenneis); shorter or less reliable (possibly draft) versions survive in the British Library, London, and Beethoven-Haus, Bonn.

In his *Beethoven-Handbuch* of 1926 (II, 124), Theodor Frimmel published the salutation and slightly altered variants of the first two sentences of this letter (up to the word "wurde" in German, "envious" in English translation), erroneously identified as having been written by Adolf Martin Schlesinger, with its date of June 9, 1817, supplied by another hand.

240. George Thomson to Beethoven

Edinburgh, Royal Exchange; June 25, 1817[1]

Monsieur L. van Beethoven
Vienna, Austria

My dear Monsieur,

I have received your last two packages of national airs[2] and a letter in which you ask for 124 ducats to compose seven overtures. I must tell you frankly that it is absolutely impossible to pay such a price, and that I really do not know how to make you a proposal. You are so *inconsistent* concerning the price of your works, because in 1815 you sent me a list of your prices, in which you indicated that the price of an overture is exactly 12 ducats.[3]

It is not of any use, here, to unite the foreign airs with prose; and not seeing any way to reap profit from the foreign airs that you have sent me, I have indulged the hope that you would be willing to render them usable to me as overtures for the piano, for the sum that I have proposed, beyond that which I had paid you to harmonize them.

But, since you did not want to accept this proposal, I shall take the liberty to make another that you will perhaps find better: you will choose 12 of the airs of various nations — those that seem to you the best adapted to be *varied;* and if you compose variations (not more than eight) on each air, for piano, in a pleasing style, and not too difficult, I shall pay you 72 ducats.[4] It will be very easy work for you to write some variations for 12 themes that are already composed. I would like the last variation, or a coda of each air or of some of the airs, to be written in the style of a waltz.

If you do not accept this proposal, it remains for me only to prove to you my regrets for having made it; for I would be imprudent to spend more on these foreign airs than I have proposed. I would have done better by not getting mixed up with them. The airs from the *Tyrol* are truly beautiful and full of vivacity; I admire them very much.

The ritornellos and accompaniments that you have sent are, in my opinion, generally composed in a perfectly delightful and absolutely inimitable style. Nevertheless, some of them are certainly too learned, too bizarre — in short, such that I dare not offer them to the public, and, consequently, I cannot make use of them.

I request you to redo the *violin* part of No. 1[5] and No. 8 of the last group or 12,[6] and of No. 12 of the previous group of 15.[7] The piano part is charming[8] in all three airs, but the violin part (and the violoncello part in No. 8) is—for the Scottish people—filled with too many notes, too difficult for the hand and for the meter[9] and too remote from the type of song. In place of the violin part (enclosed), I request that you be so kind as to supply a new part, simpler and more resembling the style of the melodies. You will oblige me by sending me these parts by mail, without any delay.

If you wish to compose an overture to be prefixed to my Scottish work for 12 ducats, in a lively and playful style, and easy to play, you can generally imitate the Scottish style, without introducing anything actually Scottish; and if you are willing to add accompaniments, you will give me pleasure; but all of this as it pleases you.

I have sent a volume of Welsh airs with your accompaniments, which I have just published,[10] to a friend in London, to be sent to you as soon as the occasion presents itself, and I hope that you receive it before long.

I have never received the package of printed music, which, I learned last year, was addressed to me and placed into the hands of Messrs. Fries.

Have you recently published anything new?

Mozart's *Don Giovanni* has been presented for the first time in London this season with unprecedented success.[11]

If you are inclined to compose some music for English words, there is an Ode on the power of music over the passions, in 94 verses or lines—an absolutely sublime poem that I would be willing to send you with a literal translation into German. It is truly worthy of your great and brilliant genius; and if you would set it to music for voices with the accompaniment of a large orchestra, I am convinced that it would be admired as much as the *Creation*.[12]

I do not need to tell you with what enthusiasm I admire your works; I am transported by them, and there is nothing in the world that I desire more than to make a pilgrimage to Vienna to see you, and to hear your Masses, your Sonatas, your Symphonies, and your Quartets performed by the great musicians of your country; for alas! most of them are too difficult for Edinburgh. In Vienna, I would believe myself in Heaven! What a pity that it is such a long way from Edinburgh to Vienna.

Your plan to visit England pleases me; I would be delighted to see you in Edinburgh.

I have the honor, etc., etc.

G. Thomson

1. Replies to Beethoven's letters of February 15, 1817 (Anderson No. 757), and January 18, 1817 (Anderson No. 736).

2. Barry Cooper has identified these as the seven items listed in n.3 of Thomson's July 8, 1816, letter (No. 226 above); as well as the four items listed in n.2 of the same letter; plus the ten items listed in n.2 of Thomson's January 24, 1817, letter (No. 238 above); plus WoO 157, No. 6 (Sicilian), and WoO 158/I, No. 1 (Danish).

3. Barry Cooper suggests that, since Beethoven was not proficient at multiplication, he possibly figured each overture at 18 ducats and then added this figure seven times, erroneously arriving at 124 ducats instead of 126.

4. Ultimately these became Opp. 105 and 107.

5. Op. 108, No. 6.

6. Op. 108, No. 21.

7. Op. 108, No. 7; these identifications courtesy of Barry Cooper.

8. Thomson originally wrote "superb."

9. That is, too difficult to count.

10. *A Select Collection of Original Welsh Airs,* WoO 155, evidently published in late May or early June 1817; entered at Stationers Hall on June 20, 1817.

11. The first professional performance of *Don Giovanni* in London took place at the King's Theatre on April 12, 1817.

12. By Haydn. It is remotely possible that Thomson's idea for setting a poem might have influenced the conception of the Symphony No. 9.

Incipit: J'ai reçu vos deux derniers paquets. . . .

Sources: Summarized in MacArdle, "Beethoven and Thomson," p. 46, and Hadden, *George Thomson,* pp. 340–341. Copy in Thomson's copybook, British Library, Add. MS 35268, pp. 8r–10r.

241. *Beethoven to Carl Czerny*[1]

[Vienna;] June 30, [probably 1817][2]

My good Herr von Czerny!

Last week, I was at your place and left behind the sum of 12 florins. Now I do not remember whether I left them for the two past weeks or for *last week and the present one.* I therefore ask you most obligingly to let me know how the matter stands. Many thanks for your trouble with my dear nephew Karl. In haste,

Your friend,

L. v. Beethoven

[Exterior:]
    For Herr von Czerny
    on June 30th.

1. Carl Czerny (1791–1857), Vienna's most prominent piano pedagogue, studied with Beethoven when young and in turn gave the composer's nephew Karl piano lessons from 1816 to 1818.

2. Beethoven wrote only the month and day, but, according to Joseph Schmidt-Görg's catalog of watermarks, the paper used is consistent with letters dating from the summer of 1817. Sieghard Brandenburg (personal communication) kindly indicated that the month has now been transcribed as June.

Incipit: Ich war die vorige *Woche.* . . .

Sources: Transcribed and edited by Martin Staehelin in Staehelin, "Unbekannte . . . Schriftstücke," pp. 57–60. Autograph in the Beethoven-Haus, Bonn, NE 108.

242. Beethoven to Nikolaus Zmeskall von Domanovecz

[Vienna; probably late August 1817][1]

My good Z!

By chance, I have gotten a servant with whom I can perhaps be happy—I was forced to dismiss the other servant because of his rudeness, which was entirely too great, even before his 14 days had passed. I requested a soldier from Ertmann,[2] and this person, after he was with me for a few days, asked me to get him a year's leave, since he wanted to devote himself entirely to me; in this manner a kind of gratitude can manifest itself, and at the same time the lot of a poor man—robbed of his freedom and almost as good as a galley slave—can be eased for a while. Thus I asked Ertmann to permit him this leave, which he immediately granted. Now I have to give you my sincere thanks for your kindness toward me, in that Breuning[3] told me that you even wanted to take care of this matter for me. Should you have the opportunity, with regard to me, whereby I can return some kindness to you, I hope that you will not let it pass. Now I have another wish, my dear Z, that you would indicate to me everything that you give with respect to the clothing of your servant, and how much that comes to, and how best I should arrange it that it does not cost me more than it would you, with your *talent for economy*.[4] I request that you send me a *statement* about this as soon as possible through your servant, for *my soldier* must now dress in civilian clothes, otherwise someone might take me for a *military man* rather than a *General of Harmony*.

Your devoted admirer,
Beethoven

[Exterior:]
For Monsieur de Zmeskall

1. Judging from the servant problem and the time element discussed in the first sentence, this letter probably follows sometime soon after Beethoven's letters to Zmeskall of August 17 and 21, 1817 (Anderson Nos. 802 and 805).

2. General (Baron) Stephan von Ertmann, husband of Beethoven's talented piano pupil Dorothea von Ertmann (1781–1849). The baroness received the dedication of the Piano Sonata, Op. 101. Ertmann was transferred to Milan in 1818 and died there as a lieutenant field marshall in 1835. For further details, see Beethoven's card, January 1, 1804 (No. 78 above).

3. Mutual friend Stephan von Breuning.

4. Beethoven means *domestic* economy here.

Incipit: Durch einen Zufall bin ich. . . .

Sources: Transcribed and edited by Martin Staehelin in Staehelin, "Unbekannte . . . Schriftstücke," pp. 60–63, with facsimile and extensive commentary. Autograph in the Handschriften-Abteilung, Zentralbibliothek, Zürich, Autographen-Sammlung Jenny Ris-Neumann RP 16.

243. *George Thomson to Beethoven*

Edinburgh; December 28, 1817[1]

Monsieur Beethoven

My dear Monsieur,

I wrote you on June 25, but I have not yet had the pleasure of a reply to it.

I ask you to redo the violin part of No. 1 of the last group of 12, and No. 12 of the previous group of 15, enclosed.[2] The piano part is charming, but the violin accompaniment (for us) is filled with too many notes, too difficult to play and too remote from the type of song. I request that you be so kind as to supply a new, simpler and easier part. And you will oblige me by sending me this part without any delay. I shall await it with impatience; the parts for the voice and the piano are printed and ready to be published.

I am also sending you three other Scottish airs[3] that are infinitely loved, and for which I would like to have ritornellos and accompaniments of your composition, in your simple and admirable style, for when you are simple, I find you completely divine.

Messrs. Fries will pay you immediately—and I urgently ask you, as well, to send them to me within a few days of having received them.

As it will be a great gift, I believe, for our flutists, I intend to have your violin accompaniments adapted for the flute. We have a great number of flutists, but alas! our violin players are rare and very weak. A musician here, who has some discrimination and is a flutist, may do all that is necessary for the passages that are presently too low for the flute, because the greater part of the violin accompaniment does not need any change.

Please give me the pleasure of informing me concerning the new music that you have recently published. I have procured your magnificent Trio in B♭ for piano, violin and violoncello.[4] I have never seen anything so charming and so marvelous; but it is terribly difficult!

I have the honor, my dear Monsieur, to be, with a great deal of esteem,

Your friend and very humble servant,

(signed) George Thomson

130

P.S. If you find that a very short ritornello in the middle of any of the three airs would have a good effect, be so kind as to insert it. You cannot make the introductory ritornellos too long, because I am convinced that they will be admirable.

1. Follows on Thomson's letter of June 25, 1817 (No. 240 above), and, in its first large paragraph, repeats material from that letter.
2. Barry Cooper has identified these, respectively, as Op. 108, Nos. 6 and 7, and further notes that Thomson no longer requests a revised version of Op. 108, No. 21, as he had in the June 25, 1817, letter.
3. Cooper has identified these three items as Op. 108, Nos. 23, 2 and 18.
4. Trio, Op. 97 (*Archduke*).
Incipit: Je vous écrivis le 25 Juin. . . .
Sources: Summarized in MacArdle, "Beethoven and Thomson," p. 46. Copy in Thomson's copybook, British Library, Add. MS 35268, pp. 15r–16r.

244. Beethoven to Joseph Blahetka[1]

[Vienna; 1817/1818?][2]

Since I know that you are already at home in the afternoon, I am coming to [see] you for certain around 5 o'clock this afternoon. In the meantime, farewell, my dear B.

Your

B.

[Address:]
To H[err] v[on] Blahetka[3]

1. Born in 1786, Joseph Blahetka had been an inspector in a paper factory at Guntramsdorf, near Vienna. His daughter, Leopoldine (1809–1877), was a child prodigy and played Beethoven's Piano Concerto in B♭, Op. 19, at a concert in Vienna on April 3, 1820 (see Thayer-Forbes, p. 771). Blahetka himself became a writer and music critic and was one of the torchbearers at Beethoven's funeral.
2. The dating of this undated letter follows Stargardt's catalog.
3. The address page bears the dedicatory inscription (in German): "Beethoven's handwriting, presented by Blahetka to Dr. Hering [Häring?], London, August 14, 1832."

Incipit: Da ich weiss, dass Sie Nachmittags. . . .

Sources: J. A. Stargardt, *Autographen aus drei alten Schweizer Sammlungen: Auktion, Katalog 66/652* (Basel, September 19, 1992), item 431, p. 220 (facsimile on p. 223); summarized in Ira Brilliant, "Music Auction Report," *Beethoven Newsletter* (San Jose) 8, no. 1 (Spring 1993), 26.

1818

245. Beethoven to Nannette Streicher[1]

[Vienna; probably late December 1817/early January 1818][2]

Here [is] the forgotten vessel with contents.[3] Now, kitchen talk—she must answer you various things in writing immediately. Ask if she is *really a cook;** if they are satisfied with her there; if she is skilled with venison, fish, etc.

Can she protect her 22-year-old virginity until we rightfully allow her to marry herself off? Boyfriends will not be allowed in the house; at most, she can go wherever she wants to with him outside the house on Sundays. It is best to examine her cooking; it would be an [appropriately] difficult trial for her to make beefsteak, etc. If she passes this examination for you, then make an appointment with her for tomorrow at noon, when you yourself are at my place—or the day after tomorrow. If she cannot easily [come] at this time, however, she can come Monday early, whereupon you [will] eat breakfast at my place. Tomorrow we see you at noon—if you find that the person is a star of the first magnitude, then one must also not make things too difficult for her.

Yours in haste.

* Or is her position subordinate to a cook? [Beethoven's footnote.]

1. Nannette (properly Maria Anna) Stein Streicher (1769–1833), daughter of an Augsburg piano maker, married Johann Andreas Streicher in 1794 and moved to Vienna, where she, her husband and brother continued in the family business with considerable success. She often advised Beethoven on household matters.
2. Beethoven gave notice to his cook Baberl (the diminutive of Barbara) on December 27, 1817. This letter was probably written shortly thereafter, very possibly early in January 1818. The new cook ultimately hired was Peppi (the diminutive of Josephine), who figures in Anderson No. 894, written to Frau Streicher in January (or perhaps as late as February) 1818: "P[eppi] is a good cook, and for this I must again express to you my infinite gratitude." Anderson No. 885 (early January 1818) indicated that the transition from Baberl to the new cook would take place the following Monday.

3. Several of Beethoven's letters during this period mention silverware, a silver sugar bowl and so on. Perhaps this vessel (presumably of tin, pewter or silver) was among them.

Incipit: Hier die vergessene Dose. . . .

Sources: Transcribed and edited by Martin Staehelin in Staehelin, "Unbekannte . . . Schriftstücke," pp. 64–69, with considerable commentary, as well as a partial facsimile on p. 65. Autograph in the Zentralbibliothek, Zürich (Handschriften-Abteilung: Autographen-Sammlung Emil Beber M 16/1).

246. Joseph Anton Bridi[1] to Thomas Broadwood, London[2]

Vienna; February 5, 1818[3]

Since Beethoven sends me this letter that is directed to you, I take advantage of the opportunity to reply to your friendly [letter] of last January 3d.[4] I have formally requested Monsieur Barraux and Co. in Trieste[5] to try[6] out the instrument in question, and to send it here. With joy in his heart, Beethoven wishes to dedicate to you the first composition that he writes [after receiving it], convinced that the new instrument can inspire him to something very fine.[7] I believe that your intention is to deliver the instrument to Beethoven without his having to pay the expenses in Trieste or our customs [in Vienna]. . . .[8] Nonetheless, please tell me how I should proceed.[9]

1. Italian-born Giuseppe Antonio Bridi (1763–1836), a partner in Bridi, Parisi & Co., Viennese import merchants, Wollzeile No. 820. Bridi is also mentioned in Beethoven's letter to Count Moritz Lichnowsky, January 1818 (Anderson No. 890).

2. Thomas Broadwood, manager of the prominent piano manufacturing firm of (John) Broadwood & Sons, London. Sometime earlier he had toured the Continent and had evidently become acquainted with Beethoven. On December 27, 1817, the firm selected from its warehouse "a 6 octave Grand Pianoforte, No. 7362, tin and deal case," and delivered it to Mr. Farlowe (London), to be shipped in "care of F. E. J. Bareaux and Co., Trieste." It had been played and signed, before shipment, by Muzio Clementi, Ferdinand Ries, John Baptist Cramer and Friedrich Kalkbrenner, among others.

3. Accompanies Beethoven's letter to Broadwood, February 3, 1818 (Anderson No. 891). In French, Beethoven expresses his great pleasure at the prospect of the gift, which he will regard as an altar on which to place the beautiful gifts of his spirit before

the divine Apollo. He promises, as soon as he receives the gift, to send Broadwood the first fruits of his inspiration on playing it.

4. Broadwood's letter to Bridi, January 3, 1818, seems to be lost, but surely it indicated that the piano for Beethoven had been shipped the week before.

5. As noted above, Broadwood's porter, Millet, spelled the name "Bareaux."

6. The original printing in Thayer reads "prouvent." Bridi probably meant "éprouvent" or possibly even "trouvent."

7. Beethoven seems never to have made good this promise.

8. Thayer places ellipses here, evidently indicating some omission.

9. The fullest account of Broadwood's gift is in Thayer-Deiters-Riemann (with letter transcriptions); subsequent editions of Thayer contain condensed accounts.

Incipit: Je profite de l'occasion. . . .

Sources: Thayer-Deiters-Riemann, IV, 86; summarized in Thayer-Krehbiel, II, 391; Thayer-Forbes, p. 695.

247. Johann Nepomuk Wolfmayer[1] to Beethoven

Vienna; April 9, 1818

Dear H[err] v[on] Beethoven!

If you are really in earnest, and, as promised, you compose the Requiem,[2] then I hereby pledge to pay you on this account 100# (i.e., One Hundred Ducats). I ask merely that a copy of the score be given to me immediately after the completion of this, your work of art; and you can otherwise dispose of the original, as your true and irrevocable property, at your discretion. Otherwise, please just notify me of your consent to this amount in writing, and accept the assurance of my great esteem.

Johann Wolfmayer

[Exterior address:]

Herr Ludwig v[on] Beethoven,

most famous composer and musical virtuoso,

Landstrasse

Gärtnergasse No. 26;

Zum grünen Baum; 2d floor.[3]

1. Wolfmayer (b. 1768) was a wealthy Viennese cloth merchant and music lover. He figures frequently among Beethoven's friends and supporters mentioned in the conversation books and ultimately received the dedication of the String Quartet, Op. 135.

2. While Beethoven may have considered such a project, he seems not to have worked on it extensively, if at all.

3. American third floor.

Incipit: Wenn es richtig Ihr Ernst ist. . . .

Sources: Frimmel, "Wolfmayer," in *Beethoven-Handbuch*, II, 466; also Theodor Frimmel, "Neue Beethovenstudien," *Deutsche Kunst- und Musikzeitung* 22 (January 15, 1895), 17–18. Autograph in the Beethoven-Archiv, Bonn, since 1935; listed in Schmidt-Görg, *Katalog der Handschriften* (1935), p. 60.

248. Johann Nepomuk Maelzel[1] to Beethoven

Paris; April 19, 1818

Best of Friends!

You surely expect from me no detailed excuses for my truly very long silence. In a nutshell, not much time for correspondence remains for someone like me, if he is busy with all types of undertakings. Meanwhile, I do not have to prove to you now through words that I always remember you; thus at least the deed speaks in my favor.

I have the pleasure of assuring you that I worked diligently on the agreed-upon hearing device for conducting and have already brought it to a happy conclusion. I promise that it will be most successful for you. Too bad that I do not have you with me now, in order to be able to try it out. You will therefore be all the more satisfied, since I was intent upon giving the item a nice shape in order to make its appearance pleasing.

Since our projected artistic tour rests upon this matter, I shall provide you with this device before you arrive, if it will bring about the actual beginning of the tour. Indeed the exact time for this may not have been determined yet, but I have already provisionally advised the local composers of your journey through Paris, without giving them the specific hope, though, that you will give a concert here.

I have had your letter to Mosel about the metronome[2] translated into French; it made an enormous sensation among the composers. Your example has had a mighty effect. As proof I am sending you here a copy of a declaration by these gentlemen, to the effect that they do not merely accept the metronomic method of [tempo] designation; rather, they want to avail themselves of this [method] *exclusively.* From this it clearly follows that they renounce the Italian words for the interpretation of tempo.

What is the situation then, my little friend,[3] with the two symphonies that you have designated for performance on our tour? Surely you are close to finishing them?[4] In order to show you how diligently I am working, for my part, I am sending you on this occasion two copies of a chart[5] that is designed to give composers a guide to the designations from which they may choose in all meters, depending upon whether the piece of music has a slow, moderate or fast tempo. This chart has just left the press; the explication is not yet printed, but you shall also receive copies of it as soon as possible. It goes without saying that I do not want to give *you* any instruction about it; you know the subject as well as anyone. But there are stupid and lazy people who must be fed the truth with a cooking ladle,[6] and who do not want to take any, not even the least trouble to learn something—and there are only too many of these in Paris. In Table 3 of this chart you will find the absurdity of the Italian words [for speed] proven metronomically, demonstrating that no composer agrees with the other about the meaning of these words.[7]

If, as I wish and hope, you write back to me soon, let me know when you actually intend to set out on your artistic tour,[8] whereupon I shall make my plans accordingly. Meanwhile I greet you from my whole heart, and remain

Your sincerest friend,
J. Maelzel

P.S. I have changed my lodging. My address is now: Carré St. Martin No. 29F.

1. Johann Nepomuk Maelzel (1772–1838), mechanic, inventor and sometime Hapsburg court engineer, who had invented an improved metronome earlier in the decade and collaborated with Beethoven in the composition of *Wellington's Victory,* Op. 91, in 1813. He and/or his brother Leonhard made several ear trumpets for Beethoven as the composer's hearing continued to deteriorate. Maelzel had recently spent two months (from November 1817 to mid-January 1818) visiting Vienna (see Günther Haupt, "J. N. Mälzels Briefe an Breitkopf & Härtel," *Der Bär* [1927], 122–145).

2. Beethoven's 1817 letter to Ignaz Franz von Mosel (1772–1844), Viennese conductor of the Gesellschaft der Musikfreunde (Anderson No. 845); the letter heartily endorsed the metronome. As early as April 8, 1816, Maelzel had unveiled his *Chronometer* to the foremost composers in Paris and created a sensation, noting that he had developed it with "insightful advice from his friend, the famous master Salieri." See Gasparo Spontini, Paris, letter to Antonio Salieri, Vienna, April 9, 1816, in Ida Marie Lipsius (La Mara), ed., *Musikerbriefe aus fünf Jahrhunderten*, 2 vols. (Leipzig: Breitkopf und Härtel, 1886), II, 23–24. Mosel had been a student of, and remained a friend (indeed became the biographer) of, Salieri.

3. Maelzel greets Beethoven above as "Bester Freund," and addresses him here as "Freundchen," but still uses the polite form *Sie*.

4. Ries's letter of June 9, 1817 (No. 239 above), had requested two symphonies for Beethoven's projected journey to London early in 1818. This reference corresponds to the verbal sketches for a pair of symphonies, ultimately leading to the Symphony No. 9, reported in Nottebohm, *Zweite Beethoveniana*, pp. 162–163, as deriving from about this time. See also Thayer-Forbes, p. 888, for summary. The phrase literally reads: "You are surely close to the finales?" From the dating of this letter, Beethoven seems to have contemplated taking Maelzel along with him to London, possibly to drum up enthusiasm for *Wellington's Victory*, Op. 91.

5. One copy of the chart (one side of a full sheet, reproduced here in different format) is housed in the Staatsbibliothek zu Berlin–Preussischer Kulturbesitz, Mus. ms. autogr. Beethoven 37, 18.

On the blank back of this chart, nephew Karl, then eleven years old, penciled some notes to Beethoven at seemingly different, but closely proximate, times: "Mother asks that, since she is very tired today, she wants me to bring Andre [*sic*] along in place of her. At this, I asked whether she could count on Ander's [*sic*] honesty, whereupon she answered yes. I therefore said that if she cannot get Ander [*sic*], she herself should come. . . ." Somewhat later, Karl noted: "Mother said that she could surely go with [us]." Below and partially mingled with these notes are further jottings: "a portion of meat" and "she does nothing." This blank side of the metronome chart therefore functioned as something of a conversation sheet, at just about the time Beethoven began using conversation books more systematically.

The "Andre" or "Ander" mentioned by Karl may be one Court Councillor Anders, who worked in the Head Customs Office in Vienna (see Anderson No. 899: tentatively identified by Otto Erich Deutsch as Bernhard Anders, Ritter von Porodin, who drew a pension as a bank official until 1825). Thus, Anders may have assisted either Johanna van Beethoven (Karl's mother), Ludwig or both in securing the interest from brother Carl's estate that was intended for young Karl's support (see Anderson, III, 1371, 1377–1378, for possible references to such activity in various legal documents).

6. Ley read the German as: "dumme und faule Leute, denen man die Wahrheit

mit dem Kuhlöffel im Mund streichen muss." Despite Maelzel's ornate handwriting, the autograph indicates that the key word in this phrase is "Kochlöffel," rendering Ley's "cow-spoon" into "cooking spoon" or ladle, a variant on a common German idiom for "spoon feeding."

7. On September 27, 1817, Maelzel sent a relatively simple chart of metronome marks and Italian verbal designations to Breitkopf und Härtel for publication in the *Allgemeine musikalische Zeitung.* By January 18, 1818, he sent additions, designating what to do with such qualifiers as *affetuoso, agitato, amoroso, animato, appassionato, con brio, brillante, capriccioso, con delicatezza, dolce, energico, con fuoco, grazioso, gustoso, legato, maestoso, marcato, mesto, con moto, pastorale, patetico, piacevole, religioso, scherzoso, sdnegnoso, sentimentale, serio, smanioso, sostenuto, con spirito, staccato, strepitoso* and *vivace.* They were not published. (Reproduced in Haupt, pp. 132–133, 136.)

The present chart, in three tables and dating from April 1818, represents a more complex concept. Table 1 presents metronome marks in ascending order, as applied to various meters, with designations of speed (in French, English, German and Italian) posted along the way. Table 2 (placed vertically on the left side of the sheet) essentially presents the layout of the increments on the physical metronome itself. Table 3 (to which Maelzel specifically refers at this point) presents the divergent and inconsistent ways in which various composers (Paer, Clementi, Cherubini, Méhul, Spontini, Beethoven, Henri-Montan Berton, Cramer, Viotti, Nicolò [Nicolas Isouard] and Charles-Simon Catel) interpreted Italian verbal tempo indications, as translated here into metronome marks. Other than the recently deceased Méhul (died October 18, 1817) and Nicolò (died March 23, 1818), all the composers listed were alive at the time. This chart was ultimately published in the *Allgemeine musikalische Zeitung* (the *Intelligenz-Blatt,* no. 8 [September 1821]) with an explanation by Maelzel, probably the explication to which this letter refers.

8. The tour never materialized.

Incipit: Sie warten von mir wohl. . . .

Sources: Ley, "Aus Briefen an Beethoven," pp. 147–149 (two-thirds of the letter); summary in Nohl, *Neue Beethoven Briefe,* p. 154. Autograph in the Staatsbibliothek zu Berlin–Preussischer Kulturbesitz, Mus. ms. autogr. Beethoven 35, 51; listed in Kalischer, "Beethoven-Autographe," p. 50, and Bartlitz, p. 134. Maelzel's chart, with Karl's jottings, listed in Bartlitz, p. 187.

TABLE No. 2

Scale of the Metronome

50	50
	52
	54
	56
	58
60	60
	63
	66
	69
70	72
	76
80	80
	84
	88
90	92
	96
100	100
	104
	108
110	112
	116
120	120
	126
130	132
	138
140	144
150	152
160	160

TABLE No. 1

Division of Musical Time, according to J. Maelzel's Metronome

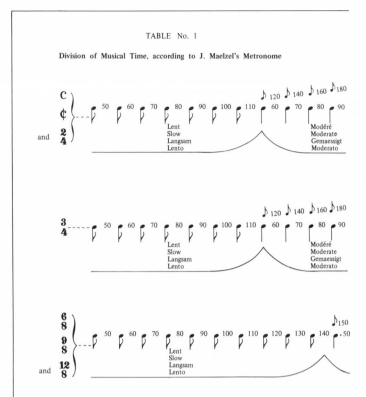

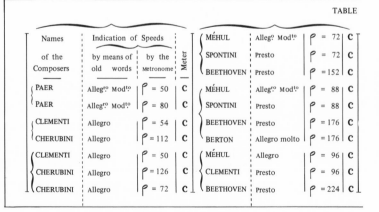

TABLE

Names of the Composers	Indication of Speeds — by means of old words	by the Metronome	Meter					
				MÉHUL	Alleg.o Mod.to	♩ = 72	C
				SPONTINI	Presto	♩ = 72	C
				BEETHOVEN	Presto	♩ = 152	C
PAER	Alleg.to Mod.to	♩ = 50	C	MÉHUL	Alleg.to Mod.to	♩ = 88	C
PAER	Alleg.to Mod.to	♩ = 80	C	SPONTINI	Presto	♩ = 88	C
CLEMENTI	Allegro	♩ = 54	C	BEETHOVEN	Presto	♩ = 176	C
CHERUBINI	Allegro	♩ = 112	C	BERTON	Allegro molto	♩ = 176	C
CLEMENTI	Allegro	♩ = 50	C	MÉHUL	Allegro	♩ = 96	C
CHERUBINI	Allegro	♩ = 126	C	CLEMENTI	Presto	♩ = 96	C
CHERUBINI	Allegro	♩ = 72	C	BEETHOVEN	Presto	♩ = 224	C

Eighth notes: ♪ 200 · ♪ 220 · ♪ 240 · ♪ 280 · ♪ 320 · ♪ 360 · ♪ 400 · ♪ 440 · ♪ 480 · ♪ 520 · ♪ 560 · ♪ 600 · ♪ 640 · ♪ 720 · ♪ 800

Quarter notes: ♩ 120 · ♩ 140 · ♩ 160 · ♩ 180 · ♩ 200 · ♩ 220 · ♩ 240 · ♩ 260 · ♩ 280 · ♩ 300 · ♩ 320 · ♩ 360 · ♩ 400 · ♩ 160 · ♩ 180 · ♩ 200

Lower notes: 100 · 110 · 60 · 70 · 80 · 90 · 100 · 110 · 120 · 130 · 140 · 150 · 80 · 90 · 100

Vite / Quick / Geschwind / Presto

Eighth notes: ♪ 200 · ♪ 220 · ♪ 240 · ♪ 260 · ♪ 280 · ♪ 300 · ♪ 360 · ♪ 420 · ♪ 480 · ♪ 540 · ♪ 600 · ♪ 660 · ♪ 720 · ♪ 780 · ♪ 840

Quarter notes: ♩ 150 · ♩ 180 · ♩ 210 · ♩ 240 · ♩ 270 · ♩ 300 · ♩ 330 · ♩ 360 · ♩ 390 · ♩ 420

Lower notes: 100 · 110 · 120 · 130 · 140 · 50 · 60 · 70 · 80 · 90 · 100 · 110 · 120 · 130 · 140

Vite / Quick / Geschwind / Presto

Eighth notes: ♪ 180 · ♪ 210 · ♪ 240 · ♪ 270 · ♪ 300 · ♪ 330 · ♪ 360 · ♪ 390 · ♪ 420 · ♪ 450 · ♪ 480 · ♪ 540 · ♪ 600 · ♪ 660 · ♪ 720

Dotted quarter notes: ♩. 160 · ♩. 180 · ♩. 200 · ♩. 220 · ♩. 240

Lower notes: 60 · 70 · 80 · 90 · 100 · 110 · 120 · 130 · 140 · 150 · 80 · 90 · 100 · 110 · 120

Modéré / Moderate / Gemaessigt / Moderato

Vite / Quick / Geschwind / Presto

Eighth notes: ♪ 180 · ♪ 210 · ♪ 240 · ♪ 270 · ♪ 300 · ♪ 330 · ♪ 360

Lower notes: 60 · 70 · 80 · 90 · 100 · 110 · 120

Vite / Quick / Geschwind / Presto

No. 3

Composer	Tempo	Value	Metre		Composer	Tempo	Value	Metre
CHERUBINI	Andantino	♩ = 76	2/4		NICOLÒ	Andantino	♩. = 52	6/8
CHERUBINI	Andantino	♩ = 104	2/4		CATEL	Andantino	♩. = 126	6/8
CRAMER	Moderato	♩ = 63	2/4		PAER	Andante	♩. = 50	6/8
CRAMER	Moderato	♩ = 116	2/4		BERTON	Andante	♩. = 100	6/8
CRAMER	Allo. non tanto	♩ = 138	2/4		CRAMER	Più tosto Modto	♩. = 92	6/8
CRAMER	Presto	♩ = 138	2/4		CRAMER	Allo. agitato	♩. = 66	6/8
CRAMER	Moderato	♪ = 100	2/4		PAER	Andante	♪ = 120	6/8
CRAMER	Moderato	♪ = 252	2/4		PAER	Lento	♪ = 120	6/8
VIOTTI	Andante	♪ = 52	3/8		PAER	Andante	♪ = 112	6/8
BERTON	Andante	♪ = 152	3/8		BERTON	Andante	♪ = 300	6/8

249. George Thomson to Beethoven

Edinburgh; June 22, 1818[1]

My dear Monsieur Beethoven,

I have received the three melodies with your letter of February 21 and your letter of March 2, in which you offer to compose for me themes with variations for the piano, etc., etc. I infinitely respect your talent, and I take inexpressible pleasure in your music; and if I were rich, or if I could be reimbursed merely for the price that I pay you, without making a single ducat more, I would be only too happy to see you always work on your own conditions, solely to serve a man of genius. But alas, my good sir! Everyone in this country finds that your works are much too difficult; there are only a very small number of masters with the greatest skill who will be able to play them. — My songs with your ritornellos and accompaniments do not sell! I recently wrote to my correspondent, one of the foremost music dealers in London, to note to him how much this surprised and distressed me, and here is his response: "Although a great and sublime artist, Beethoven *is not understood,* and his arrangement of your songs is *much too difficult* for the public. After all your announcements in the journals, people do not buy any of the volumes with his accompaniments."

You see, then, that my zeal for your composition has produced nothing but loss for me. But, despite a blind public, I shall say that I find several of your latest ritornellos and accompaniments sufficiently simple and easy, and entirely charming. And I flatter myself that the time is coming when the English will be able to comprehend and truly perceive the great beauties of your works.

I have been thinking, however, that if an accompaniment for the flute were added to my songs, it would probably make them noticed by the flutists. I am not speaking of an additional accompaniment, written to be played along with the violin accompaniment; rather of an accompaniment for the flute to be played *instead* of the violin part when there is no violin. A flutist of this city has arranged an accompaniment for the flute from your violin part, and I believe that I really would be able to publish it for the marketplace. But I should publish it with more confidence if you were so kind as to look over it and make the changes or the corrections that you approve. In this case, not only shall I be very grateful for your benevolence, but in return I shall agree to your proposition to compose for me twelve themes with variations for the piano. I shall send you eight more Scottish airs for your ritornellos and accompaniments.

And for the twelve themes with variations, I shall pay you the sum that you ask in your letter, 100 ducats;[2] and for the ritornellos and accompaniments of the eight airs, 40 ducats more, that is to say the round sum of *one hundred forty ducats in cash.*

Following the advice of my correspondent in London, I would like you to choose the themes from among the *Scottish* airs that you have harmonized for me, and to take two or three of them from among the Tyrolean airs, if they seem to you to be pleasing and well adapted for the themes. One would also like an accompaniment for *flute ad libitum* for all the themes, if you please, and that you write the variations in a *familiar* and *easy* and a bit *brilliant* style, so that a greater number of our young ladies may play them and enjoy them. I need one copy, written correctly and distinctly for the engraver.

Regarding the eight melodies, I request that you pay particular attention when making the ritornellos and accompaniments, that they be simple and easy so that the [female] singer will not be embarrassed *while accompanying herself.* And one would love for the melody, or something resembling it, to be indicated delicately in the piano accompaniment. In addition to giving me the score, have the kindness to send me separate parts to them for the violin, *the flute* and the violoncello.

Believing that you will give me the pleasure of examining and correcting the flute accompaniment, I shall send it to you with each volume to which it applies, as the occasion presents itself. First I shall send you the newest volume, which you have not yet seen, and which I greatly desire to present to you.[3] I hope to have the package transported to Vienna by means of my banker in London before long. I shall place in it the superb English poem with the literal translation into German, of which I have already told you.[4] If you become acquainted with the meaning and the pronunciation of the English words with the aid of the translator of which you speak, if you compose the music in the style of an oratorio, if you yourself bring it to England and have it performed in London under your own supervision, then in my opinion, you will secure for yourself not only a great deal of money but an increase of your reputation in England.

You made mention of the name of some person as the means of having a large package reach Vienna promptly, but the writing was so indistinct (and it did not have any address) that I was not able to make out any of it.

More than a year ago, Messrs. Fries wrote to my banker that they had a package of printed music to send me when they found the occasion to do so. *I have never received it.*

Have you published any trios or quartets of late? I have only twice had the extreme pleasure of hearing the Quartets dedicated to Count Rasumovsky[5] played well, although I have had them for several years. Our professors do not play them because of the intense study and the great work that they demand. I infinitely regret this, because I admire them with enthusiasm.

But tell me, my dear sir, is it not possible for you to demonstrate the enchanting power of your art in a simpler form? Could your genius not lower itself to compose music equally superb, but less difficult as to execution, so that amateurs could partake of so delicious a feast?

Is it not true that in all the fine arts the greatest beauty is found, in general, combined with the most perfect simplicity? And do such works not find the most lasting and most universal admiration?

I would very much like to see a volume of quartets and a volume of trios for violin, viola and violoncello, obligati, composed by you with all the richness of your genius, but easy to play, particularly the first violin. They would be a great gift to our amateurs, and for that matter to our connoisseurs themselves. I have heard the most distinguished professors express their regret that you do not consider this. I also say [this] because of the solicitude that I feel for your welfare, and for that of music: this is why I am sure that you will be very grateful to me for it, although you [may] not share my opinion.

Your memory has deceived you, no doubt, concerning the sum that I received from you [*sic*][6] for the last three airs. My banker has sent me the memorandum from Messrs. Fries, where they have noted 12 ducats paid by them to you. Consequently I have paid this sum to my banker, and he has given me *your own receipt* to Messrs. Fries for *12 ducats.*

Several things have prevented me from writing to you sooner: I have been ill, but am beginning to be restored.

I have the honor to be, etc., etc.

Pierre Rode (1774–1830), French violinist who gave the first
performance of Beethoven's Sonata, Op. 96. Engraving, artist
unidentified. See No. 169. Source: Bekker (suppl.), p. 67.

Große musikalische Akademie,

welche

auf hohes Verlangen

heute Dienstag den 29 November 1814 im großen k. k. Redoutensaale,

zum Vortheile

des Herrn Ludwig van Beethoven

abgehalten wird.

Die dabey vorkommenden Musikstücke,

sämmtlich von der Composition des Herrn L. van Beethoven, sind folgende:

Erstens: Die neue große Symphonie.
Zweytens: Eine neue Cantate: Der glorreiche Augenblick, von Dr. Aloys Weissenbach.
Drittens: Eine große vollstimmige Instrumental-Composition, geschrieben auf

Wellingtons Sieg

in der Schlacht bey Vittoria.

Erster Theil: Schlacht.   Zweyter Theil: Sieges-Symphonie.

Die Solostimmen der Cantate werden vorgetragen von Mad. Milder, Dlle. Bondra, Herrn Wild und Herrn Forti. Hr. Umlauf hat den Platz am Klavier übernommen.

Die Eintritts-Preise sind auf dem Parterre 3 Gulden, auf der Gallerie 5 Gulden.

Die Eintritts-Billete sind heute am Eingange des Saals an der Casse zu haben.

Die Zu- und Abfahrt ist wie gewöhnlich bey den Redouten.

Der Anfang der Akademie ist Mittags mit Schlag 12 Uhr.

Der Text von der Cantate ist an der Casse für 12 kr zu haben.

Ankündigung der Akademie
vom 29. November 1814

Announcement for the concert,
November 29, 1814, featuring Beethoven's cantata
Der glorreiche Augenblick. See Nos. 193 and 194.
Source: Bekker (suppl.), p. 81.

Joseph Hammer (1774–1852), colorful orientalist who sought to interest
Beethoven in a libretto. Engraving by Friedrich John after Johann
Peter Krafft. See No. 199. Source: Historisches Museum der Stadt Wien,
I.N. 103.619; Deutsch, *Schubert: Leben in Bildern*, p. 509.

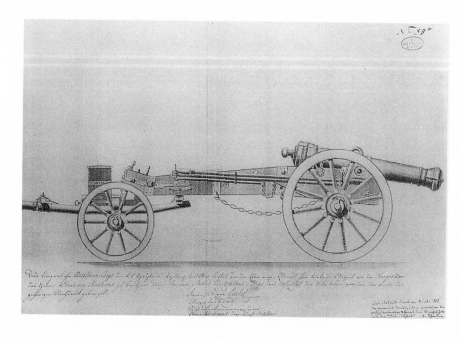

Above: Full sheet with cannon, under which is Franz Xaver Embel's letter to Beethoven, sometime before June 3, 1816. See No. 225. Source: Staatsbibliothek zu Berlin–Preussischer Kulturbesitz.

Top right: Dr. Wilhelm Christian Müller (1752–1831), leader of a group of Beethoven enthusiasts in Bremen. Lithograph, unidentified artist. See Nos. 266 and 81. Source: Focke Museum, Bremen, A 398; H. M. Hauschild, *Alte Bremer,* p. 43.

Bottom right: Count Joseph Sedlnitzky (1778–1855), chief of police who conducted an investigation of Beethoven and nephew Karl in 1820. Lithograph, artist unidentified. See No. 270. Source: Eismann, p. 93.

Carl Friedrich Peters (1779–1827), Leipzig publisher, was disappointed
in the small-scale works Beethoven sent him. Portrait, unidentified artist,
after 1820. See Nos. 286, 290, 294, 295, etc. Source: Homburg, *Spohr,* p. 88.
© Reprinted with permission of C. F. Peters, Frankfurt.

Count Moritz Dietrichstein (1775–1864), administrator of the Hapsburg court's musical establishment. Lithograph by Joseph Kriehuber (1828). See Nos. 128, 311 and 314. Source: Österreichische Nationalbibliothek; Deutsch, *Schubert: Leben in Bildern,* p. 214.

Johann Nepomuk Schelble (1789–1837), conductor of the Cäcilien-
Verein in Frankfurt. Lithograph, artist unidentified. See No. 315.
Source: Historisches Museum der Stadt Frankfurt am Main,
N42.125; Homburg, *Spohr,* p. 88.

Ferdinand Georg Waldmüller (1793–1865), genre and landscape artist who painted Beethoven's portrait in 1823. Print (source unidentified). See Nos. 316 and 318. Source: Historisches Museum der Stadt Wien, I.N. 75.689; Lütge, "Waldmüllers Beethovenbild" (1927), facing p. 36.

Johann Schickh (1770–1835), editor of the *Wiener Zeitschrift für Kunst,
Literatur, Theater und Mode.* Lithograph by Joseph Kriehuber (1835).
See No. 323. Source: Österreichische Nationalbibliothek; Deutsch,
Schubert: Leben in Bildern, p. 397.

Franz Schoberlechner (1797–1843), Viennese pianist who solicited a recommendation from Beethoven in 1823. Lithograph by Joseph Teltscher (1827). See Nos. 324 and 330. Source: Österreichische Nationalbibliothek; Deutsch, *Schubert: Leben in Bildern*, p. 363.

Ein Brief des Erzherzogs Rudolph an Beethoven

Archduke Rudolph (1788–1831), letter to Beethoven,
July 31, 1823. See No. 332. Source: Staatsbibliothek
zu Berlin–Preussischer Kulturbesitz; Bekker
(suppl.), p. 101.

[Thomson's note (in English) concerning the music sent and his annotations of them (originally in French):]

The following are the eight airs included in the above letter, to be arranged as trios, with his ritornellos and accompaniments, with the words prefixed [*sic*] to each in French, in order to convey to him a proper idea of the general character of the melodies, chiefly as derived from the verses with which they stand associated.

[1.]   "From thee Eliza I must go," Vol. 1, p. 15.[7]
        (The tender farewells between a girl and her beloved.)
[2.]   "Sweet Annie from the sea beach came," or rather the English verses "To fair Fidele's grassy tomb," which last words are to be set to the trio [*sic*], Vol. 1, p. 24.[8]
        (Lamentation on the death of a beautiful girl.)
[3.]   "Duncan Gray," Vol. 1, p. 48.[9]
        (A shepherd, enamored of a village flirt, is rebuffed and becomes disdainful in turn; but the village girl repents her folly, is pardoned, and they are married.)
[4.]   "She's fair and she's fause," or rather the second stanza, "Wha e'r ye be that woman love," which are fitted for a plurality of voices, Vol. 1, p. 40.[10]
        (Oh charming, angelic woman, but to my misfortune, inconstant and perfidious.)
[5.]   "Auld lang syne," Vol. 2, p. 68.[11]
        (A reunion of friends after several years of separation, recalling with delight the innocent pastimes of their youth.)
[6.]   "Blythe have I been on yon hill," Vol. 2, p. 58.[12]
        (My mistress is so beautiful, but so cold, that neither cheerfulness nor singing can give me pleasure.)
[7.]   "Low doon in the broom," Vol. 2, p. 86.[13]
        (My father is sullen, and my mother lowborn, but never mind, for my lover is constant.)
[8.]   Manuscript air of the Strathspey kind, to be attached to Burns's beautiful verses, "Now Spring has clad the groves in green," Vol. 2, [p. 91,] instead of the meager air to which [they] are at present set.[14]
        (Song of the most constant and the most devoted love.)

The following lines [writes Thomson] were prefixed to the eight Scottish airs before enumerated:

> Eight Scottish melodies, for which Monsr. B[eethoven] will be so kind as to compose ritornellos and accompaniments for piano, violin, flute and violoncello, in a *cantabile* manner and with great simplicity. Monsr. Beethoven will be so kind also to arrange seven of the airs as *terzetti*, by adding a second part and a bass to each one. Perhaps he will be able to give a little bit of *simple* imitation in the second [voice] or in the bass of some of them, but only if he finds it entirely fitting and proper. Probably homophonic harmony is more agreeable for our simple airs. In this case, while requesting that Mr. B[eethoven] introduce them in the voice parts, he should be the judge of it. Mr. B. may introduce little ritornellos in places, where he thinks that they will be to good effect, or to give a little respite to the voice.
>
> N.B. We would like the accompaniment to be interrupted from time to time, to give the singer time to take a breath, instead of running without interruption from beginning to end, thereby forcing the singer to keep time strictly, without any *ad libitum*.

1. Replies to Beethoven's letters of February 21, 1818 (Anderson No. 892; MacArdle & Misch No. 234), and March 2 (or 11), 1818 (Anderson No. 896; MacArdle & Misch No. 237). MacArdle's editions of both these letters (as was his custom) contain copious notes on the identification and background of the works discussed. See also Beethoven's receipt to Fries, February 1818 (MacArdle & Misch No. 235).

2. Items in Opp. 105 and 107. Thomson had placed a large X before this paragraph, for some reason no longer apparent.

3. *A Select Collection of Original Scottish Airs*, vol. 5, including Op. 108 and five Haydn settings, published in June 1818.

4. Thomson mentioned this, briefly, in his June 25, 1817, letter (No. 240 above).

5. String Quartets, Op. 59.

6. Surely Thomson meant "that you received from me."

7. WoO 158/III, No. 5. Barry Cooper has identified all the songs given in this list. The volume numbers cited refer to Thomson's earlier publications of Scottish songs.

8. WoO 156, No. 9.

9. WoO 156, No. 2.

10. WoO 156, No. 8.

11. WoO 156, No. 11.

12. WoO 156, No. 12.

13. WoO 156, No. 4.

14. WoO 156, No. 7.

Incipit: J'ai reçu les 3 melodies avec votre lettre. . . .

Sources: Summarized in MacArdle, "Beethoven and Thomson," p. 47, and Hadden, *George Thomson,* pp. 335–336, 343. Copy in Thomson's copybook, British Library, Add. MS 35268, pp. 21v–25r.

250. *Hans Georg Nägeli to Beethoven*

Zürich; July 3, 1818

Permit me, my highly honored friend, to make herewith a revelation to you! Upon the establishment of my expanded music business, I intend to compile a thematic catalog. To this end, I wish to obtain from you a complete list of your hitherto published works, with annotations concerning the original publisher for each opus; and if, among your many arranged works you notice some of which you approve, or even some of which you disapprove, I would likewise ask a short annotation to that effect.

At the same time, I recommend to your well-disposed attention the undertaking of the Bach Mass,[1] and request your obliging intercession with the art lovers there.

One of my favorite plans is to produce the score of a major church work each year, and if this undertaking succeeds, perhaps I will be so fortunate in the future also to be able to acquire one of yours.

Have you received, my friend, the letter that I enclosed last winter in one to Herr von Collin?[2]

1. Nägeli advertised his edition of J. S. Bach's Mass in B Minor in 1818, but it was not actually published until 1833. Beethoven evidently did not know this when, on September 9, 1824, he ordered a copy from the Zürich publisher. See Anderson No. 1306.

2. Nägeli's letter of winter 1817/1818 seems not to have survived. The Collin meant here was not the poet Heinrich von Collin, who had died in 1811, but probably his brother Matthäus (1779–1824), author and professor of the history of philosophy in Vienna.

Incipit: Erlauben Sie, mein hochverehrter Freund! . . .

Sources: Nohl, *Briefe* (1865), p. 269; quoted in Staehelin, *Nägeli und Beethoven,* p. 40; letter cited briefly in Kalischer (German), V, 50–51. The autograph of this letter and a once-extant copy made by Nägeli's son Hermann seem not to have survived.

251. Dr. Karl Witte, the Elder,[1] to Beethoven

Vienna; July 12, 1818

Most highly honored Herr *Kapellmeister!*

I most ardently wished for the happiness of [making your] acquaintance. I am told by many, however, that you are often not at home,[2] and my visit here is for only a very short time yet. I am still staying for a little while in Baden, though, and venture perhaps from there to pay you my respects. Otherwise I belong to the great number of those who most sincerely admire you and your splendid compositions. For that very reason, I venture to send you a few poems, with the submissive request that you set one or two of them, for I would consider myself very fortunate if my text were elevated by your beautiful music.[3]

My son is the young man who, in his eighth year and, thank God, continuously since then, attracted the attention of the learned and cultivated world. He is now 18 years old, a doctor of philosophy and a doctor of jurisprudence, as well as a member of four learned societies, and now, at the expense of the King of Prussia, is making a scholarly journey through Europe. He joins with me in paying you his honor.

With deepest respect,

Your most obedient,

Dr. Karl Witte, the Elder

[P.S.] I request that you address your reply either to Baden, in care of Doctor von Schenk, or to Vienna, in care of the Prussian chargé d'affaires Count von Pirot.[4]

1. The author of this letter, as he explains during its course, is the father of Karl Witte (born, Lochau near Halle/Saale, July 1, 1800; died, Halle, March 6, 1883), future jurist as well as Dante and Boccaccio scholar.

2. Beethoven spent most of the summer of 1818 in Mödling.

3. In the hope that Beethoven might set his poetry, Witte is one of the more personally unassuming authors who approached the composer. Seven poems are preserved with the autograph of this letter: "Frühlingsgefühle," "Klage" (Rundgesang), "Mein Eintritt ins Tirol," "An Emma," "Der Sommerabend in der Schweiz," "An die Liebe" and "Die Freiheit."

4. The name could also be read Picot.

Incipit: Sehnlichst wünscht ich das Glück. . . .

Sources: Autograph in the Staatsbibliothek zu Berlin–Preussischer Kulturbesitz, Mus. ms. autogr. Beethoven 37, 32; listed in Kalischer, "Beethoven-Autographe," p. 66, and Bartlitz, p. 188.

252. *Thomas Broadwood to Beethoven*

London; July 17, 1818

My dear Monsieur Beethoven,

My friend Mr. Stumpff (bearer of this letter)[1] intends to go to Vienna. I do not need to tell you that all who have ever heard [your] music generally envy him [the opportunity] of making your acquaintance, or even only of seeing you and speaking to you. Please permit him to tune and regulate the piano[2] that I had the pleasure of sending you, and that I hope has merited your approbation. I am extremely sorry to hear this past week that you have been ill again—but I hope that the next news that I receive from you, or from my estimable friend Mr. Bridi,[3] will tell me that you are well again. I remain forever, my dear Monsieur Beethoven,

Your sincere friend,

Thomas Broadwood

[P.S.] Please pass my respectful compliments on to Mr. Bridi.

1. Born in Thuringia (or Saxony), Johann Andreas Stumpff (1769–1846) went to London in ca. 1792 and worked for Broadwood. Later he became a harp manufacturer, and in this capacity was reintroduced to Beethoven by Tobias Haslinger (through a letter from Johann Andreas Streicher) in September 1824 (Thayer-Forbes, p. 919, amplified by Köhler et al., *Konversationshefte*, VI, 359).

2. Broadwood used the term *piano* here, rather than *pianoforte* or *fortepiano*, in reference to his firm's product.

3. See Bridi's letter to Broadwood, February 5, 1818 (No. 246 above), for background.

Incipit: Mon ami Mon^r Stumpff (porteur. . . .

Sources: Thayer-Deiters-Riemann, IV, 90; Kastner (1910), pp. 523–524; Kalischer (German), III, 270; Kalischer-Shedlock, II, 102. Autograph in the Staatsbibliothek zu Berlin–Preussischer Kulturbesitz, Mus. ms. autogr. Beethoven 35, 58; listed in Kalischer, "Beethoven-Autographe," p. 51, and Bartlitz, p. 136.

253. *George Thomson to Beethoven*

Edinburgh, Scotland; December 28, 1818[1]

To Monsr. Beethoven
Vienna

My dear Monsieur,

I have had the pleasure of receiving the twelve themes with your variations for piano and an accompaniment for flute;[2] but I regret that I have not received the flute part for the volume of songs. Nonetheless, you will, without doubt, be so kind as to correct it and to send it to me as soon as possible.

I find the majority of the variations to be full of beauty and genius, and entirely worthy of your talent. I have heard six of them played with great pleasure; I regret to say that there are two others that would not be successful here,[3] and I want to tell you about these:

I have not yet heard the last four of the twelve.

In order that I have the full number of twelve in a style that will please the public, permit me to ask you to do me the favor of composing two others, in place of those of which I have just spoken. And I ask you to do these in a pleasant and *cantabile* style, brilliant for the right hand as much as you please, but *easy* to play: this is what you have done in a charming manner in some of the themes that you have sent me, for example, in No. 7:[4]

I am sending you two themes, enclosed, to be varied, but I give you complete freedom to choose from among our national airs those that you prefer, although I admire both of them. I am also sending you another air for your ritornellos and accompaniments for piano, violin, flute and violoncello.

(Charlie he's my darling.)[5]

I have written to Messrs. Fries to pay you twenty-one ducats in gold, when you deliver the manuscripts to them, for I suppose that you will not give me the new themes in exchange for the two of which I spoke above.

I hope that you will take the greatest possible care not to permit anyone to have a copy of my Themes and Variations, etc., before they are published here. For it has been decided in our supreme court of law that if a musical composition is published in Vienna or elsewhere before being published in England, this negates the proprietary right in England and gives everyone the freedom to publish the music.

I hope to publish six of the Themes and Variations in three months and shall send you a copy, if you want it.[6]

My friends in London write me that you ought to be there soon. I hope that this is true.

I have the honor, my dear sir, to be

Your friend and very humble servant,

(signed) George Thomson

1. Replies to Beethoven's bill of sale, November 18, 1818 (MacArdle & Misch No. 240), although Thomson sent it back to Fries for a seal. MacArdle, "Beethoven and Thomson," pp. 47–48, provides the sequence with explanations.

2. Items in Opp. 105 and 107.

3. Op. 107, Nos. 8 and 10, respectively.

4. Op. 105, No. 4.

5. "O Charlie is my Darling," WoO 157, No. 3.

6. Items from *Twelve National Airs with Variations,* Op. 105, published in July 1819. *Incipit:* J'ai le plaisir de recevoir les 12 Themes. . . .

Sources: Summarized in MacArdle, "Beethoven and Thomson," p. 48. Copy in Thomson's copybook, British Library, Add. MS 35268, pp. 33r–34v.

254. Beethoven to Tobias Haslinger

[Vienna; 1818][1]

My good Provisional General Adjutant![2]

We appreciate you, etc., and once again appreciate you, *et cetera.*

I request first the three pieces still overdue yesterday, but the piano arrangement of the 6th Symphony in C minor[3] has been forgotten by the General Adjutant (Chief Rascal, etc.); and for just this reason I could be run into prison (for debt), as formerly happened to the Roman people—meanwhile you are also the Master of the Cavalry[4]—

The old year follows—the reply is to be entered in the yearbook, and the surplus credited to us.[5]

Yours, etc.

L. v. Beethoven

[Exterior:]
To the General Adjutant (Chief Rascal)
as well as the Master of the Mules[6]

1. The letter bears the inscription "Beethoven, 1818," in Haslinger's hand.

2. In this letter, Beethoven seems to call Haslinger "Provisional General Adjutant" and "Master of the Cavalry," with senior publishing partner Sigmund Anton Steiner called, as usual, the "General Adjutant" and "Chief Rascal" (*Hauptlump*). Beethoven's calling Haslinger "*Provisional* General Adjutant" may indicate Steiner's absence from Vienna, possibly for some event like Leipzig's spring trade fair.

3. Actually the Symphony No. 5 in C Minor, Op. 67, whose number was reversed with No. 6, the *Pastoral* Symphony in F, Op. 68, at their premiere performance on December 22, 1808.

4. *Magister Equitum* in the original. In letters such as Piringer's jocular message of July 25, 1822 (No. 297 below), soldiers or similar low-ranking military personnel

represent a monetary unit. This sentence, therefore, may indicate that, in Steiner's absence, Haslinger was in charge of the publishing firm's coffers.

5. During this period, Steiner & Co. provided what amounted to banking services (loans, savings, etc.) to Beethoven.

6. *Magister Mulorum* in the original. The relation of these mules to the horsemen or horses mentioned above is unclear. A pun on *mulier* (woman or wife, in this case plural) is also not out of the question.

Incipit: Wir erkennen dero etc. . . .

Sources: Transcribed and edited by Alan Tyson in Staehelin, "Unbekannte . . . Schriftstücke," pp. 69–72, with facsimile. Autograph in the Biblioteca Estense (Autografoteca Campori), Modena.

1819

255. George Thomson to Beethoven

Edinburgh; January 8, 1819[1]

Monsieur Louis van Beethoven
c/o Messrs. Fries & Co.
Vienna (Austria)

My dear Monsieur,

Since I wrote to you on the 28th of last month, I have heard all the themes and variations, in which I experienced, for the most part, a great pleasure.

But in addition to the two themes of which I spoke in my last letter, I find another that is not suitable for the young ladies of this country: I speak of the Tyrolean air, No. 11,[2] which begins thus:

As the two hands, in this piece, are together in continuous movement, it is much too difficult for persons who amuse themselves with themes and variations; and I assure you that it would be entirely useless for me to publish it.

You will pardon me this frankness, because it is necessary. I therefore request that, in place of the air of which I have just spoken, you would be willing to choose some other national air—[of] Russia, Germany, or of any other country that pleases you—and to compose variations in a beautiful and brilliant style, but if it please you, not too difficult, for the ladies of Scotland may not be as strong as those in your country where music is so cultivated.[3]

I also request you to give me a new variation for one of the themes:[4]

to be substituted in place of the variation that begins thus:

The effect that this variation produces does not satisfy me; it is, so to speak, too *meager*, and would not be appreciated by the public. I therefore request that you give me another one, in a more singing manner and in a style more brilliant, or flowing; and since the theme is a very favorite air, that you give me the pleasure of adding another variation, since the piece is a bit short.

For this trouble, regarding No. 9, and for the three new themes with variations that you still have to do—and for the air of which I spoke to you in my last letter, Messrs. Fries will pay you thirty-one ducats in gold when you show them this letter, notwithstanding my letter of the 28th.

I shall have the great pleasure of hearing your news. Please accept my sincere wishes during this season, and for many happy years to come. I have the honor, etc.

(signed) G. Thomson

1. Continues Thomson's message of December 28, 1818 (No. 253 above).

2. Op. 107, No. 1.

3. In a letter to George Farquhar Graham, January 25, 1817, Thomson relates that his daughter Anne plays through these materials for him: "Tho' not a great player, [she] is on a footing at least with nine tenths of the Scottish ladies in ready reading and execution"—therefore, Thomson's daughter was the measure by which Beethoven's work was judged!

4. Op. 107, No. 4. The variation that Thomson illustrates does not appear in the printed *Gesamtausgabe*.

5. Thomson's letter of December 28, 1818, offered only twenty-one ducats.

Incipit: Depuis que je vous ai écrit. . . .

Sources: Summarized in MacArdle, "Beethoven and Thomson," p. 48, and very briefly in Hadden, *George Thomson*, p. 343. Copy in Thomson's copybook, British Library, Add. MS 35268, pp. 35r–36r.

256. Antonie Brentano[1] to Johann Michael Sailer, Landshut[2]

Frankfurt [am Main]; February 22, 1819

Dear Delightful Friend!

May it not unpleasantly surprise you that I bother you again so soon with a letter,[3] but having been selected as a go-between in order to ask a favor of you (in fact, a good deed because the question concerns the welfare—even the salvation, I believe—of a human being), I do not hesitate, with all the confidence *you* inspire so sincerely, to call upon you for your counsel and action.

Vienna, my glorious and beloved home city, is full of great merit, etc., etc., but has—to some extent especially now, owing to the great uncertainty of *pecuniary* conditions—unforeseeable evil consequences upon *morality* throughout all classes. This great disadvantage makes it most difficult, indeed almost impossible, to bring up a normal boy suitably, and the trouble is compounded for one who is born under an unlucky *constellation*—like the one whose rescue could be achieved by removing him [from such circumstances].

He is an ardent boy, 10 to 12 years old,[4] the only son of parents without means—his father dead, his mother publicly [known] as a thief,[5] with a very low style of living, full of intriguing and the most vulgar links in the chain of life, and with her maternal rights set aside by the courts. [The youth appears] to me to be very talented and of great aptitude; he learns with ease—a model boy with an indescribable frivolity. His father's death, three years ago, resulted in his care being left to his uncle, his father's brother.

This great, excellent man, whose name I have enclosed here,[6] is even greater as a human being than he is as an artist. He has made it the greatest concern of his life to provide the best conditions possible. But with his tender heart, glowing soul, faulty hearing, with his very demanding profession as an artist, and [with] the few pure resources that stand at the command of the educator there, with the isolation of the boy in his *uncle's house*, and with the imperfection of public institutions, with the eternally active and dangerously intriguing spirit of the mother, etc., etc., not a single tolerable patchwork has resulted up to now.

He [the uncle] wishes to send this talented, lighthearted boy to a Catholic university that is not too expensive, where, besides the Invisible Spirit to protect him, a visible spirit would lovingly care for his salvation and preservation. Heaven has suggested Landshut to him, and since he learned through one of my relatives that I was fortunate enough to know you personally—you, whom he has already venerated in spirit for a long time.[7] He very ardently desired that I would introduce the matter to you, and inquire if the boy would find well-being there; whether he, who is in the third school,[8] can also learn *drawing* and *French* there upon continuing his studies; and how much it might cost for boarding such a student.

Since you, dear Sailer, know very well how everyone feels,[9] you also know very well how you have to answer a person like this one, who asks you with such warm will, such sincere confidence and with such needful expectations as befits this B[eethoven]. He is natural, simple and wise, with pure intentions; and the finest and surest approach would be if *you* write him as he deserves—that is, as if *you* had known him for a long time, this singer of pious songs. The fastest way is for the letter to go *directly;* he is expecting it, because I have indicated to him that one can predict kindness from you. . . .

The children kiss your hands, whose blessings may rest upon me.

Your devoted,

Winkler Hausfrau[10]

1. Antonie Brentano, née von Birkenstock (1780–1869), born in Vienna, moved to Frankfurt in 1798 on her wedding to Franz Brentano, returned to Vienna (followed by her husband), 1809–1812, to care for her father and settle his sizable estate, then moved back to Frankfurt. Maynard Solomon posits convincingly that she was the "Immortal Beloved" (*Beethoven,* pp. 158–189), and Susan Lund, hypothesizing further, believes that Beethoven may have fathered the Brentanos' last child, Karl Josef, born March 8, 1813 ("Beethoven: A True 'Fleshly Father'?" *Beethoven Newsletter* [San Jose] 3, no. 1 [Spring 1988], 1, 8–11; 3, no. 2 [Summer 1988], 25, 36–40).

2. Johann Michael Sailer (1751–1832), Bavarian orator and educator, later archbishop of Regensburg, was in 1819 professor of philosophy at the University of Landshut, forty miles northeast of Munich.

3. Antonie had most recently written Sailer on February 12; therefore, Beethoven's request for assistance must have arrived between February 12 and 22 (Sandberger,

"Antonie Brentano an Johann Michael Sailer," p. 253). On ca. February 1, 1819, Beethoven had written to the lawyer Johann Baptist Bach (1779–1847), entrusting him with his nephew Karl's welfare (Anderson No. 937). Antonie Brentano wrote in run-on sentences and phrases, their precise meanings sometimes clouded by the stream of words.

4. Beethoven's nephew Karl had been born on September 4, 1806.

5. Beethoven's brother Carl had died on November 15, 1815; for more details about Johanna's activities as a thief, see Solomon, *Beethoven,* pp. 232–233.

6. The slip of paper that must have borne Beethoven's name had disappeared by the time Sandberger examined the document in ca. 1914. The contents listing for Sailer's correspondence, however, noted "[Antonie Brentano] requests in the name of Beethoven, Vienna," etc.

7. Possibly about this time, Beethoven procured two of Sailer's works in editions published in Graz during the course of 1819: *Kleine Bibel für Kranke und Sterbende* and *Friedrich Christians Vermächtnis an seine lieben Söhne, deutschen Jünglingen an die Hand gegebenen von einem ihrer Freunde.* For Beethoven, the latter especially pertained to his nephew. See the inventory of the mostly non-musical books in Beethoven's library (No. 483 below).

8. It is not entirely clear whether Antonie meant that Karl was in his third school or that he was in the third class (grade) at school. Count Joseph Sedlnitzky's report to Emperor Franz I, June 20, 1820 (No. 270 below), however, states that Karl was then in the "third grammatical class," thus indicating that the latter interpretation is more likely to be correct.

9. Possibly a veiled reference to the "Immortal Beloved" affair and its consequences on the Brentanos' family life.

10. The Brentanos' country residence was at Winkel am Rhein, and it was there that Sailer had most recently visited them, in the fall of 1818. The signature may have been written in this manner to maintain some anonymity for Antonie, but it is difficult not to read a tone of sad resignation in the term "housewife from Winkel."

Incipit: Möge es Sie nicht unangenehm befremden. . . .

Sources: Adolf Sandberger, "Antonie Brentano an Johann Michael Sailer wegen Beethovens Neffen," *Jahrbuch der Musikbibliothek Peters* 21–22 (1914–1915), 43ff., reprinted in his *Ausgewählte Aufsätze zur Musikgeschichte II* (Munich: Drei Masken, 1924), pp. 251–257; Maynard Solomon, "Antonie Brentano and Beethoven," *Music and Letters* 58, no. 2 (1977), 168–189, expanded in his *Beethoven Essays* (Cambridge, Mass.: Harvard University Press, 1988), pp. 178–180. When Sandberger examined it, the letter was in the Archiv des bischoflichen Ordinariats, Regensburg.

257. *Philharmonic Society, Laibach,*[1] *to Beethoven (Diploma)*

Laibach; March 15, 1819[2]

The Philharmonic Society here, whose aim it is to promote refinement of feeling and cultivation of taste in the domain of music, and who strive, by their ceaseless efforts, to impart greater value, solidity and distinction to the Society both inwardly and outwardly by the judicious selection of new members, are universally animated by the desire to see their list of Honorary Members adorned by your name. The spokesmen of this Society, the undersigned directors,[3] in fulfilling the universal wish of the Society, thus perform *their most agreeable duty,* in that they, by appointing you one of their Honorary Members, ask you, sir, to accept the strongest proof of their most profound admiration, and at the same time to accept the enclosed copies of their Bylaws and current Membership List.

1. The Philharmonic Society, Laibach (Ljubljana, then in Hapsburg territory), had been founded in 1702 and finally dissolved in 1921. In 1800, the society named Haydn an honorary member, and he sent a copy of his *Missa in tempore belli* in return. In 1808, they asked one Dr. Anton Schmith (*sic*), apparently a native of Laibach living in Eisenstadt, whether he thought that the election of Beethoven and of Johann Nepomuk Hummel (1778–1837; son of Johannes Hummel, sometime conductor at the Theater auf der Wieden, Vienna) would contribute to the advancement of the society. They also seemingly desired a canon by Haydn on this occasion. Schmith replied: "I, for my part, with such an object in view, would cast my vote only for the latter, namely Hummel's son, who is Second *Kapellmeister* to the reigning Prince Niklas Esterhazy (Haydn is the First). Beethoven is as full of moodiness as he is devoid of obligingness [*Beethoven hat ebenso viele Launen als wenig Dienstfertigkeit*]. I have not seen Father Haydn for a long time, since his residence is very far away; he is weakly and hardly ever writes. I shall, however, visit him soon and make an attempt to get a canon from him" (see Nohl-Wallace).

Schmith's evaluation of Beethoven may have reflected general opinion or, more likely, mirrored the estimation in which Beethoven was held in Eisenstadt after the September 1807 failure of the Mass, Op. 86. In 1819, however, the Laibach society considered Beethoven's name again, resulting in the present document as a greatly altered form of diploma.

2. Beethoven replied on May 4, 1819 (Anderson No. 943). Although he promised the society an unpublished composition, he seems instead to have sent a copy of the Symphony No. 6 in another hand, with "Sinfonia pastorale" in his own hand on the cover. Among the pencil corrections in the score, two appeared to have been entered by the composer. The copy survived in the society's archives at least until the 1860s. In 1978, Dorfmüller (*Beiträge,* p. 320) listed the copy in the Library of the Academy for Music, Ljubljana; in 1991, Cooper (*Compendium,* p. 191) gave the location as the university library there.

3. The directors' names are not cited in the available literature.

Incipit: Die hiesige philharmonische Gesellschaft. . . .

Sources: Nohl, *Briefe* (1865), p. 192; Nohl-Wallace, II, 40–41; Thayer-Deiters-Riemann, IV, 159; Kastner (1910), p. 564. For further background, see also Friedrich Keesbacher, *Die philharmonische Gesellschaft in Laibach seit den Jahre ihrer Gründung 1702 bis zu ihrer letzten Umgestaltung 1862: Eine geschichtliche Skizze* (Laibach, 1862), pp. 25, 49–52; Landon, *Haydn: Chronicle and Works,* IV, 567–568; and Kinsky-Halm, p. 162.

258. George Thomson to Beethoven

Edinburgh; April 5, 1819

Monsieur Louis van Beethoven
c/o Messrs. Fries & Co.
Vienna, Austria

My dear Monsieur Beethoven,

The three last themes with variations that I received the other day give me more pleasure than I can express.[1] I am so delighted by your manner of treating the Austrian theme in particular that I cannot resist the desire to have another theme on a *foreign* air varied by you, and I shall leave to you the choice of the air. Permit me only to ask you to make it as pleasant, singing and brilliant as the Austrian theme, and as easy. And I hope that you will make it as long as the Russian theme, with a small Adagio Cantabile.

I am also sending you four Scottish airs,[2] and ask that you do me the favor of composing ritornellos and accompaniments for these, for the piano — and violin, flute and violoncello — also adding parts for a second voice and a bass voice. Messrs. Fries will pay you 25 ducats when you deliver the manuscripts of the theme with variations and the airs.

I am very displeased that you have not sent me the flute accompaniment to the last volume of our national airs,[3] revised and corrected by you. I urgently request that you send it with the theme, etc. Messrs. Fries will pay your copyist for making a small copy of the flute accompaniment, [suitable] for the mail.

I am very sorry to tell you that one of the best [female] pianists here, one of my friends, has tried with much effort to play the Tyrolean themes:[4]

 and

and that she has given up in despair, having found them too studied, chromatic and terribly difficult. She is convinced that our amateurs will neither be able to play them nor to appreciate them. I particularly like the final air, but it will probably be useless to ask you to make the variations for it simpler and easier, to make them suitable for the taste of the public here. I fear that this trouble would not be pleasant for you, and in this case it will be useless for me to publish it. What a great pity.

You do not write to give me the pleasure of your news! On what works are you occupied at present? And when are you coming to England? Have you composed other trios for the violin, etc., easier than the trios that you have previously published [and] suitable for ordinary amateurs? I wish that you would find such work pleasant; for me it would be entirely delightful, because I love to play the viola part if it is not too difficult. What would you ask for three trios of this description, and of ordinary length?

You have offered me twelve overtures for the piano, etc. If it pleases you, at your convenience, to send me three of the overtures, with those accompaniments that you judge proper, for my examination, I would then be able to judge if they suit me and if I have the means to give you one hundred twenty-four ducats for the twelve.

I have the honor to be, etc.

[Thomson's note to himself:]

The Scottish airs sent to be harmonized were as follows:

The following titles [in French] were prefixed to the four melodies:

No. 1: The words refer to the pleasures of country life and invite one to enjoy the morning in the fields.

No. 2: Friends taking leave of one another for a long time.

No. 3: The return, or the tender and happy reunion of lovers and friends.

No. 4: The jolly miller.

1. Although he had shipped songs and variations in the meantime, Beethoven's most recent letter seems to date from March 1818 (Anderson No. 896; MacArdle & Misch No. 237). A frustrated Beethoven replied to this and other interim Thomson letters in an epistle dated May 25, 1819 (Anderson No. 945; MacArdle & Misch No. 248; and Hadden, *George Thomson,* p. 344). Although Thomson would reply on November 23, 1819, and June 14, 1820 (Nos. 265 and 269 below), Beethoven seems never to have written again after May 25, 1819. The Austrian theme mentioned is probably Op. 105, No. 3.

2. In the order in which they are presented below, the songs are "Up! quit thy bower," WoO 156, No. 3; "Oh! tell us, Harper" (Glencoe), WoO 156, No. 10; "From the brown crest of Newark" (The Banner of Buccleuch), WoO 156, No. 1; and "There was a jolly miller" (The Miller of Dee), WoO 157, No. 5.

3. *Scottish Airs,* vol. 5 (including Op. 108), published in June 1818.

4. Op. 107, Nos. 1 and 5.

Incipit: Les trois derniers Thèmes Variés. . . .

Sources: Summarized in MacArdle, "Beethoven and Thomson," pp. 48–49, and Hadden, *George Thomson,* p. 343. Copy in Thomson's copybook, British Library, Add. MS 35268, pp. 39r–40v.

259. *Domenico Artaria*[1] *to Beethoven, Mödling*

Vienna; July 24, 1819

Dear Sir!

Enclosed I am sending the proofs, which I believe are free of errors.[2] In the catalog of your works, the following numbers are missing, and despite every effort, I have never been able to find them: Opp. 46, 48, 51, 65, 71, 72, 87, 88, 89 and 103.[3]

On the other hand, the following works have no numbers or opus designations at all:[4]

Fidelio [Op. 72]
The overture to *Leonore*[5]
Finale from the *Singspiel Die Ehrenpforten* [WoO 97]
Polonaise for Piano, published by Mechetti [Op. 89]
Finale from the *Singspiel Die gute Nachricht* [WoO 94]
Rondo in C ⎱ published by Artaria [Op. 51]
Rondo in G ⎰
Six Songs by Gellert, Artaria [Op. 48]
Adelaide by Matthisson, Artaria [Op. 46]
Variations for 4 hands in C [WoO 67]
Grand Trio for 2 oboes and English horn, Artaria [Op. 87]
Grand Quintet for 2 violins, 2 violas and violoncello, E♭ major, Artaria [Op. 4]
Prelude for piano in F minor, Riedel [WoO 55]
12 German [Dances] for the Redoutensaal ⎱ Artaria [WoO 8 and 7]
12 Minuets for the Redoutensaal ⎰
Quintet in C for 2 violins, 2 violas and violoncello, Mollo[6]
Scene and Aria, "Ah, Perfido," Peters [Op. 65]
Variations on a March by Dressler, Steiner [WoO 63]
Variations for piano on the air "La vie est un voyage," Paris, Janet[7]

Sextet for 2 clarinets, 2 horns and 2 bassoons, Breitkopf [Op. 71]
Songs by Goethe and Matthisson, Riedel[8]
Italian and German songs, 4 folios, Peters[9]
And other unnumbered works described in the catalog on the back.[10]

Please consider this, sir, and let us know which of these works we may assign within the missing numbers.

We also respectfully ask that you return the enclosed proofs as soon as possible.

In anticipation of your prompt answer,[11] we remain most respectfully, etc.

1. Domenico Artaria (1775–1842), controlling partner in the family publishing firm located in the Kohlmarkt.

2. Schindler noted that these were proofs for the Piano Sonata, Op. 106 (*Hammerklavier*); see also Beethoven's letter to the firm concerning the title page (August 31, 1819, Anderson No. 962).

3. In the catalog of Beethoven's works that Artaria published as part of the second printing of the Sonata, Op. 106, at the end of October 1819, all the unused numbers listed in this letter except Op. 103 were assigned to specific compositions. In most cases the numberings were those used today, but the following exceptions were noted by MacArdle:

51: Artaria used this number for the Sextet, Op. 71, and used the number 71 for the Prelude, WoO 55. The two rondos received the number 51 in the *Thematisches Verzeichnis* issued by Hoffmeister in 1819.

71: See the comment for 51 above. In the 1832 edition of the Artaria catalog, the sextet was listed twice: as Op. 51 and as Op. 71.

72: In his first catalog (1819), Artaria used this number for the *Ehrenpforten* finale, WoO 97, and in his second catalog (1832) for the song "Andenken," WoO 136. The opus number 72 for *Fidelio* was suggested by Härtel in his letter to Beethoven, September 24, 1810 (No. 152 above), along with numberings (Opp. 73–86) that were in fact used. MacArdle could locate no actual use of Op. 72 to designate *Fidelio* earlier than the Breitkopf und Härtel *Thematisches Verzeichnis* of 1851. Jahn's vocal score of the 1806 version (published in 1851) gives no opus number.

87: Artaria assigned this opus number to the *Waldstein* Variations, WoO 67; Hoffmeister assigned it to the wind trio in his 1819 catalog.

103: In both editions of his catalog, Artaria left this number unassigned. Presumably it was first used for the wind octet in the Breitkopf und Härtel catalog of 1851.

4. Opus numbers or WoO designations now assigned to the following works are given in brackets, unless a more extensive (or obtrusive) explanation is required in the notes.

    5. Schindler noted that Artaria doubtless meant the *Leonore* Overture No. 3, which had been published in 1810.

    6. Probably an arrangement of the Symphony No. 1, published by Mollo without opus number in ca. 1810–1811.

    7. Variations on Mozart's "Ein Mädchen oder Weibchen" from *Die Zauberflöte*, for Piano and Violoncello, Op. 66 (see Kinsky-Halm, p. 157).

    8. WoO 136 and 137; Op. 75, Nos. 1 and 2.

    9. Op. 32; WoO 124; six songs from Op. 52, published 1806–1812 (see Kinsky-Halm, pp. 82, 123 and 587).

    10. This further list seems not to have survived.

    11. Schindler says that at this time Beethoven was in Mödling working on the *Missa solemnis* and answered immediately, although his reply is apparently lost.

    Incipit: Beiliegend übersende ich die Correctur. . . .

    Sources: Schindler, 3d ed. (1860), pt. 1, pp. 203–204; Schindler-MacArdle, pp. 175–176. The present editing of this letter owes much to Schindler-MacArdle. Autograph in the Staatsbibliothek zu Berlin–Preussischer Kulturbesitz, Mus. ms. autogr. Beethoven 35, 68; listed in Kalischer, "Beethoven-Autographe," p. 52, and Bartlitz, p. 139.

260. Carlo Boldrini (Artaria & Co.) to Archduke Rudolph (Draft in Beethoven's Hand)[1]

[Vienna; Summer 1819][2]

Whereas we have learned from B[eethoven][3] that Y[our] I[mperial] H[ighness] has brought such a masterly work into the world, we wish to be the first to have the great honor of bringing this work to the light of day, in order to make the world acquainted with the excellent talent of such a great prince. May Y.I.H. indeed grant our submissive request.

Falstaff, Chief Rascal

1. Referring to himself as "B." in its body, Beethoven drafted this letter for recopying and signing by another person. On the basis of the "Falstaff" signature designation

below, the draft was surely intended for the "authorship" of Carlo Boldrini, a partner in the Artaria publishing firm from 1811 to ca. 1824. Like the violinist Ignaz Schuppanzigh, Boldrini was heavyset and thus earned Beethoven's Shakespearean epithet. (See Anderson Nos. 1017 and 1036.) The autograph shows corrections in the hand of one Wuister, a bookkeeper for Artaria & Co.

2. During the summer of 1819, Beethoven tried to interest several publishers in taking Archduke Rudolph's Forty Variations on Beethoven's "O Hoffnung," WoO 200. On July 29, 1819 (Anderson No. 955), Beethoven referred to Rudolph's "competing for the laurels of fame"; on August 31 (Anderson No. 963), he discusses Rudolph's Forty Variations, ultimately published by Steiner in December 1819 and evidently delivered to Steiner by October 15 (Anderson No. 978). In still another letter from Beethoven to Artaria in 1819 (Anderson No. 1003), Beethoven denies his own fault that Steiner and not Artaria received the archduke's variations for publication. The present letter, drafted for Boldrini's adaptation and signature (on behalf of Artaria), seems to vindicate Beethoven. For an account of the genesis, publication and style of the Forty Variations, see Kagan, *Archduke Rudolph*, pp. 68–118.

3. Earlier transcriptions (all citing Nohl) indicate "von Hrn. B." here, but Schmidt reads no title, rendering this passage "von B."

Incipit: Indem wir von B. vernommen haben. . . .

Sources: Nohl, *Briefe* (1865), No. 219; Kalischer (German), No. 787; Kalischer-Shedlock, II, 153; Prelinger, Nos. 607 and 1140; Kastner (1910), p. 602; Kastner-Kapp, pp. 505–506 (all citing Nohl). In 1865, the draft autograph was in the possession of Artaria & Co., Vienna. The Beethoven-Archiv, Bonn (BH 74), acquired it in 1956 as part of the collection of H. C. Bodmer, Zürich. See Schmidt, "Beethovenhandschriften," p. 33.

261. Karl Friedrich Zelter[1] to Beethoven

Vienna; September 18, 1819[2]

To look once more in this life upon the face of the man who brings joy and edification to so many good people, among whom I freely and gladly number myself—that was the reason, worthy friend,[3] why I wanted to visit you in Mödling.

You met us from the opposite direction,[4] and my purpose was at least not entirely frustrated, for I have seen you face-to-face.

I have learned of the malady that afflicts you; and I sympathize with you, for I suffer from something similar.[5]

The day after tomorrow, I leave here and return to my duties, but I shall never cease to hold you in high esteem and love.

Your,

Zelter

1. Zelter (1758–1832) was conductor of the Berlin *Singakademie* and *Liedertafel*; they had met during Beethoven's journey to Berlin in 1796. Originally a mason by profession, he composed in smaller forms, especially songs, and his musical tastes often influenced those of his longtime friend and correspondent Goethe. At the time Beethoven composed music to Goethe's *Egmont*, Zelter was lukewarm in his opinion of the Viennese composer, but, in the ensuing decade, his admiration had grown considerably.

Zelter spent from July until September 20, 1819, in Vienna. On September 12, accompanied by publisher-dealer Steiner, Zelter set out in a carriage to visit Beethoven in Mödling, where he was spending the summer. At the same time, Beethoven was driving in to Vienna from the country resort. As Zelter wrote to Goethe on September 14: "The day before yesterday I wished to pay a visit to Beethoven in Mödling. He was going to Vienna, and so we met in the Landstrasse, stepped out of our carriages and cordially embraced one another. He is unfortunate in being almost deaf, and I could hardly refrain from tears. I drove on to Mödling and he to Vienna" (see Kalischer-Shedlock). The two had agreed to meet again that afternoon in Steiner's shop, but neither made an appearance. They accidentally saw each other from a distance that same evening at the theater, but (perhaps out of mutual embarrassment) did not speak. This, then, is the context for Beethoven's letter to Zelter, August 19, 1819 (Anderson No. 972).

2. In answer to the letter from Beethoven on the same day (Anderson No. 972). Although Zelter penned this draft on Beethoven's letter, it is not known whether he made a slightly more coherent fair copy and sent it to Beethoven.

3. Zelter's subtle tone of patronizing superiority (possibly due to the fact that he was eleven years older than Beethoven) in this context struck Schottländer as "almost naive."

4. The circumstances under which the two met on the Vienna-Mödling road (described in n.1, this letter) add dimension to the phrase "Sie kamen uns entgegen."

5. As a result of his activities as a mason, Zelter suffered from "gout" (possibly arthritis) in his fingers and had complained about it to Goethe in a letter of August 16, 1819, at the same time recounting what he had heard in Vienna about Beethoven's deafness. Goethe, in return, complained of his own weak eyes. This furthered Zelter's

identification with suffering because, after a bout with smallpox as a seventeen-year-old, the Berliner suffered from weak eyes and was forced to use glasses.

Incipit: Den Mann noch einmal. . . .

Sources: Thayer-Deiters-Riemann, IV, 165; Thayer-Krehbiel, III, 18; Thayer-Forbes, p. 739; Kalischer (German), IV, 34–35; Kalischer-Shedlock, II, 143; Johann-Wolfgang Schottländer, "Zelter und die Komponisten seiner Zeit," *Jahrbuch der Sammlung Kippenberg* 8 (1930), 201–202; Anderson No. 972. Autograph (draft) in the Kippenberg Collection, Goethe Museum, Düsseldorf.

262. The Vienna Commercial Society[1] to Beethoven

Vienna; October 1/3, 1819[2]

[Two complementary items:]

[Decree, partially printed, partially handwritten, dated "Vienna, October 1, 1819," naming Beethoven an "Honorary Member" (*Ehrenmitglied*) of the society.][3]

[Invitation/admission card, engraved, with Beethoven's name entered by hand, dated "October 3, 1819," with signatures of society directors "Jos. R. v. Henikstein"[4] and "J. von Wayna."[5] On the reverse, the society's address is noted by hand: "Bauernmarkt, Prince Lichtenstein's building, No. 626, 1st floor."][6]

1. Frimmel, *Beethoven-Handbuch,* calls the organization *der Kaufmännische Verein.*

2. The *Führer* gave the date as October 13, probably a typographical error resulting from two documents dated October 1 and October 3.

3. Frimmel (1895) hypothesized that cloth merchant Johann Wolfmayer (who commissioned a requiem from Beethoven on April 9, 1818, No. 247 above) may have been directly or indirectly responsible for the composer's receiving this honor. Possibly so, but the two signers of the accompanying invitation card also figure in the Beethoven literature, albeit somewhat later.

4. Joseph Henikstein (or Henickstein), the eldest son of banker Adam Albert Henikstein, possessed a fine bass voice and was among the earliest members of the Gesellschaft der Musikfreunde (Thayer-Deiters-Riemann, III, 204). During the 1820s, the Henikstein firm handled Beethoven's banking transactions with Prince Galitzin in St. Petersburg.

5. Wholesale merchant Joseph von Wayna, among the signers of the petition to Beethoven, before February 26, 1824 (No. 344 below).

6. American second floor.

Incipits: Unavailable.

Sources: Frimmel, "Neue Beethovenstudien" (1895), p. 18. Summarized less extensively in Vienna Historisches Museum, *Führer,* item 484, p. 101. Briefly discussed (along with other honors) in Frimmel, *Beethoven-Handbuch,* I, 122. In 1895, this *Ehrenmitgliedskarte* was in the collection of wholesale merchant Franz Trau, Vienna; in 1927, it was still in a Viennese private collection but was loaned for the centennial exhibition.

263. Georg Christoph Grosheim[1] to Beethoven

Cassel; November 10, 1819[2]

Herr *Kapellmeister!*

A dedication[3] is the recognition of a debt of gratitude. In that I thus dedicate the works of my muse to you, I want thereby to express before the public my esteem and my thanks associated with it for the manifold delights that your labors have given me.

With all the praise due you, Herr *Kapellmeister,* there would be no excuse for it if I didn't want to go into detail and enumerate the happy hours that your muse has given me. I therefore urgently ask you to accept my modest thanks with patience.

Your letter, which I received in its time [1811–1812], told me many good things, but unfortunately also the sad fact that you were not as well off as the friends of music might wish. I hope that the maladies about which you complained then are now relieved.

You wrote me that you had placed yourself among the admirers at Seume's grave.[4] He deserves your esteem. He was a great man. He was a fortunate man. He was permitted to express aloud his *vitam imponere vero* — and was loved; Rousseau, for his motto — was stoned.[5]

It is still a wish of mine that is not too suppressed, that you, Herr *Kapellmeister,* might impart to the world your marriage with Seume (I mean the Fantasia in C♯ minor and *Die Beterin*).[6]

Our simple-minded brethren recall the dead often enough; what pleasure it would give us all to hear *Die Beterin* with your music, and the inconceivable joining of hands that Beethoven and Seume give one another in spirit!

I bid farewell in friendship and love, and ask you to accept the assurance of my deep respect.

G. C. Grosheim

Doctor of Philosophy

P.S. In case I should have the pleasure of an answer from you, the Electoral Legation's secretary Weissenborn, who brings this, would gladly take care of it; and you need only send it to him. He is staying in the home of the Electoral Ambassador Baron von Münchhausen.[7]

1. Grosheim (1764–1841) was a music teacher in Cassel (Kassel); earlier in his life, he had composed and now wrote music treatises.

2. Beethoven must have written to Grosheim in 1811 or 1812 as well as in 1816 or 1817; he is also mentioned in Beethoven's letter to Spohr, July 27, 1823 (Anderson No. 1213). From the 1823 reference, it seems that this letter of Grosheim's may never have been answered.

3. Kalischer and Bartlitz agree on the reading "Zueignung" here; Thayer prints "Zuneigung" (affection), possibly a typographical error. It is not clear what Grosheim is dedicating to Beethoven.

4. The poet Johann Gottfried Seume (born 1763) had died in Teplitz on June 13, 1810. Beethoven spent the first three weeks of August 1811 and a brief period during the summer of 1812 at Teplitz. In a note in the *Cäcilia* 8 (1828), 257, Grosheim wrote: "Beethoven's thoughts at Seume's grave, which I still protect like a noble jewel, give an exact report of his magnanimous outlook on the world's misfortune." At the time of his own death in 1827, Beethoven possessed two volumes of Seume's works.

5. Jean-Jacques Rousseau (1712–1778). Like Rousseau, Seume wrote about social consciousness, although a generation later than the Frenchman.

6. Grosheim thus advocates Beethoven's applying Seume's poem *Die Beterin* to the *Sonata quasi una fantasia* in C♯ Minor, Op. 27, No. 2 (later dubbed the *Moonlight*). The poem describes a maiden kneeling at the high altar, praying for the recovery of a sick father. Possibly Grosheim meant only the first movement. Some critics believe that Grosheim here implies that the association of the sonata and the poem originated with Beethoven, but he may have urged Beethoven to such an adaptation in an 1816 or 1817 letter (presumably lost). See Philip Robinson, "Grosheim," *New Grove*, VII, 741.

7. Münchhausen was an old North German noble family, best known for the daring (and often fictitious) exploits of Baron Carl Friedrich von Münchhausen (1720–1797). In ca. 1790, Grosheim had written a sacred drama, *Die Sympathie der Seelen*, with a libretto by one C. A. von Münchhausen.

Incipit: Eine Zueignung ist das Erkenntniss. . . .

Sources: First published by A. C. Kalischer in *Neue Berliner Musikzeitung* 47, no. 49 (December 7, 1893), 50; further information on Grosheim in his "Ein Kopierbuch," *Zeitschrift der internationalen Musikgesellschaft* 4 (1903), 533–534. Full text in Thayer-Deiters-Riemann, IV, 173–174; mentioned and briefly excerpted in Thayer-Krehbiel, I, 292–293, and Kastner (1910), p. 230 (derived from Thayer). Autograph in the Staatsbibliothek zu Berlin–Preussischer Kulturbesitz, Mus. ms. autogr. Beethoven 35, 52; listed in Kalischer, "Beethoven-Autographe," p. 50, and Bartlitz, p. 134.

264. Dr. Alois Weissenbach[1] to Beethoven

Salzburg; November 15, 1819[2]

Intimate Friend!

You would have received the first letter from me if I had been able to follow the order of rank that the matter occupied in the Court of my Heart; but during the three months when I was absent,[3] my heart became a stranger from my house, and my house almost likewise from my heart;[4] and I am only now beginning again, little by little, to feel at home in my quiet cottage. I wrote the same to friend Bernard,[5] and conveyed through him my greetings to you. I am hoping for an answer from him.

I have already thought a thousand times about you and about your misunderstood heart, stifled by high society. When the snow has gone again from our mountains, I shall allow you no rest until you come here. You will lead a carefree life in our grand and glorious nature, and not allow the world to trouble you any more. Like the songbird of the mountains, you will come every year with the blossoms, seeking out only the quiet dark foliage in the ravines. In the days of Spring, you will draw near to the mountain brooks and lodge in rock cottages. Mödling will never see you again. To be sure, nature is also beautiful there, but in comparison to ours it is only excrement.[6] What kind of comfort does a stay there really bring you? Essentially Mödling is only one of the retreat places where, in the summer, the Imperial City deposits its winter detritus.[7] Truly it is not refreshing to meet on the hills and in the pastures the sinful people from the city, who are no more suitable to Nature in this environment than are their false hearts and false manor houses.

Therefore, be sure to come, and bring with you your nephew—without whom your soul is never free on earth. Here and hereafter, the ways and means will be found at all events. I would indeed like to learn how matters stand that concern your heart. Have you not turned, through the father confessor, to the Empress? Have you not challenged the Magistrat of Vienna concerning the crime that violates the majesty of God, [committed] against one of his most dedicated people on earth?[8] I intend to do so publicly if you do not get satisfaction. Just write me a few words about it.

I have had your picture[9] enclosed in a golden frame, and have thus done what kings should have done. It is a crime against the *Jus Regum* to mint coins with your portraits on them; therefore the portraits that God has clearly marked are otherwise at liberty.

My wife kisses and greets you sincerely. She can hardly wait for the hour when she can see you face-to-face, for your wings have so often transported her to heaven.

Give my greetings to our Bernard.

> Always,
> Your
> Weissenbach

[Exterior address:]
From Salzburg.
To Herr Louis van Beethoven
Vienna

1. Alois Weissenbach (1766–1821), physician and poet from Salzburg, had, five years before, written the text for *Der glorreiche Augenblick,* Op. 136. Like Beethoven, he suffered from hardness of hearing, and the two became good friends. Despite the salutation (*Herzensfreund!* in German), Weissenbach used the polite rather than the familiar form of the second-person pronoun.

2. Weissenbach's letter had probably arrived in Vienna by November 20, 1819, when Bernard wrote in Beethoven's conversation book, "When will you write to Weissenbach?"

3. Weissenbach had recently spent some time in Vienna, evidently (as can be deduced later in the text of this letter, as well as from references in Anderson Nos. 968 and 976) while Beethoven was living in Mödling. In 1819, Beethoven moved to Mödling on May 12 and returned ca. October 16. Weissenbach seems to have been present in August.

4. Conversation book entries, discussing Weissenbach in late November and December, seem to indicate that he was fond of flirting with the ladies.

5. Joseph Karl Bernard (1775–1850), editor of the *Wiener Zeitschrift* and close friend and adviser of Beethoven's during this period, especially in matters concerning

his nephew Karl's education. Weissenbach was trying to get a play of his own produced and evidently asked Bernard to intercede for him. Bernard's entries in the conversation books indicate that the play was not very good and had been rejected by the censor by ca. December 20, when Bernard sent a report to Salzburg.

6. *Excrement* in the original German.

7. Weissenbach continues the bathroom metaphor: *Retiradenwinkel* can also refer to a latrine, and the allusion is certainly to excrement, which a constipated Vienna has kept in during the winter.

8. References to the painful and protracted litigation over the guardianship of Karl. The *Beichtvater* (father confessor) may be Archduke-Cardinal Rudolph.

9. Probably the engraving by Blasius Höfel, which Beethoven was fond of giving to his friends.

Incipit: Sie hätten wohl der erste. . . .

Sources: Unger, "Beethovens Konversationshefte als biographische Quelle," pp. 384–385. For background material, see Frimmel, *Beethoven-Handbuch,* II, 413–417; and Köhler et al., *Konversationshefte,* I, 83, 87, 95, 99, 149, 159 and 168. Autograph in the Beethoven-Haus, Bonn, since 1896; listed in Schmidt-Görg, *Katalog der Handschriften* (1935), p. 59.

265. *George Thomson to Beethoven*

Edinburgh; November 23, 1819[1]

Monsr. L. v. Beethoven
c/o Messrs. Fries & Co.
Vienna, Austria

My dear Monsieur Beethoven,

It pains me to be obliged to tell you that your variations on the air:[2]

are not in a style that will be successful in England; and that this is the fifth theme with variations that I have been obliged to eliminate because they are too studied and too difficult for the ladies of this country. What a pity that your admirable genius cannot accommodate in these pieces the ability of those [persons] for whom they are composed. I suffer greatly for it.

I have had eleven of the themes engraved, of which nine have been published for some time, but to my great disappointment people do not buy them! As I have announced in the journals, however, that I shall publish *twelve* themes, I wish to complete this number; and for the twelfth, I propose to take one of the five of which I have already spoken, and which begins thus:[3]

I am choosing this one because it is the easiest. It is, however, *excessively short*, not being half as long as any of the others. This is why I hope that you will make it of an acceptable length, and add to it some variations, in a singing and brilliant style, but not difficult. When you see that you have only sent *two* variations, you will agree that I only ask what is reasonable.

I am sending you, enclosed, two other airs,[4] for which I request you to compose ritornellos and accompaniments (adding also parts for a second voice and a bass voice) with a great deal of simplicity. Messrs. Fries will pay you eight ducats for these airs, and whatever you ask for your copyist, when you show them this letter.

We recently had a superb Music Festival in Edinburgh, which lasted for a week. In the orchestra, we have seen assembled all of the best artists in Great Britain, and in engaging Sir [George] Smart as the conductor, we have had the good fortune to hear your *Mount of Olives*.[5] This is a sublime work, which alone would suffice to make you immortal. We also had the *Creation* by Haydn, the *Messiah* by Handel (with the accompaniments by Mozart), the *Requiem* by Mozart, etc., etc. Also given were a Mass of your composition,[6] your grand Symphony in D,[7] and your Overture to *Egmont*;[8] all were received with enthusiasm, and the audience demanded the last piece to be played a second time with their acclamation. In short, we were in *Paradise* for a week. Since I was one of the [board of] directors, I spent a great deal of time in the company of Mr. Smart, and we talked a great deal about you and about your inimitable works. Since he is a very active member of the celebrated Philharmonic Society of London, and has a great deal of influence in that society, I believe that you will receive a proposal on their part that will be worth accepting. There is nothing I desire more than to see you engaged to visit London, because this visit, I hope, would have the effect of procuring for you a great deal of money, and, at the same time, of improving the musical taste of our country.

My friend Mr. Smith told me, and your letter, which he brought to me, indicated to me that you find it amusing that I beg you to compose in a simple and easy style.[9] I am upset about that, as much on your behalf as on mine, because the difficulty in playing your works is the true and the only cause for their few sales in this country.

I have the honor, Monsieur, to be

Your friend and very humble servant,

(signed) G. Thomson

[The airs mentioned in paragraph 3, above:]

No. 1: Scottish air — for ritornellos and accompaniments — and two other voices in the chorus. (A girl sighs for the return of her beloved.)

Allegretto

No. 2: for ritornellos and accompaniments and two other voices *through-out*. (Serenade: or the tender invocation of a lover to his mistress.)

Andante con moto ed con espressione

P.S. Permit me to send you two more airs with accompaniments by Haydn, and to request you to add parts for two other voices.[10] I shall not give you any more trouble of this sort, and I hope that you will excuse me for that which I am giving you now. Be so kind as to have your copyist write them in the same size with the others, for the mail.

[Thomson's note to himself:]

The foregoing letter was sent to C. R. Broughton, Esq., S[ecretary] of State's Office, London, with the request that he would enclose it to one of his friends in the Embassy in Vienna.

1. Beethoven seems never to have written a letter to Thomson again after May 25, 1819 (Anderson No. 945; MacArdle & Misch No. 248; and Hadden, *George Thomson*, p. 344), although he did set the new songs sent in the present letter and eventually sent them, along with the variations for Op. 107, No. 8, to Thomson at some time before Thomson's letter of June 14, 1820 (No. 269 below).

2. Op. 107, No. 3.

3. Op. 107, No. 8

4. In the order in which they are presented below: "My Harry was a gallant gay" (Highlander's Lament), WoO 157, No. 9, and "Mark Yonder Pomp," WoO 158/III, No. 3.

5. Op. 85, probably in Smart's English translation. For an account of Smart's activities as an omnipresent festival conductor during these years, see Percy A. Young, *Beethoven: A Victorian Tribute, Based on the Papers of Sir George Smart* (London: Dennis Dobson, 1976), pp. 8–11.

6. Mass in C, Op. 86.

7. Symphony No. 2, Op. 36.

8. Op. 84.

9. John Smith of Glasgow, a friend of Thomson's to whom Beethoven entrusted letters to Thomson and Ferdinand Ries (London), both dated May 25, 1819 (Anderson Nos. 944 and 945).

10. Barry Cooper indicates that Beethoven actually complied with this request in one instance, possibly more.

Incipit: Il me fait peine d'etre obligé. . . .

Sources: Summarized in MacArdle, "Beethoven and Thomson," p. 49, and briefly in Hadden, *George Thomson*, p. 344. Copy in Thomson's copybook, British Library, Add. MS 35268, pp. 44v–46r.

266. Dr. Carl Iken and Elise Müller[1] to Beethoven

Bremen; [shortly before December 17,] 1819

To Herr
Ludwig van Beethoven
for his 49th Birthday[2]
on December 17, 1819,
From several of his Admirers
in Bremen.

[Literary gifts:]

Die Rhein- und Donau-Nixe[3]

[poem, signed by Iken]

Das Leben der Menschen

[prose essay, signed by Iken]

Erkennen deinen Freund [poem, with a note by Elise Müller:

"Our young friend, who knows of our congratulatory

address, just brought this sheet. I could not refuse

to enclose it."]

1. Iken was the editor of the *Bremer Zeitung* and the author of several far-fetched literary interpretations of Beethoven's works. Largely through the efforts of Dr. Wilhelm Christian Müller (1752–1831), the music director of the city's cathedral and organizer of a series of concerts that regularly included Beethoven's music, Bremen had become the center of a Beethoven cult some years before. Iken's interpretation of the Seventh Symphony, sent to Beethoven early in 1819, possibly through Müller, aroused the composer's ire. Müller and his pianist daughter Elise (d. 1849) seemingly corresponded occasionally with Nannette Streicher during this period (see Anderson Nos. 738, 807 and 1035), sending messages to the composer through this intermediary.

2. The Müllers had sought information about Beethoven's birth date from historian-theologian Ernst Moritz Arndt (1769–1860), who had been appointed professor at the University of Bonn in 1818. Arndt gave them information gleaned from the baptismal record, although the term *Geburtstag* is used in the present document.

3. The various adulatory poems and essays total ten well-filled pages and will not be reproduced here.

Incipit: Dem Herrn Ludwig van Beethoven zu seinem 49sten Geburtstage. . . .

Sources: Autograph in the Staatsbibliothek zu Berlin–Preussischer Kulturbesitz, Mus. ms. autogr. Beethoven 38, 18; listed in Kalischer, "Beethoven-Autographe," p. 76, and Bartlitz, p. 193. Information about Iken and the Müllers may be found in Schindler-MacArdle, pp. 398–400; Thayer-Forbes, pp. 765–766; and Frimmel, *Beethoven-Handbuch,* I, 231, 436–437.

1820

267. Archduke Rudolph to Beethoven

[Vienna; ca. January 1, 1820][1]

[Canon:] Dear Beethoven,[2] I thank you for your good wishes upon the New Year; please accept mine in return with indulgence.[3]

1. Although Rudolph had been Beethoven's student since ca. 1803–1804, the composer's surviving correspondence with the archduke begins in 1810 (Anderson No. 290, a questionable item), or at least by late March 1811 (Anderson No. 301), therefore after Rudolph became one of the guarantors of Beethoven's stipend. Anderson includes three letters by Beethoven that contain New Year's wishes to his patron: December 31, 1816 (No. 688), December 31, 1817 (No. 840), and January 1, 1819 (No. 933) — thus three successive years — the last of which makes references to the archduke's musical talents. The next year, on January 1, 1820, Beethoven sent Rudolph a musical greeting in the four-voiced canon "Seiner kaiserliche Hoheit . . . Alles Gute! Alles Schöne!" (WoO 179), whose text in translation reads: "His Imperial Highness! the Archduke Rudolph! Spiritual Prince! All good things! All beautiful things!" Since the archduke certainly copied its style (essentially a homophonic salutation, followed by a canonic setting of the message proper), this reply probably also originated on New Year's Day 1820 or shortly thereafter. Kagan likewise dates the canon as 1820.

2. The musical setting of Beethoven's name indicates that the Viennese (including the composer's closest acquaintances) already pronounced his name incorrectly, with the stress on the second syllable.

3. Rudolph is asking Beethoven's indulgence for this composition.

Incipit: Ich danke für Ihre Wünsche. . . .

Sources: Excerpt in "Die Wiener internationale Ausstellung für Musik und Theaterwesen," *Neue Zeitschrift für Musik* 59, no. 47 (November 23, 1892), 525–526. Full musical text in Paul Nettl, "Erinnerungen an Erzherzog Rudolph, den Freund und Schüler Beethovens," *Zeitschrift für Musikwissenschaft* 4 (1921–1922), 98–99. See also Kinsky-Halm, pp. 683–684. Autograph draft in the Fürsterzbischofliche Bibliothek, Schloss Kremsier (today: Státni Zámek, Hudební Archiv, Kroměříž), A4376, transcribed in Susan Kagan, *Archduke Rudolph,* pp. 253, 255. While Kagan examined Rudolph's draft, Nettl and the *Neue Zeitschrift* reporter probably examined the copy Rudolph sent to Beethoven (which must have differed from the draft in details). This version essentially follows Nettl; in neither Nettl nor Kagan does the full verbal text continue to the end of the composition.

* Both Kagan and *Neue Zeitschrift* give this note as B.

zum neu - en Jah - re für Ih - re

an mit Nach - sichtan und neh -men Sie auch mei - ne

an mit Nach-sicht an mit Nach-sicht an mit Nach-sicht und neh-men Sie auch auch

mei - ne mit Nach - sicht an und neh-men Sie auchmei-ne an

268. *Archduke Rudolph to Beethoven*

Olmütz; March 25, 1820[1]

Dear Beethoven!

Since it was my duty to come here, I had to leave Vienna quickly,[2] otherwise I would never have been able to separate myself from so many things that I valued. Therefore you see that even from a distance, I am thinking of them, and so I am writing you these few lines.

I was sorry that I did not see you before my departure, but convinced of your sentiments, I hope that you will compose diligently for me.[3] If only I were also capable of doing something worthy of you! Since I already have several proofs of your indulgence, when I have finished something (until now I have not had a single moment for it), I shall send it off to you for your correction and my instruction.[4]

If only my wish were granted that your health, as well as your spirit, could find peace. I was very fortunate and arrived safely; with God's assistance, I have fortunately gotten through the rather straining ceremonies of my installation and am well.[5]

Since music always remains my most gratifying recreation, I have already attended several Dilettante Concerts and, to my astonishment, have heard some very skillful talents. Since they know my justified predilection for your compositions, they treated me to a performance of your Symphony in A Major,[6] remarkably good for Olmütz. I have heard many passages performed worse in Vienna, especially the first Allegro; since I love this work very much, I was completely delighted by it.

I shall be happy to receive good news from you soon; and if I get through Holy Week (which for me is rather troublesome) fortunately enough, I shall try to place my thoughts into notes and send them to you as new proof of how much, even from a distance, I am

Your devoted,

Rudolph

1. Answered by Beethoven's letter of April 3, 1820 (Anderson No. 1016). This letter and its contents render Anderson's n.2 invalid.

2. Rudolph's installation as archbishop of Olmütz (Olomouc) had taken place on March 9, the festival of Moravia's patron saints Cyrillus and Methodius.

3. Beethoven was still working on the *Missa solemnis,* originally intended for Rudolph's installation.

4. As Beethoven's pupil in composition, Rudolph possessed a considerable talent for writing pleasant, if not profound, music.

5. Rudolph suffered from occasional attacks of epilepsy.

6. Symphony No. 7, Op. 92; see also Letter No. 172, note 2, above.

Incipit: Da ich hierher bestimmt bin. . . .

Sources: Ley, *Beethoven als Freund,* pp. 256–257; slightly abbreviated English translation in Marek, *Beethoven,* p. 324. Autograph in the archduke's hand in the estate of Gerhard von Breuning.

269. George Thomson to Beethoven

Edinburgh; June 14, 1820[1]

My dear Monsieur Beethoven,

You have unfortunately made a mistake concerning the air that begins thus:[2]

Andante con moto ed espressione

You have arranged it for a solo voice, but if you reread my letter of last November 23, you will find that I asked you to harmonize it for *three* voices. Be so kind, then, to send me the parts for a second voice and a bass; for without these it is completely useless to me: Haydn arranged it long ago for a solo voice.

You have entirely overlooked the postscript at the end of my last letter, but perhaps you do not find it pleasing to be vexed with this trifle to serve me.[3]

No one makes any requests for the themes with variations that I have published; *I would lose all my expenses for them!* If you could sell the six Themes that I still have in manuscript (Tyrolean, Russian and Scottish) to some music dealer in Vienna, I would willingly give them to you; and I would really like to take in exchange some airs that you would compose for six of the English songs that I sent you some years ago.[4]

I have the honor to be, with great esteem,

Your friend and very humble servant,

(signed) G. Thomson

[Thomson's note to himself:]

The above sent to C. R. Broughton, Esq., Downing Street, to be sent by him to Vienna.

1. Although Beethoven seemingly never wrote a letter again to Thomson after May 25, 1819 (Anderson No. 945; MacArdle & Misch No. 248; and Hadden, *George Thomson*, p. 344), he did send the materials requested in Thomson's letter of November 23, 1819 (No. 265 above), although not entirely to the Scot's satisfaction. This letter marks the end of the surviving correspondence between Beethoven and Thomson.

2. "Mark Yonder Pomp" (alternately called "Sleep'st thou or wak'st thou"), WoO 158/III, No. 3.

3. With his November 23, 1819, letter Thomson had sent two airs as set by Haydn, for Beethoven to add two more voices. Beethoven did one of these as WoO 158/III, No. 4.

4. Thomson's copybooks indicate that he had already approached Breitkopf und Härtel, Leipzig, with a similar proposition, but seemingly to no avail.

Incipit: Vous avez malheureusement fait une meprise. . . .

Sources: Summarized in MacArdle, "Beethoven and Thomson," p. 49, and Hadden, *George Thomson*, pp. 344–345. Copy in Thomson's copybook, British Library, Add. MS 35268, pp. 51v–52r.

270. Count Joseph Sedlnitzky[1] to Emperor Franz I[2] (Report)

Vienna; June 20, 1820[3]

It is evident that this boy, now 13 years old, even before the death of his father (a treasury official) seven [sic] years ago, ran wild to some extent under the influence of his uneconomical mother, who did not have the best reputation. For a year now, at his uncle's expense, he has been in the private school of a certain Blöchinger [sic] in the Josephstadt,[4] and is now in the third grammatical class. His talent and his application are praised, and if he commits many thoughtless and youthful pranks immediately afterward, they are ascribed much more to his imprudence, combined with a passionate temperament and the habit of doing violence to obedience and decorum in outbreaks of irresponsibility and mischievousness, than to ill will; and therefore, in this respect, there is cause to expect his improvement.

1. Sedlnitzky (1778–1855), chief of the Imperial Royal Police and Censor's Office, held this position from 1817 to 1848. Earlier in 1820, he had overseen an investigation into the suspicious activities of the student Johann Senn and his friend Franz Schubert.

2. Franz I (1768–1835), emperor of Austria and, earlier, the Holy Roman Empire.

3. On April 8, 1820, the Appellate Court ruled that Beethoven (and not his nephew Karl's mother Johanna) was to be guardian of the youth. Johanna van Beethoven (ca. 1784–1868) was the widow of the composer's brother Carl, who died on November 15, 1815. On learning of the Appellate Court's decision, Johanna applied to Emperor Franz for a ruling in her favor (see Thayer-Forbes, p. 754).

As a result, Franz, through his cabinet director, von Neuberg, had Count Sedlnitzky commissioned to make inquiries about young Karl. The present report was based on the following material, gathered from "reliable sources":

Karl van Beethoven was born here [Vienna], is 13 years old and the only child of the I[mperial] R[oyal] Income Tax Treasury Official Carl van Beethoven, who died seven [sic] years ago. His mother, a woman of 35 years, draws an annual pension of 333 florins, 20 kreuzer, lives in the city at Tiefer Graben No. 238 and, with regard to her conduct, does not have the best reputation. After the death of her husband, the debt-laden house in the Alservorstadt No. 139 fell to her with the condition that she bear the responsibility for the education of her son. Since she accrued more debts after the passing of her husband, she was finally forced to sell the house two years ago for 20,000 florins W.W., of which, however, only a limited portion remained to her. She always complained that her pension and the limited estate did not suffice to take care of the education of her son. The uncle and guardian of the boy [i.e., in one person—Ludwig] took him away from his mother since he feared that unless he did so, the morals of his nephew would be ruined by the careless supervision of the mother, and placed him in an educational institute [run by Giannatasio del Rio] in the Landstrasse. A year ago, however, he transferred the boy to the schoolmaster Blöchinger [sic] in the Josephstadt, in Count Chotek's building, No. 26, where he now receives instruction in the subjects of the third grammatical class. His uncle pays 1,200 florins W.W. for it annually. The mental abilities and diligence of the boy are very much praised, only his educator is less satisfied with his mischievousness and youthful disposition, in which, however, his uncle, who loves him very much, seems to find pleasure. But, owing to his youth and pliability, improvement on his part is all the more to be expected, as he himself demonstrates much goodwill in wanting to come up to justified expectations.

4. Joseph Blöchlinger von Bannholz (1788–1855), in whose school Beethoven placed Karl on June 22, 1819. The nephew remained there until August 1823.

Incipit: Es geht daraus hervor. . . .

Sources: Theodor Frimmel (?), "Kaiser Franz und Beethoven's Neffe," *Neue Freie Presse* (Vienna), December 25, 1907, p. 13. The excerpts translated here represent the extent of the materials given in this source.

271. *Beethoven to Karl van Beethoven (Draft)*

[Vienna; ca. June 20, 1820][1]

Little by little you have become accustomed to horrible deeds. The judges over you would tell you that you must be acquainted with your mother, for you are here given the best example, and without leniency, you will. . . .

Now, when you are more than 13 years old, goodness must establish itself anew in you. You should not hate your mother, but you cannot view her as another good mother. This is evident, and as long as you are guilty of further violations against me, you cannot become a good person; that is the same as if you rebelled against your father.

Karl, you know my special situation: all I must earn in order to care for you I do with joy, and I wanted to bring you here once, upon Blöchlinger's[2] dissatisfaction and your recently running away to your mother.

The errors to which you pretend to be misled by your mother are no longer excusable; you are old enough to know good from bad; moreover, it is a question of whether you have to be removed from her, regard [her] as an irrational person. . . .

You must also do well at your mother's. . . .

Your mother, however, has not counseled you to study poorly, but you yourself understand enough that you must realize your senselessness; but it is your own tendency, as I also recall that you ran to her the first time. . . .[3]

1. The dating follows the chronology of the conversation books; it is not clear whether this draft and the two following were written in Vienna or in Mödling, where Beethoven spent much of the summer of 1820.

2. Joseph Blöchlinger, headmaster of Karl's boarding school, to whom Beethoven also drafted a letter at this time (No. 272 below).

3. Following this draft in the conversation book are a few jottings concerning a daily work regimen, which Beethoven may have meant for himself or for Karl: "In the early morning at 4 o'clock, go for a walk or study; or ['afternoon' crossed out] after breakfast, in case of study, go for a walk."

Incipit: Du gewöhnst dich nach u. nach. . . .

Sources: Köhler et al., *Konversationshefte,* II, 155–158, 415 (© Deutscher Verlag für Musik, Leipzig). Autograph in the Staatsbibliothek zu Berlin–Preussischer Kulturbesitz.

272. Beethoven to Joseph Blöchlinger[1] (Draft)

[Vienna; ca. June 20, 1820]

I believe that the facts, as they were represented to you, are not so. Go through these two incidents with Karl; listen to his remarks against his mother. Say that you are just as impartial as I am, and that you are just as little pleased about it as I am that he said something against his mother that is not so.

Ask him, though, how he was then instructed in a Socratic manner in my home; how, with his comings and goings, he [ran away] from me twice later. [Ask him:] Tell me the truth in everything; also if you have to offend me, I can care for you, and I want to restore your soul to health.[2] How have you found your mother [to be] since your childhood?

Then lead back to the pain that he has caused me; say that others have already said that you would have completely divested yourself of him [if you were] in my place — go through various periods of his childhood with him. [Tell him that] each detrimental association with his mother is of detrimental consequence for you.[3] However, if Karl places these actions by his mother in a favorable light to you. . . .

It would be the greatest depravity, and out of love also does not allow his being reconciled with her.

Moreover, to me the foundation of his moral improvement is to be based upon the recognition of his mother's true nature, for the sake of his getting. . . .[4]

1. Headmaster of Karl's boarding school.
2. Crossed out: "Your uncle will, unnoticed by you. . . ."
3. Crossed out: "Because of [your] hotheadedness. . . ."
4. It is difficult to determine which message elements of these and the following conversation book pages were intended for Blöchlinger and which for Bernard (No. 273 below).
Incipit: Ich glaube, dass das *Factum.* . . .
Sources: Köhler et al., *Konversationshefte,* II, 155–156 (© Deutscher Verlag für Musik, Leipzig). Autograph in the Staatsbibliothek zu Berlin–Preussischer Kulturbesitz.

273. Beethoven to Joseph Karl Bernard[1] (Draft)

[Vienna; ca. June 20, 1820]

[Fragmentary indications of letter contents:][2]
Concerning the bank note.
Concerning Karl—best that Blöchlinger comes here alone with Karl, where we can speak. . . .
I want to take [?] you, until the beginning of this month, as. . . .

1. Coeditor of the *Wiener Zeitschrift* (1818) and editor of the *Wiener Zeitung* (from 1819), Bernard (or Bernhard), 1780–1850, often counseled Beethoven concerning the education of his nephew Karl.
2. These sketchy indications of the contents of a projected letter to Bernard are interspersed among draft phrases for Beethoven's letter to Karl, ca. June 20, 1820 (No. 271 above). It is difficult to determine which message elements of this and the preceding conversation book pages were intended for Bernard and which for Blöchlinger (No. 272 above). There is also a jotted note that Beethoven intended to write a letter to C. F. Peters that day but, since he indicated no contents, it will not be included here.
Incipit: Wegen der *Banknote.* . . .
Sources: Köhler et al., *Konversationshefte,* II, 157 (© Deutscher Verlag für Musik, Leipzig). Autograph in the Staatsbibliothek zu Berlin–Preussischer Kulturbesitz.

274. Beethoven to Adolf Martin Schlesinger, Berlin[1]

Vienna; June 28, 1820[2]

Dear Sir,

I wrote to you on the 31st of last month, and told you in answer to your last esteemed letter that I could let you have the Scottish songs[3] and three completely new Sonatas[4] for the price that you suggested of 60 ducats for the songs and 30 ducats for each sonata—however, only to do business with you [this way] once, since I would have to stipulate higher prices in future dealings. I tried, furthermore, to propose a firm here at which I could deposit the manuscripts and collect the sums of the fees [due me] in return, as I have usually done in my dealings with foreign publishers. Further, I asked you for a reply on these matters by return post; to my surprise, I have not received it as yet. Meanwhile I have had the Scottish songs copied, and have also had offers from other parties for the aforesaid works; for that reason I have repeated above the contents of my letter, which perhaps may not have reached you,[5] and request you to inform me of your decision concerning this matter by return post. I repeat to you that I would gladly give you preference over other [publishers], but in return I expect at least that you would not prevent me from exploring other alternatives by delaying your answer in any way. Therefore, be so kind as to write me immediately. If you agree with my suggestions, as I should not doubt from your proposals, I shall send you the songs immediately, together with one sonata that also already lies finished; the other two sonatas will follow, as I told you, by the end of next month. I repeat to you that your answer must be received without delay, because I am under pressure from the publisher of the recently mentioned Variations[6] and from others regarding both the songs and the sonatas.

In this expectation, I remain,

Yours very respectfully,

L. v. Beethoven

[Exterior:]
[From] Vienna
To the Schlesinger Art and Book Shop
Berlin

1. Adolf Martin Schlesinger (1769–1839), Berlin book dealer and, after 1810, music publisher. In the summer of 1819, his eldest son, Moritz Adolf (1798–1871), met Beethoven in Steiner and Haslinger's office in Vienna and then visited him in Mödling. Beethoven wrote the younger Schlesinger a follow-up letter about taking some of his works on March 25, 1820 (Anderson No. 1015). The elder Schlesinger evidently replied on April 11 (letter lost, but known from the publisher's annotation on Beethoven's March 25 letter), and, for some time thereafter, Beethoven corresponded with the father (letters of April 30 and May 31, 1820, Anderson Nos. 1021 and 1024). In 1821, Moritz moved to Paris and opened a French branch of the firm under the name Maurice Schlesinger. Thereafter, Beethoven maintained a separate correspondence with him, as the occasion warranted.

2. Follows and confirms Beethoven's letter of May 31, 1820 (Anderson No. 1024), whose text is largely lost but is known through an apparently inaccurate description and brief quote by the Paris dealer Gabriel Charavay in May 1881. A close reading of the content and intent of the present letter and the surviving earlier correspondence provides more accurate speculation about the terms specified on May 31: for instance, Charavay read the letter as offering Schlesinger the rights to sell the Scottish Songs, Op. 108, *in* England, when Beethoven in fact offered him the right to sell them everywhere *except* England (the domain of Edinburgh publisher George Thomson). From Schlesinger's annotation on the exterior, it seems that this June 28 letter was received on July 4 and was answered immediately.

3. Op. 108, which had been published (with rights for Scotland and England) by George Thomson, Edinburgh, in June 1818. Schlesinger published a Continental edition of the songs in July 1822.

4. Piano Sonatas, Opp. 109, 110 and 111, all three ultimately published by Schlesinger and his son in various editions (see Kinsky-Halm for details).

5. The essential contents of the incomplete May 31 letter may be reasoned by this statement and the material to which it refers.

6. Basically items from the Scottish, Russian and Tyrolese themes with variations, Op. 107, published by Thomson (Edinburgh) in July 1819 and offered by Beethoven in his letter of March 25, 1820 (Anderson No. 1015). By mid-April, however, he had sold the Continental rights to Simrock in Bonn (see Beethoven to Simrock, April 23, 1820, Anderson No. 1019) and reported that sale to Schlesinger on April 30 (Anderson No. 1021).

Incipit: Ich schrieb Ihnen am 31. . . .

Sources: Alan Tyson, "New Beethoven Letters," in *Beethoven Studies 2*, ed. Alan Tyson (London: Oxford University Press, 1977), pp. 22–23, with translation and extensive annotation. Another translation in William R. Meredith, "The Sketches for Beethoven's Piano Sonata in E Major, Opus 109" (Ph.D. diss., University of

North Carolina, 1985), I, 125–126 (with documentation on pp. 115 and 175). In 1977, the autograph was in the possession of Sir David Ogilvy, Scotland (Tyson).

275. Beethoven to the Chief Cashier of Prince Franz Joseph Lobkowitz's Estate[1]

Vienna; September 30, 1820

For one hundred seventy-five gulden, f[ull] w[eight], which I the under-signed have received in cash as quarterly [payment] from July 1 through the end of September 1820 from the annual stipend of 700 fl. [*sic*] granted me by His Highness, Prince Franz Joseph von Lobkowitz, from his Pupillary Chief Cashier — received.

Vienna, September 30, 1820

L. v. Beethoven

Herr Oliva as Recipient[2]

    1. Prince Lobkowitz had died on December 15, 1816. Along with Prince Ferdinand Kinsky and Archduke Rudolph, he had been one of the guarantors of the stipend, begun in March 1809 as an inducement for Beethoven to remain resident in Vienna.
    2. Beethoven's friend, the bank clerk Franz Oliva, occasionally served as his business representative during this period.
    Incipit: Über ein hundert siebenzig fünf gulden v.w., welche. . . .
    Sources: Gutiérrez-Denhoff, " 'o Unseeliges Dekret': Beethovens Rente," pp. 137 (facsimile), 144. Autograph in the Státni oblastní v Litoměřicích, pobočka Žitenice.

276. Franz Oliva to Beethoven (Receipt in the Name of Artaria & Co.)

Vienna; October 27, 1820[1]

Received by Herr Artaria & Co. three hundred gulden W.W. as the remainder of the six hundred [gulden] transferred to him for the account of Herr van Beethoven.

Franz Oliva

1. This oddly worded receipt is complemented by another signed by Beethoven and dated October 26, 1820 (Anderson No. 1036). Essentially, Beethoven, who was moving back in to Vienna after a summer at Mödling, asked his bank clerk friend Franz Oliva (1786–1848) to deliver a repayment of cash advances that he seems to have received from either the publisher Artaria or his partner Carlo Boldrini.

Incipit: Von H. Artaria et Co. drey hundert. . . .

Sources: Thayer-Deiters-Riemann, IV, 205. Anderson makes no mention of this item.

277. *Nikolaus Simrock to Franz Brentano,*[1] *Frankfurt am Main*

Bonn; November 12, 1820[2]

Between Herr van Beethoven[3] and me there existed a slight misunderstanding concerning the price of a new grand Mass[4] set in music, which he wanted to sell me for 100 Louis d'ors. I agreed to these 100 Louis d'ors, but understood them in the sense in which they are understood here, in Leipzig and in all Germany, as equal to Friedrich d'ors or Pistoles. In order to have no unpleasantness after the receipt of the Mass, however, I explained myself clearly about this, and repeated in my letter of September 23 that I understood Louis d'ors to be the same as Friedrichs d'ors but in my position I could not give more, [and] that pending the receipt of the new grand Mass, in which H[err] v[an] Beethoven also promised to place the German text under the Latin, I would hold this sum in readiness here. I believe that I have also noted that I expect his decision by return post, because I cannot let my money lie unused in Frankfurt. I must confess that, since I received no answer after four weeks, I did not count on it [receiving the Mass] any more, and disposed of my money. Now, after your valued letter of the 8th, where it appears that Herr van Beethoven transfers the Mass to me, I am in an awkward position lest I run out of Louis d'ors in gold again. Since, however, you make no mention in your letter that you have received the music, I shall take care to collect these Louis d'ors in the meantime, in case you could not accept the value at 9 florins, 36 kreuzer per piece.

I ask you, however, to send me news of the receipt of the music, so I may inform Herr Heinrich Verhuven to take delivery of it from you for the designated sum.

I greet you

Most sincerely,

N. Simrock

1. Franz Brentano (1765–1844), Frankfurt businessman and husband of Viennese-born Antonie Brentano, who in 1812 was probably Beethoven's "Immortal Beloved."

2. Beethoven wrote letters to Simrock and to Brentano on November 28, 1820 (Anderson Nos. 1037 and 1038), and otherwise put off writing to each several times (Anderson, passim) before writing to both again on March 10, 1823 (Anderson Nos. 1152 and 1153).

3. "von" in original.

4. *Missa solemnis*, Op. 123, destined to be completed only early in 1823.

Incipit: Zwischen Herrn von Beethoven und mir. . . .

Sources: Thayer-Deiters-Riemann, IV, 215–216; copied from the original then in the possession of Dr. von Brentano, Offenbach am Main. Schmidt, *Beethoven-Briefe*, pp. 46–47; Kalischer (German), IV, 204–207; Kalischer-Shedlock, II, 234; Müller, "Beethoven und Simrock," pp. 52–53.

278. *Sigmund Anton Steiner*[1] *to Beethoven*

Vienna; December 29, 1820

Most Highly Honored Sir! and Friend Beethoven![2]

Enclosed are the three overtures in score[3] with the request that you look through them, as you yourself so obligingly offered to do, and correct any errors that have crept in. Immediately after the receipt of these corrections, we shall then proceed to engrave and print them in order to publish these original works as quickly as possible.

I am not and cannot be content with your remarks about the bill I sent you, for I have charged you 6% on the cash money lent you, whereas I paid you 8% for your money that you deposited with me, and this amount punctually in advance, and also repaid your capital promptly. What is fair for one is therefore equitable for the other;[4] besides, I am not in a position to lend money without interest. I helped you as a friend in need; I relied upon and believed your word of honor, and neither have I been importunate, nor have

I ever plagued you in any other way, and must therefore solemnly protest the reproaches made against me. If you consider that part of my loan made to you is already going into its fifth year,[5] you yourself will confess that I was not an impatient creditor. I would spare you even now and wait patiently, if, on my honor, cash money were not now necessary for my business undertakings. Were I less convinced that you really are in a position to lend me your helping hand now and able to keep *your word of honor,* I would very gladly remain patient a while longer, as difficult as it would be for me; but when I remember that I myself paid back to you 4,000 florins C.M., or 10,000 W.W., as capital seventeen months ago, and upon that repayment, at your request, did not immediately deduct the amount due me, it is now doubly painful to me to be embarrassed because of all my goodwill and from my trust in your word of honor. Everyone knows best where the shoe pinches him, and I find myself also in this position. Therefore I implore you again not to let me down, and to find the means for settling my account as quickly as possible.

Otherwise I ask you also to accept my best wishes for the New Year, with the request that you continue to give me your goodwill and friendship. It will also give me pleasure if you keep your word and honor me soon with a visit, but it gives me even more pleasure that you have fortunately withstood your illness and are now well again. May God long keep you in health, contentment and pleasure; this is the wish of

Your most completely devoted

S. A. Steiner[6]

[Exterior:][7]
  To Monsieur
  Louis van Beethoven
  Doctor of Music and
  Very Renowned Composer, etc., etc.

1. Viennese publisher (1773–1838), active from 1803 to 1826 in his firm in the Paternostergasse.

2. Steiner's laudatory and yet friendly salutation is preserved here.

3. The overtures *The Ruins of Athens,* Op. 113 (published in February 1823), *King Stephan,* Op. 117 (July 1826), and *Namensfeier,* Op. 115 (April 1825).

4. "Was also dem einen recht ist . . ." is usually translated "What is sauce for the goose . . . ," but I prefer the above translation.

5. Original: "in's fünfte Jahr."
6. On this letter Beethoven made various pencil remarks:

Sums	
	1,300
	750
	70
	300
	2,420

The 1,300 florins W.W. were probably received in 1816 or 1817; the 750 florins W.W. still later, perhaps 1819; the 300 florins are debts that I assumed for Frau [Johanna] van Beethoven and can be carried only a few years; the 70 florins may also have been charged for me in 1819.

Payment of 1,200 florins per year may be made in semiannual installments.

On the cover of the letter another hand has written: "Herr von Steiner says he will accept the lump sum of 1,200 florins W.W., which would be paid so that half is paid by April 15 of this year [1821], the other half by October 15 of this year." A letter that Beethoven wrote to an unknown person on September 27, 1821 (Anderson No. 1057), indicates that the composer contemplated selling one of his bank shares at about this time.

7. This unnecessarily flowery address is in French and must have been meant humorously.

Incipit: Beiliegend folgen die 3 Ouverturen. . . .

Sources: Neue Freie Presse (Vienna), August 17, 1900, p. 6; *Allgemeine Musik-Zeitung* 27 (1900), 493–494; O. Bn., "Beethoven et son éditeur Steiner," *Le Ménestrel* 66 (1900), 269–270 (French translation of whole); Unger, *Beethoven und seine Verleger,* pp. 79–80, 107; Thayer-Deiters-Riemann, IV, 213–214; Thayer-Krehbiel, III, 38–39 (largely translated into English); Thayer-Forbes, p. 767 (letter fully translated, torso taken from Krehbiel). In 1900, the letter was in the possession of Dr. V. Miller von Aichholz, Vienna.

279. William Gardiner[1] to Beethoven

[Leicester; late 1820/early 1821][2]

To Louis van Beethoven

Dear Sir,

At the house of Lady Bowater in Leicestershire in 1796, I met with your Trio in E♭ (for Violin, Viola and Bass).[3] Its originality and beauty gave me inexpressible delight; indeed it was a new sense to me. Ever since I have anxiously endeavoured to procure your compositions as much so as the war could permit. Allow me to present to you the first volume of my "Sacred Melodies"[4] which contain your divine Adagios appropriated to the British church. I am now engaged upon a work entitled "The Oratorio of Judah,"[5] giving a history of that peculiar people from the Jewish scriptures. The object of this letter is to express a hope that I may induce you to compose an Overture[6] for this work upon which you can bring all the force of your sublime imagination (if it please you) in the key of D minor. For this service my friend Mr. Clementi[7] will accept your draft upon him for one hundred guineas.

I have the honour to be, dear Sir,

Your faithful servant,

William Gardiner

1. William Gardiner (1769 [not 1770]–1853), a Leicester hosiery manufacturer, amateur composer, editor, violist and writer on music. See Syer, p. 256, for his corrected birth date.

2. Since *Judah* was first performed in 1821, this undated letter must have originated earlier that year or, as Thayer believed, in 1820. In his *Music and Friends* (London, 1838–1853), III, p. 337, Gardiner said that that letter to Beethoven was forwarded to Vienna through Baron Neumann of the Austrian Embassy. Gardiner complained that he never received a reply.

3. The trio may safely be identified as Op. 3. Syer, pp. 256–258, relates how it came into Frances Bowater's (died 1827) household through the Abbé Dobeler (or Döbler) (died 1836), their residence in Bonn until October 1794, their emigration

on the French invasion and their lodging in Leicester for a few weeks in October or November 1794. With the abbé as violinist, Gardiner as violist and Valentine (a local musician) as violoncellist, the trio was certainly performed in 1794 rather than 1796, probably the first performance of a Beethoven work in England or, indeed, outside Germany, the Netherlands and Austria.

4. *Sacred Melodies* (London, 1812–1838), eventually reaching six volumes, adaptations of works by Haydn, Mozart, Beethoven and others into hymns, reflecting a practice common at the time.

5. Performed in London in 1821, it contained arranged excerpts of works by Haydn, Mozart and Beethoven (the theme from the Allegretto of the Symphony No. 7, quickening into the March of the Philistines), with connecting material by Gardiner.

6. Beethoven never responded, although plenty of material in the desired D minor was certainly available in his sketchbooks at the time. Gardiner's amateurish request probably struck Beethoven as uncomfortably reminiscent of similar passages in Edinburgh publisher George Thomson's letters, to which he had only recently ceased to respond.

7. Doubtless the publisher Muzio Clementi, with whom Beethoven had had extensive dealings in the past.

Incipit: At the house of Lady Bowater. . . .

Sources: Letter printed in Thayer-Deiters-Riemann, IV, 216–217; edited version in Thayer-Krehbiel, III, 40 (on which the text above is based). For background, see Jonathan Wilshere, "William Gardiner," *New Grove* (1980), VII, 164; Geoffrey Syer, "Beethoven and William Gardiner," *Musical Times* 128 (May 1987), 256–258.

1821

280. Beethoven to Prince Rudolph Kinsky's Treasury, Prague[1]

Vienna; September 30, 1821[2]

Receipt

for six hundred gulden, contribution for subsistence due for the semiannual period from April 1 until the end of September 1821, which, as part of the annual stipend of 1,200 florins granted to me by the I[mperial] R[oyal] Bohemian Landrecht's decree, dated Prague, January 18, 1815, No. Exhib. 293, I the undersigned hereby note as having duly received today in cash from Prince Rudolph Kinsky's Pupillary Chief Cashier in Prague.

Vienna, on the last day of September 1821.

He lives.
Kreitsch [?]
Pastor[3]

Ludwig van Beethoven

1. This receipt represents a form statement evidently required in the recipient's hand or at least signed by the recipient. It is almost identical (except for appropriate dating) with the April 1, 1821, item noted below and (except for several variants) another surviving receipt, dated March 30, 1824 (No. 351 below).

2. Beethoven received his stipend from Prince Kinsky's estate in semiannual installments.

3. In the case of a lifetime annuity, such as that from the Kinsky estate, it was customary for a priest or some other reputable person to attest that the recipient was actually alive when payment was made.

Incipit: Quittung über Sechshundert Gulden vom 1-ten April. . . .

Sources: K. Bárdos, "Eine späte Quittung Beethovens in Ungarn," *Studia Musicologica* 16, nos. 1–4 (1974), 257–259 (facsimile on p. 258). Autograph, from the collection of Lajos Szimonidész, in the Hungarian State Archives (Országos Levéltár), Rszeckió, Szimonidész-Nachlass, 13 fol.

In 1974, the Beethoven-Archiv, Bonn, possessed four of these semiannual receipts: October 31, 1815 (No. 212 above); October 2, 1818; April 1, 1821; and April 3, 1822.

The April 1, 1821, item has been published in Thayer-Deiters-Riemann, IV, 221; and MacArdle & Misch No. 316.

Facsimile of another receipt, for 600 gulden, October 15, 1822 (owned by the Stadtbibliothek, Vienna), in Bory, p. 135; also in MacArdle & Misch No. 335.

281. Carl Schwencke[1] to Beethoven

[Hamburg; 1821 or 1822][2]

Capellmeister Louis van Beethoven
Vienna

Herr *Capellmeister!*

If the world is peculiar, what miserable philosophers, then, are today's composers, how commonplace, how alike they style themselves!

Thus I lamented to Apollo, when he took me into his service as an apprentice several years ago, whereupon he assigned me the study of your compositions,[3] which, to my most gratifying satisfaction, yielded the result that, among his thousand candidates, he still found one worthy to send from his cathedra as a doctor.[4] At the same time, this gave rise to a wish within me, which compelled me to appeal to your kindness—and that was to possess something in your handwriting.[5]

I am very well aware that this wish is nothing less than peculiar, and that in expressing it I fall into the same damnation as the above-mentioned philosophers. But the hope that you, like Apollo when he created you a doctor, could also be disposed one time to make an exception to the rule has inflamed me to venture this attempt to attain my purpose.

As proof that I know music, I enclose the following little concoction.[6]

Most respectfully,

Carl Schwencke

Address [c/o]:
C. F. G. Schwencke[7]
Music Director, Hamburg

198

1. Carl Schwencke (Hamburg, 1797–Nussdorf, near Vienna, 1870?), pianist, composer and arranger. A son of C. F. G. Schwencke, he began the life of a traveling musician at age nineteen and seems never to have put down permanent roots again. Even the place and date of his death are shrouded in some mystery. Possibly an indication that he, too, was *originell,* Schwencke wrote this letter using the Latin cursive rather than the customary Gothic.

2. Kalischer gives the date as ca. 1821, Bartlitz as 1821 or 1822. In any case the letter must have been written before October 27, 1822, when Schwencke's father (whose address is given below) died.

3. In the original German, for the words "style" in the first paragraph and "compositions" in the second, Schwencke adopts terms from Art: *zeichen* (to draw, design or sign) and *Zeichnungen* (drawings or designs), respectively.

4. With the exception of some theoretical instruction from his father, Schwencke, an extraordinarily talented youth, seems to have been largely self-taught.

5. In 1824, Schwencke visited Vienna and met Beethoven, who wrote for him a canon on the pun "Schwenke dich ohne Schwänke!" WoO 187. According to a copy with a superscription by Leopold Sonnleithner, the canon was written on November 17, 1824. It was one of two such items that Beethoven sent to Schott on January 22, 1825 (see Anderson No. 1345), for publication in the *Cäcilia.*

6. The following six pages were devoted to an untitled piano composition by Schwencke, a Moderato in $\frac{2}{4}$ followed by a Prestissimo in $\frac{6}{4}$, in A minor/major, with modulations and other devices to demonstrate his capabilities.

7. Christian Friedrich Gottlieb Schwencke (1767–1822), the letter writer's father, had been encouraged by C. P. E. Bach as a youth and in 1788 succeeded Bach as *Stadtkantor* in Hamburg.

Incipit: Wenn die Welt originell ist. . . .

Sources: Thayer-Deiters-Riemann, V, 139–140; Thayer obtained his copy through Nowotny. Autograph in the Staatsbibliothek zu Berlin–Preussischer Kulturbesitz, Mus. ms. autogr. Beethoven 35, 66; listed in Kalischer, "Beethoven-Autographe," p. 52, and Bartlitz, p. 139.

1822

282. The Music Society of Steiermark to Beethoven (Diploma)[1]

Graz; January 1, 1822

The Music Society in the Steiermark
Most Graciously authorized by His I.R. Majesty

which, through the development and perfection of the art of music, strives, on the flower-strewn path of spiritual pleasures,[2] to attain the sublime objective of moral refinement [and] of the religious elevation of minds in the Fatherland, has the honor to appoint you, Herr Ludwig van Beethoven, recognized through highest merit as the greatest composer of the present century, as a nonresident Honorary Member, herewith made known through the present diploma.

Count Ignaz von Attems   Johann Ritter von Kalchberg
President   Representative

Johann Baptist Jenger[3]
Secretary

1. Lithographed diploma, with Beethoven's name in gold script; vignettes (musical symbols) above and on both sides; seal.

2. Thayer read this word accurately as *Vergnügungen* (pleasures); Kastner misread it as *Verjüngungen* (rejuvenation). Sieghard Brandenburg, Beethoven-Archiv, Bonn, kindly confirmed this detail.

3. For identification of Jenger, see Marie Pachler-Koschak to Beethoven, August 15, 1825 (No. 416 below).

Incipit: Der von Sr. k.k. Majestät allergnädigst. . . .

Sources: Thayer-Deiters-Riemann, IV, 240–241; Kastner (1910), pp. 672–673; Frimmel, "Verzeichnisse," p. 111. Thayer copied the document while it was in the collection of the artist Friedrich von Amerling (1803–1887), Vienna; Frimmel listed the diploma as then in the Bibliothek und Museum der Stadt Wien (Städtische Sammlung), today's Stadt- und Landesbibliothek.

283. Beethoven for Adolf Martin Schlesinger, Berlin

Vienna; January 11, 1822

Receipt

for 30 full-weight imperial ducats in gold as fee for a piano sonata[1] for Herr Schlesinger in Berlin, which I have duly received from the firm of Messrs. Tendler and Manstein here.[2]

Vienna, January 11, 1822

Ludwig van Beethoven

[On the verso:]
Receipt from Herr L. v. Beethoven

1. Op. 110, whose autograph is dated December 25, 1821.
2. Tendler and Manstein was a Viennese book dealership that Beethoven and the publisher Schlesinger used as a medium in correspondence and shipping.

Incipit: Quittung. Über 30 vollwichtige kaiserl. Dukaten. . . .

Sources: Alan Tyson, "New Beethoven Letters and Documents," in *Beethoven Studies 2,* ed. Alan Tyson (London: Oxford University Press, 1977), pp. 25–26. In 1977, the autograph was in the collection of Sir David Ogilvy, Scotland.

284. Nikolaus Zmeskall von Domanovecz to Beethoven

Vienna; May 4, 1822

Dear Beethoven,

With astonishment I discovered today that in my attic were items that belong to you, and about which I never knew anything, except for two plaster busts,[1] which I thought had been taken back to you long ago by the same two servants to whom you had entrusted them. I am now sending back to you everything that was found, and that I think belongs to you. Also you are receiving herewith your book by Weissenbach[2] and raven quills,[3] which you sent to me a long time ago.

The day after tomorrow I leave for Carlsbad and Teplitz, where I shall still seek a cure. I wish you uninterrupted good health and the joys of the most fortunate men.

Zmeskall

[P.S.] With this, there follow four bottles of Ofner wine; the freight is entirely covered.

1. Possibly busts of Beethoven by Anton Dietrich (1796/7–1872). Dietrich made two versions of his plaster busts, in "contemporary" and "classical" styles, depicted and discussed in Alessandra Comini, *The Changing Image of Beethoven* (New York: Rizzoli, 1987), pp. 43–46, 55–58, color plate 2.

2. Probably Aloys Weissenbach's *Meine Reise zum Congress* (Vienna: Wallishauser, 1816). Weissenbach, a Salzburg physician, also authored the libretto to *Der glorreiche Augenblick,* Op. 136.

3. *Rabenfedern:* either Zmeskall or someone in his employ was adept at cutting quill pens; the clumsy Beethoven often asked the "Count of Music" to send him some. In this case, Beethoven might have supplied the raw materials from which the pens were to be crafted. It is also possible that Zmeskall was returning a copy of *Die Rabenfeder: Eine Geschichte zum Ostergeschenk für Kinder,* which underwent many printings by Schneider in Basel; Beethoven might have bought such a book for his nephew Karl.

Incipit: Mit Erstaunen entdeckte ich. . . .

Sources: Thayer-Deiters-Riemann, IV, 269, n.1; Frimmel, "Ein ungedruckter Brief Zmeskalls an Beethoven," pp. 85–86, with considerable commentary. In Thayer's time, the letter was in the possession of Beethoven's nephew Karl's widow, Caroline; when Caroline died in 1891, the letter passed to their daughter Gabriele. Gabriele's husband, Viennese bank clerk Robert Heimler, in turn supplied a copy of the letter to Frimmel some years before its 1906 publication.

285. Nikolaus Simrock to Beethoven

Bonn; May 13, 1822[1]

Herr Louis van Beethoven!
in Vienna!

It is now a year since you promised me for certain that I would receive the Mass[2] completely finished at the end of April. Since October 25, 1820, I have had 100 Louis d'or on deposit in Frankfurt, so that you could receive your payment immediately.[3] On March 19, [1821,][4] you wrote me explicitly that you had been confined to your bed for six weeks and still were not completely well. I was supposed to be completely reassured; [you said that] you only wrote this so that I should not think otherwise.[5] Then I inquired of Herr Brentano[6] at the Fall Fair, and again at the Easter Fair[7] this year, but as always, it had not arrived; I am asking you now, finally, to write me a few words about it; I [myself] am writing, therefore, so that you do not believe that I have died, which nearly happened this past winter!

For the present I have undertaken to publish your 6 symphonies in score, which should have been done several times already. [They] were even publicly advertised [as such], but were never done because there was no profit to be gained from it. I know this very well indeed, but I wanted to dedicate to my worthy old friend a worthy monument, and I hope that you will be satisfied with the edition, since I have done my utmost for it! I have had the first two [symphonies] appear at the same time,[8] and will send copies for you along with the first shipment to Vienna!

We thought that we might see you here with us this past summer, as you had promised in your letter of March 19, but that also did not come to pass.[9]

We all greet you sincerely.

N. Simrock

1. The address reads: "Herrn Louis van Beethoven, Josephstädter Glacis, Fürstlich Auersberg'schen Hause, gegenüber Nr. 16 im Hause des Freiherrn von Fingerlin in Wien." To this, a postal official added: "Presently in Döbling." For further commentary on Beethoven's addresses during this period, see Anderson No. 1076, p. 945, n.1.

2. *Missa solemnis,* Op. 123.

3. Beethoven had requested such a deposit, available on delivery of the Mass, on August 30, 1820 (Anderson No. 1029).

4. Anderson No. 1051 dates this letter as March 14, 1821.

5. Beethoven had written: "As I am up to my eyes in work, I am merely sending you this information so that you may not imagine that things are different from what *they really are*" (Anderson No. 1051).

6. Franz Brentano, Frankfurt merchant, husband of Antonie Brentano.

7. Frankfurt was, and remains today, the site of major trade fairs.

8. Although Cianchettini & Sperati (London) had issued Beethoven's first three symphonies in score in 1808–1809, Simrock's was the first such project to be realized on the Continent. The Symphonies Nos. 1 and 2 were evidently ready by the time this letter was written; the Symphony No. 3 would follow during the course of 1822, No. 4 in 1823.

9. Beethoven on August 5, 1820: "I cherish the hope of being able perhaps to set foot next year on my native soil and to visit my parents' graves" (Anderson No. 1028). And on March 14, 1821: "I am still hoping to return to Bonn this summer" (Anderson No. 1051). Beethoven never revisited Bonn; for a discussion of his desired "return," see Solomon, *Beethoven,* pp. 275–293.

Incipit: Jetzt ist es ein Jahr. . . .

Sources: Thayer-Deiters-Riemann, IV, 242–243; Schmidt, *Beethoven-Briefe,* pp. 53–54; Müller, "Beethoven und Simrock," pp. 56–57; Thayer-Forbes (English), p. 784. Briefly excerpted in Nohl, *Neue Briefe* (1867), p. 210; mention in Nohl, *Beethoven's Leben* (1877), III, 262, 871. In 1867, the letter was in the possession of the artist Amerling, Vienna; by 1877, it belonged to W. Künzel, Leipzig.

286. Carl Friedrich Peters[1] to Beethoven

Leipzig; May 18, 1822[2]

[A summary of this letter, with quotes:][3]

Peters stated that since taking over the publishing business from Hoffmeister und Kühnel he had zealously endeavored to issue excellent works in good printings and had long since wished to enter into an association with Beethoven. He had refrained from doing so out of consideration for the Viennese publishers, so as not to make them angry "if I were to take you away from them, and I would rather offend no one and leave each to his own."

Now, however, Peters sees that Beethoven has begun to allow his compositions to be published outside of Vienna again and even gives them "to the Jew
Schlesinger" (about whom he speaks very disparagingly). Thus he no longer
restrains himself and asks Beethoven to let him have his compositions. He
[Beethoven?] and his admirers would rejoice if his works appeared from
him [Peters] in better editions than those of that Berliner. If "this Jew, who
is nowhere respected," gets Beethoven's works, then it would be foolish to
hold the Viennese [publishers] in regard any longer. Also Steiner, to whom
he had spoken about this concern at the last Fair, assured Peters that he had
nothing against it and would even rejoice if Peters instead of Schlesinger
got his works.[4] Steiner had even offered to intercede with Beethoven on his
behalf and had even requested a list of works that he [Peters] wished to
have. Peters therefore gave him such a list and on it mentioned: symphonies
for orchestra, quartets and trios with piano, solo pieces for piano ("among
which could also be smaller works"), songs with piano accompaniment and
similar things. Whatever Beethoven sends him would be welcome, "for I
seek your association not from self-interest, but rather from honor."

1. C. F. Peters (1779–1827), a Leipzig bookseller, bought the firm Hoffmeister und
Kühnel in 1814, after the death of Ambros Kühnel, the surviving earlier partner, in
1813. Peters was prone to periods of severe depression, for which he was subsequently
committed to an asylum. In July 1822, Peters deposited money in Vienna against
Beethoven's delivery of manuscripts for publication; when they did reach him in late
February or on the first day of March 1823, Peters was disappointed and returned
them (see his letter of March 4, 1823, No. 313 below). Beethoven, however, did not
return to Peters the money he had received for them until December 1825.

2. Answered by Beethoven's letter of June 5, 1822 (Anderson No. 1079).

3. Thayer seemingly made a copy of this letter, then in the possession of Karl van
Beethoven's widow, Caroline. His copy of the long epistle was then summarized,
with quotes interspersed, in Thayer-Deiters-Riemann. Likewise, Nohl also copied
the letter before 1867 and summarized it in a footnote in his *Neue Briefe*. Because
these summaries were based on firsthand examinations of the original rather
than reconstructed from inferences elsewhere, they are combined here in an order
suggested by subject elements. Furthermore, this letter initiates and sets the tone
for the remainder of the Peters-Beethoven correspondence and reflects important
facets in Beethoven's association with Steiner and Schlesinger.

4. Beethoven's letter to Schlesinger of November 14, 1821 (Anderson No. 1061),
reflects the composer's dissatisfaction with the quality of the Berlin publisher's

work; other correspondence corroborates this. Moreover, at some time between May 22 and August 31, 1822, Beethoven felt himself shortchanged through some perceived inequity in Schlesinger's manner of payment (see Anderson No. 1095). This may account for Beethoven's unkind remark to Peters on June 26 (Anderson No. 1083) that Schlesinger had "played me a Jewish trick." Beethoven's relationship with Steiner was cooling during this period: Beethoven owed Steiner money, for which Steiner was charging him interest; on the other hand, Steiner had bought several compositions from Beethoven but had not yet issued them, a fact that caused much friction. Steiner evidently carried the gossip (about Beethoven's dissatisfaction with Schlesinger — as much as had transpired by then — as well as the fact that Beethoven was nonetheless considering selling Schlesinger the *Missa solemnis*) to the Easter Fair in Leipzig and imparted it to Peters. Thus the groundwork was laid for, and many allusions explained in, Beethoven's letter to Peters of June 26, 1822. These maneuvers on the part of publishers and would-be publishers of Beethoven's works lend credence to Anton Schindler's seemingly paranoid remark that the composer had "to resort to subterfuge" because so many "regarded him cynically as their fatted calf" (Schindler-MacArdle, pp. 239–240).

Incipit: Unknown.

Sources: Thayer-Deiters-Riemann, IV, 248–249 (see n.3, this letter); this summary further abbreviated (slightly) in Thayer-Krehbiel, III, 57–58, and Thayer-Forbes, pp. 787–788. Another summary in Nohl, *Neue Briefe* (1867), p. 199. In Thayer's and Nohl's time, the autograph was in the possession of Beethoven's nephew Karl's widow, Caroline in Vienna. Sieghard Brandenburg, Beethoven-Archiv, Bonn, confirmed in 1995 that the location of the autograph was unknown.

287. Nikolaus Simrock to Franz Brentano, Frankfurt

Bonn; May 29, 1822

Herr Franz Brentano, Frankfurt

I thank you very much for your kind communication of Beethoven's letter.[1] I am very sorry that illness is the cause of [his] delay.

Over a year ago I deposited the fee for the Mass[2] with Herr Heinrich Verhuven, because I expected it daily and did not want the good Beethoven to wait a [single] day for the payment.

Upon arrival of the Mass, please inform Herr Verhuven, who then will immediately, upon receipt of the same, pay you the 100 Friedrichs d'or, or equivalent value.[3]

With great esteem,

Your

N. Simrock

1. Probably Beethoven's letter and postscript of May 19, 1822 (Anderson Nos. 1076 and 1077), which must have traveled swiftly indeed from Vienna to Frankfurt am Main and then to Bonn! The only other letter to which Simrock might refer is Beethoven's letter of November 21, 1821 (Anderson No. 1059), by then six months old. Both letters concern the composer's illness. See Thayer-Deiters-Riemann, IV, 244, for commentary.

2. *Missa solemnis,* Op. 123. See Simrock's letter of November 12, 1820, for clarification.

3. The exchange rates of the *Louis* versus the *Friedrich* and other currencies seemed a great cause of consternation in post-Napoleonic Europe.

Incipit: Ich danke sehr für die gütige Mittheilung. . . .

Sources: Thayer-Deiters-Riemann, IV, 244; Kalischer (German), IV, 204–207; Kalischer-Shedlock, II, 234; Müller, "Beethoven und Simrock," p. 58. When Thayer copied it, the autograph was in the possession of Dr. von Brentano, Offenbach am Main, southeast of Frankfurt.

288. Tobias Haslinger, for Sigmund Anton Steiner, to Beethoven (Price List)

[Vienna; ca. June 5, 1822][1]

Instrumental Music

	Ducats
Symphonies for the whole orchestra	60–80
Overtures " " " "	20–30

For the Violin

Concertos for violin, with orchestral accompaniment	50
Octets for various instruments	60
Septets " " "	60
Sextets " " "	60

Quintets for two violins, two violas and violoncello 50
Quartets for two violins, viola and violoncello 40
Trios for violin, viola and violoncello 40

For the Piano

Concertos for piano, with orchestral accompaniment 60
Fantasia   "   "   "   "   30
Rondo   "   "   "   "   30
Variations   "   "   "   "   30
Octets   for piano, with accompaniment of various instruments 50
Septets   "   "   "   "   "   50
Quintets "   "   "   "   "   60
Quartets "   "   "   "   "   70
Trios for piano, viola and violoncello 50
Duets for piano and violin 40
Duets for piano and violoncello 40
Duo for piano, for four hands 60
Sonata (Grand) for piano solo 40
Sonata for piano solo 30
Fantasia for piano 30
Rondo for piano 15
Variations for piano, with accompaniment 10–20
Variations for piano solo 10–20
Six Fugues for piano solo 30–40
Divertimentos, Airs, Preludes, Potpourris, Bagatelles, Adagio,
Andante, Toccatas, Capriccios, etc., etc.
for piano solo, at 10–15

Vocal Music

Grand Mass .... 130[2]
Smaller Mass 100
Greater Oratorio 300
Smaller Oratorio 200
Graduale 20
Offertorium[3] 20
Te Deum Laudamus 50

Requiem 120
Vocal Pieces with orchestral accompaniment 20
An Opera Seria 300
Six Songs, with piano accompaniment 20
Six Shorter Songs, with piano accompaniment 12
A Ballade 15

[Beethoven's annotation, beginning in the margin at the top of the list (first sentence), and continuing in the blank space at the end of the document:][4]

Perhaps reserve the rights for London and Paris; therefore write to Schlesinger[5] about it. One could also reserve the right sometimes to change prices or to designate new ones; if one considers that these [conditions] were only for Austria, or at most for France, and [if] England were left to me, then this could be acceptable. In the case of several [items by genre], one might reserve the right to designate the price himself. Concerning the publication of collected works, England and France should perhaps be reserved for the author. The sum paid by the publisher would be 10,000 florins C.M. Since they are also interested in the publication of the collected works, such a contract would, in my opinion, be the best.[6]

1. This price list contains neither heading, signature nor date. Schindler's marginal annotation indicates that it is from Steiner and Haslinger, in the hand of the latter. It obviously concerns a projected publication of Beethoven's collected works and contains provisions for genres in which Beethoven ultimately never wrote (a requiem and miscellaneous religious vocal forms, for example). In 1840, Schindler dated this document from the period 1821–1822, placing it within his discussion of 1822 in the 1860 edition of the *Biographie*. C. F. Peters's letter to Beethoven, May 18, 1822 (No. 286 above), indicates that Peters had met Viennese publisher Steiner at the recent Leipzig Trade Fair and that Steiner had offered to intercede on Peters's behalf in asking for genres of compositions. Beethoven's letter to Peters, June 5, 1822 (Anderson No. 1079), however, says that he (Beethoven) had met with Steiner a few days before and that Steiner had mentioned neither Peters nor his commission but had urged him to contract for present and future works. At this time, Beethoven was still corresponding with publishers Adolf Martin Schlesinger in Berlin and his son Moritz (Maurice) Schlesinger in Paris (thus the allusion in Beethoven's own marginal note), but that relationship must have soured temporarily by the time Beethoven wrote Peters again on June 26, 1822 (Anderson No. 1083). Therefore, this document seems to date from a week or two on either side of June 5, 1822.

2. Directly above this price of 130 ducats, in the autograph, is the monetary figure of 1,000; the denomination is unclear: it could be read as fl. (florins) or an incomplete ducat sign (#, without the lower horizontal slash). In any case, its presence is not explained, nor does the amount seem to tally as a sum with anything above or below.

3. Count Moritz Dietrichstein's letter to Beethoven, March 10, 1823 (No. 314 below), confirms that Beethoven seriously considered composing Proper movements, specifically the Gradual and Offertory, as indicated here. Since the *Missa solemnis* was complete by March 1823, these movements would have been set independently or incorporated into still another Mass, possibly a simpler setting, written to imperial taste (see Dietrichstein to Count Moritz Lichnowsky, February 23, 1823, No. 311 below).

4. All editions of Schindler reverse these elements. The presence of the word "also" (*auch*) in the second sentence, as presented above, confirms the correct sequence of Beethoven's thoughts.

5. As noted above (see n.1, this letter), Adolf Martin Schlesinger in Berlin or his son Maurice in Paris, both publishers who were courting Beethoven's favor at this time, and with whom he had contracted to publish several of his works. Beethoven was obviously concerned about international copyright, or the lack thereof, during this period.

6. A similar statement, in draft, is printed in Anderson, III, 1450–1451, and still another follows in the present collection (No. 289 below).

Incipit: Instrumental-Musik: Sinfonien für ganzes Orchester. . . .

Sources: Schindler (1840), pp. 246–247; Schindler-Moscheles, pp. 171–172; Schindler (1860), pt. 2, pp. 39–40; Schindler-MacArdle, pp. 255–256. Autograph in the Staatsbibliothek zu Berlin–Preussischer Kulturbesitz, Mus. ms. autogr. Beethoven 35, 69; listed in Kalischer, "Beethoven-Autographe," p. 52, and Bartlitz, p. 140.

289. Beethoven to Tobias Haslinger
and Sigmund Anton Steiner (?)[1]

[Vienna; ca. early June 1822?][2]

If the gentlemen[3] were to consider themselves as co-holders of the [copy]-rights to each new large-scale work, that would be the viewpoint to which I would be the first to subscribe, and in that manner the appearance that I receive a fee for [doing] nothing would disappear.[4]

1. This memo may have been written for dispatch to some publisher (perhaps Steiner and Haslinger, as in the foregoing document), or it may simply have represented a marginal note (again, like the annotation on the foregoing price list).

2. This note is not dated and seemingly bears no discernible watermark. Landon correctly likened it to Beethoven's "Draft Statement about a Complete Edition of His Works," ca. 1822 (Anderson, III, 1450–1451) — thus its placement after the price list of ca. June 5, 1822 (No. 288 above), in this collection.

3. By "the gentlemen," Beethoven means more than one publishing firm.

4. In the absence of international copyright protection, Beethoven had often attempted to arrange simultaneous publication of his works by publishers in several European economic markets. History has been unjustly critical of Beethoven for these machinations, and here he indicates that such a perception existed as early as his own day and that he was sensitive to it.

Incipit: Wenn die Herrn sich als die Miturheber. . . .

Sources: Landon, "Two New Beethoven Letters," pp. 217–218. In 1983, the autograph was in a private collection in north Wales. Sieghard Brandenburg, Beethoven-Archiv, Bonn, indicates that the letter is presently in a private collection in Belgium.

290. *Carl Friedrich Peters to Beethoven*

Leipzig; June 15, 1822[1]

Herr L. von Beethoven, Vienna

Your honored reply has given me much pleasure, not only because you showed yourself therein inclined to the fulfillment of my wishes, but also because your language was so friendly and trustful that in you I have become acquainted with the human being whom I venerate so much as an artist. Yet how seldom is something perfect, for as much as I was gladdened by your letter, I was likewise pained to learn from it Herr Steiner's[2] really cunning dealings.

[Peters then related that Steiner had told him that Beethoven had invited him to accept orders for him, since it appeared greatly preferable to him (Steiner) that Beethoven's works should go to Peters and not to "the Jew Schlesinger."][3]

Herr Steiner's faithless action is very offensive to me, not so much because of the issue itself (for through your goodness I can now work against his cunning), but rather because he has destroyed for me the belief in a friend, for I regarded him as such, and such was I to him; and a sad experience in friendship is as painful to me as any other loss.

I am glad to be honest and sincere; I am often that way too much and to my disadvantage; I would not have believed that I would have had such an experience with Steiner as well; but all sinners are forgiven, and I want to let him, too, go in peace — The knowledge of his guilt may punish him, and my continuing honest and honorable method of doing business may shame him, for he shall learn *nothing* of what has transpired because you wish it thus. But I shall be cautious with him in the future. . . . Now I want to hope that, as much as everything speaks to the contrary, Steiner dealt falsely with me not so much intentionally as out of weakness.

What I wish to have, for the present, from among your compositions, and for which I commissioned Steiner, were:

1 Quartet for piano, violin, etc.

1 Trio for piano, violin, etc.

1 Concert Overture for large orchestra

Songs with piano accompaniment

Small *solo* pieces for piano, such as capriccios, divertissements, etc.[4]

[Peters then proceeded to the selection of works that Beethoven had already offered.]

The most exquisite among them is your grand Mass, which you wanted to give me, together with a piano reduction, for one thousand gulden, Conventions Münze, and whose acceptance at this price I hereby acknowledge.

As a truth-loving man, I assure you that undertakings of this kind are the most unprofitable that we can make, not only because they cost a great deal and cannot have great sales, but rather because, in the long and costly time needed for the production, we could print many other, more marketable works. I chose this work, however, first, for your sake; second, for the honor of my business, which I see as valuable as any profit; third, because Steiner told me that Schlesinger is also bargaining for it, and a Christian Mass composed by a Beethoven cannot come into the hands of a Jew, and especially such a Jew.[5]

Between honest men like us there need be no contract, but if you want one, send it to me, and I will return it *signed.* If not, however, please oblige me in writing merely that I am to receive the *stated Mass,* along with the *piano reduction* for *One Thousand Gulden* at the 20 florin rate, and indicate when I should be able to receive it and that it is to be my *exclusive* property *forever.* I wish the first so that I can consider this transaction as *settled,* and I wish the time so I can arrange the publication.

If I were a rich man I would pay you entirely differently for this work, for I suspect that it is very excellent, especially since it was composed for a specific occasion; but for me 1,000 florins for a Mass is a great expense, and the entire undertaking, I tell you truthfully, has been entered into only so I may show myself to you and to the world as a publisher who does something for art.

But I must place one condition on you regarding this, namely that *no one* learn how much I have paid you for the Mass, at least that no one learn it for a considerable time. I am not a man of great means, rather I must drudge and worry; still I pay artists as well as I can and, in general, better than other publishers. I know that people talk about it, and I prefer not to get into any arguments because of this Mass.

[Peters, for the present, did not wish to take any further large-scale vocal works from Beethoven, but he also did not wish to bring out the Mass entirely alone; rather, he wanted it to appear in conjunction with several works, in order to place Beethoven in a position whereby he could declare to the Viennese publishers that he had reached an agreement with Peters and was continually obliged to send him something. Therefore Peters asked Beethoven for individual songs with piano accompaniment, several bagatelles for piano solo, the four military marches for Turkish music and. . . .]

Finally, I would very much like to have, as well, your new Quartet for two violins, but 50 ducats might indeed exceed my capabilities, for the highest that I have paid for a quartet before now was 150 florins C.M., and I have to make that back before I make any profit.[6]

[Peters had already often thought about an edition of Beethoven's complete works but would keep a statement about that for a later letter. He allowed that Beethoven could tell Steiner the truth, in moderation, since he (Peters) had turned to Beethoven with Steiner's knowledge and consent and the composer had promised him his works in the future.][7]

1. The postmark of this letter, however, bears the date June 17. Answers Beethoven's letter of June 5 (Anderson No. 1079); answered by Beethoven's letter of June 26, 1822 (Anderson No. 1083). The present text is a composite of excerpts and paraphrases of identical and differing passages found in Nohl and Thayer-Deiters-Riemann.

2. Viennese publisher Sigmund Anton Steiner; see Peters's letter of May 18, 1822 (No. 286 above), about those dealings and also Beethoven's letter of June 5.

3. Berlin publisher Adolf Martin Schlesinger. This paragraph, with its string of pronouns, reflects a paraphrase found in Thayer-Deiters-Riemann.

4. These seem to be largely exclusive of the works offered by Beethoven on June 5.

5. In the early nineteenth century, a Christian like Peters could protest that he was "honest" and "truth-loving" and still make a statement such as this. While it is true that on June 26 (Anderson No. 1083) Beethoven replied that "[Schlesinger] too has played me a Jewish trick," the composer seems not to have been fundamentally anti-Semitic. He was merely dealing in tasteless stereotypical remarks that, although mildly prejudicial, do not reflect deeper intent. Ultimately Beethoven did not sell the *Missa solemnis* to Schlesinger, but he did favor father and son with several of his late works, while Peters published nothing of his.

6. Beethoven scribbled with pencil around the price of the piece and made an extra list of pieces, using them for the next letter, June 26 (Anderson No. 1083).

7. Closing material is lacking in both Nohl's and Thayer's transcriptions.

Incipit: Ew. Hochwohlgeborn geehrte Antwort hat mir viel Vergnügen gemacht. . . .

Sources: Excerpts (some in common, others different, but sufficient to reconstruct the above sequence) transcribed and summarized in Nohl, *Neue Briefe* (1867), pp. 199–200, and Thayer-Deiters-Riemann, IV, 252–254. Further summarized and/or partially translated in Thayer-Krehbiel, III, 59–60, and Thayer-Forbes, pp. 789–790. In 1867, the letter was in the possession of Beethoven's nephew Karl's widow, Caroline, in Vienna.

291. Georg August von Griesinger[1] to Beethoven, Döbling

Vienna; June 17, 1822[2]

Herr Ludwig v. Beethoven
Döbling

Honored Sir!

Herr Härtel wrote to me from Leipzig asking if you could not find and set a libretto worthy of your art before you completely hang up your harp. He regrets that he did not resume his earlier relationship with you again,[3] and he very much wishes to renew it again.

If you will give me the honor of visiting me (I live facing the courtyard of Grosse Weintraube No. 329, 2d floor)[4] or designate a location to me where I can meet you, then I will show you Herr Härtel's letter. I have to believe that Herr Härtel is ready to make you more agreeable conditions than anyone else, but I request that, for the present, you keep his proposal entirely to yourself.

With extreme admiration,
Your most obedient servant,

von Griesinger
Royal Saxon Embassy Councillor

[On the exterior, Beethoven's annotation in pencil:]
The 7 bank shares, 196 florins C.M., 490 fl. in W.W.[5]

1. Griesinger had come to Vienna in 1799 and was a trusted friend of Beethoven's by 1802 (see Beethoven's brother Carl's letter to Härtel, December 5, 1802, No. 50 above). By 1822, he had risen far beyond his initial position as tutor in the household of the Saxon ambassador.

2. Beethoven replied from Döbling on ca. June 20 (Anderson No. 1082). The composer also refers to this contact in his letter to his brother Johann, July 22–26, 1822 (Anderson No. 1086).

3. Beethoven wrote fairly regularly to Gottfried Christoph Härtel about publication matters until September 1812. Their correspondence seems to have waned until Härtel attempted to resume it early in 1815 (see Anderson No. 533), after which the correspondence lay dormant again until this attempt to revive it. Härtel frequently tried to interest Beethoven in one libretto or another.

4. American third floor.

5. Thayer's copy gave the number of bank shares as seven; Nohl's copy did not record this number.

Incipit: Herr Härtel schrieb mir. . . .

Sources: Nohl, *Neue Briefe* (1867), p. 208; Thayer-Deiters-Riemann, IV, 281; Hans Volkmann, *Beethoven in seinen Beziehungen zu Dresden* (Dresden: Deutsche Literatur-Verlag, 1924), p. 170, quoting Nohl. Nohl and Thayer both seem to have made copies of the letter, at that time in the collection of the artist Friedrich von Amerling (1803–1887) in Vienna.

292. Adolf Martin Schlesinger[1] to Beethoven

Berlin; July 2, 1822

Dear Herr van Beethoven!

I had the pleasure of receiving, one after another, the three letters with which you honored me, dated April 9, May 29, and May 1.[2] In reply to them I must beg a thousand pardons, dear sir, that my answer did not follow earlier. To explain, I was in Leipzig at the Fair, where I became ill, and after my return was very indisposed for several weeks. During this time many business matters had accumulated; thus I cannot send you my letter any earlier than today.

Concerning the Mass,[3] we are entirely in order, and I request you to send it, along with the two songs[4] as soon as possible, and then draw on me 650 R[eichs] T[haler] at 14 days' sight. I shall promptly honor and pay it, for I have no opportunity to make payment to you there [Vienna]; although several of your music dealers there are considerably in my debt, one can never count on their paying promptly. These gentlemen have two very ugly traits: 1, they do not respect property rights, and 2, it is only with difficulty that they are induced to pay their accounts. In comparison, the book dealers there are more respectable by far.[5]

According to your wish, I am sending as an enclosure a copy of your Sonata, Op. 109, to Dr. Wilh[elm] Chr[istian] Müller in Bremen, with a note that it is a gift from you.[6] The following sonatas[7] will be engraved in Paris, so that they will be truly superlative when they appear. One of them is being proofread by Herr Moscheles.[8] Therefore, please designate for me to whom you wish to dedicate the second sonata.[9] I thank you very much for sending the dedication of the third sonata.[10] How is it going with the four-voiced songs and quartets?[11] My son, who is in Paris, has instructed me to greet you sincerely.[12] With special esteem, I have the honor, in expectation of receiving an obliging answer soon, to be

Your entirely devoted,

Ad[olf] M[artin] Schlesinger

1. With Schlesinger's alleged letter of June 9, 1817 (No. 239 above), shown to be by Ferdinand Ries, the present document is his first to Beethoven whose text has survived.

2. The April 9 letter survives as Anderson No. 1074, May 1 as Anderson No. 1075. Despite the strange order in which these letters are enumerated, the May 29 letter seems not to have survived.

3. *Missa solemnis*, Op. 123, in which Beethoven was trying to interest as many publishers as possible. C. F. Peters's letter to Beethoven of June 15, 1822, indicates that he (Peters) and possibly the Viennese publisher Steiner were alarmed that the Mass might fall into the hands of a Jew. Beethoven was likewise offended at Schlesinger for some reason; see the composer's letter to Peters, June 26, 1822 (Anderson No. 1083), perhaps partially explained in Beethoven's letter to Moritz Schlesinger of August 31, 1822 (Anderson No. 1095).

4. Beethoven had first mentioned these two unidentified songs in his letter of April 9 and again on May 1.

5. The original says "bei weitem"; Thayer's copy read "bei meisten."

6. Müller (1852–1831) was a church musician and promoter of Beethoven's works. He and his pianist daughter Elise had visited Beethoven in 1820. The Piano Sonata, Op. 109, was first published in November 1821.

7. Opp. 110 and 111.

8. Ignaz Moscheles (1794–1870), pianist, sometime student of Beethoven's and Salieri's. According to Kullak, the sonata he checked was presumably Op. 110 (Kinsky-Halm, p. 316).

9. Op. 110 bears no dedication, although Beethoven had originally intended both Op. 110 and Op. 111 to be dedicated to Antonie Brentano.

10. Op. 111 was dedicated to Archduke Rudolph; as can be surmised from Beethoven's May 1 letter, he evidently identified Rudolph as the dedicatee in his May 29 letter, now lost.

11. Evidently Beethoven had mentioned this material in his May 29 letter. Its identification is uncertain. On June 5, 1822 (Anderson No. 1079), he had offered a string quartet, presumably a projection for Op. 127, to C. F. Peters. One also might consider the *Elegischer Gesang*, Op. 118, for four (mixed) voices accompanied by string quartet, also offered to Peters on June 5, 1822.

12. Moritz Schlesinger, who had met Beethoven in the summer of 1819, the author of the next letter in this collection.

Incipit: Drey [Drei] Ihrer mir stets geehrten Zuschriften. . . .

Sources: Thayer-Deiters-Riemann, IV, 245–246; Unger, *Beethoven und seine Verleger* (1921), p. 94; excerpted briefly in Thayer-Krehbiel, III, 55, and Thayer-Forbes, pp. 785–786; mentioned in Ludwig Nohl, *Beethoven's Leben* (1877), III, 289, 877. When

Thayer and Nohl examined it, the letter was in the collection of the artist Friedrich von Amerling (1803–1887), Vienna.

293. *Moritz Schlesinger to Beethoven*[1]

Paris; July 3, 1822

Herr v. Beethoven, Vienna

I was infinitely gladdened when I was in Berlin most recently, to see that you are in an active association with my father,[2] and that several of your masterworks are appearing from his press. As you have already learned, I am now established in Paris and will have them engraved here, to their better distribution and so that they will also be endowed externally according to their inner value.

The second sonata is already finished and will be offered very soon.[3] Since I had the pleasure, a few days ago, of receiving your third sonata,[4] which contains so many beauties that could only have been created by the great master, I take the liberty, before I have it engraved, to ask you most submissively if you wrote for the work only one Maestoso and one Andante, or if perhaps the [final] Allegro was accidently forgotten by the copyist.[5] I consider it an obligation to ask you about this: since every masterwork must be published strictly according to the will of its creator, it would therefore be an injustice to publish this work without asking you beforehand.

I would be very happy if you would kindly write several quartets and quintets, however it might best suit you, for my father or me.[6] For some time you have given the world so few works in these genres of music that my request will surely not alienate you, and probably many [of these] already lie finished in your portfolio. How is it going with the one- or multi-voiced songs that you were kindly going to write for my father?[7]

One more request: would you be so kind as to supply for me in your reply the metronome markings forgotten in all three sonatas? Since admirers are accustomed to performing pieces according to the wish of the master in this way, all the world is asking for them.[8]

I shall always remember the hours that I was fortunate to spend with you; I prize the beginning of a Canon that you gave me then[9] like a sacred relic and protect it with the greatest care, to the joy of all who have never had the good fortune of seeing something written in your hand. How happy I would consider myself if, through some chance, a small Romance or some little musical piece of your composition came into my hands, if only to be preserved for me and my friends.

Since I would be happy for the occasion to do something useful or pleasing for you here, I await your command and am

Your devoted,

Maurice Schlesinger
Rue de Richelieu No. 107

[Note:] The enclosed letter lay for you at the post office and, since it was not franked, could not be forwarded.[10]

[Exterior:]
Monsieur
L. de Beethoven
Celebrated Composer
c/o Messrs. Steiner & Co.
Merchants of Music
in the Graben, Paternostergässchen
Vienna, Austria

1. Moritz Adolf Schlesinger (1798–1871) called himself Maurice after he moved from Berlin to Paris, sometime between 1819 and 1821. Here he established a publishing firm associated with his father's business in Berlin (see No. 292 above). Beethoven seemingly replied to this letter on August 31, 1822 (Anderson No. 1095).

2. Adolf Martin Schlesinger.

3. Piano Sonata, Op. 110.

4. Piano Sonata, Op. 111.

5. The two movements of the sonata are Maestoso and Arietta. Adagio molto semplice e cantabile. There is no Allegro third movement, of course. Maurice's father asked virtually the same question in his letter of July 13, 1822 (No. 296 below).

6. This remark may foreshadow the late quartets and possibly even the string quintet on which Beethoven was working when he died almost five years later.

7. See a similar question in (and also n.11 to) Adolf Martin Schlesinger's letter of July 2, 1822 (No. 292 above).

8. Beethoven did not comply with this request.

9. "Glaube und hoffe," WoO 174, dated September 21, 1819.

10. Beethoven's part-time sojourn in Döbling during May and June extended into July (see also Piringer to Beethoven, July 25, 1822, No. 297 below), possibly occasioning this annotation.

Incipit: Unendlich erfreut war ich. . . .

Sources: Theodor Frimmel, "Neue Beethoven-Studien," *Wiener-Zeitung,* December 16, 1888, citing Robert Holz as owner of the original; Thayer-Deiters-Riemann, IV, 246–247; Unger, *Beethoven und seine Verleger,* pp. 95–96; briefly noted in Thayer-Krehbiel, III, 55, and Thayer-Forbes, p. 786. Autograph in the Beethoven-Archiv, Bonn, since 1903; listed in Schmidt-Görg, *Katalog der Handschriften* (1935), p. 57.

294. Carl Friedrich Peters to Beethoven[1]

Leipzig; July 3, 1822

[Peters opens his letter[2] saying that he awaits the Mass[3] as well as the three songs[4] and four marches;[5] for the latter two items Beethoven had estimated a fee of 40 ducats, which he will pay.]

Should you wish to receive a part of my obligation in the meantime, just write to me, for although I have already had many unpleasant experiences with artists on account of advance payment, I shall still do it very gladly in your case, for I see from all indications that you are a good honest man, from whom nothing is to be feared, and that you will thus always be as frank with me as I shall be with you.

. . . One instance of frankness begets another, and therefore I also communicate to you a part of a letter that I received from Steiner[6] a couple of days ago, but ask that when you have read this paper you burn it so that no one catches a glimpse of it; likewise I would really be pleased if you would destroy the part of my letter that discusses this topic, for it is certain that Steiner has dealt unfaithfully with me and has repaid my friendship with ingratitude, but as much as it sickens me, it may still be *forgiven* him, for I cannot imagine that he is so evil at heart; rather I am convinced that he was merely led to that ignoble action by base greed, and perhaps now regrets it. . . .

If, through our new association, I can contribute to your economic situation, it will make me very happy; furthermore, it is unjust that a man like you has to consider his economic circumstances; the great ones of the Earth should long ago have placed you in a completely worry-free position, so that you would no longer have to live *from* Art, but only *for* Art. It will doubtless go for you as it has for many deceased great artists, whom people left in grief during their lifetime, and sought to make amends for it by erecting monuments after their death. Now temporal possessions will not reward you as you deserve, so if heaven grants you at least health and a clear mind, then the artist is as satisfied as everyone, and satisfaction is the finest good fortune.

 With true great esteem, I remain

Your entirely devoted,

F. Peters

[On a separate sheet, enclosed:]
[Excerpt from Steiner's letter to Peters of June 22 (or 26)][7]

 We have postponed answering your honored letter of May 26 for so long because we believed that we would be able to write you a decision concerning Herr v. Beethoven—but the good man has already been in the country for two months[8] and was, *until this hour,* absolutely not to be spoken with. As is generally known, he is increasingly seldom in a good mood, and refuses to see callers if one wants to visit him, or also is really not at home. We hope, however, to see him at our establishment in the city at the earliest opportunity, and then we shall speak to him concerning the compositions. In the meantime, however, perhaps you will be more fortunate than we have been in [dealing with] him and, upon your direct letter to Herr v. Beethoven, will have already received an answer, which will sincerely gladden us. [Steiner.]

[Annotation by Peters:]
 Should something in the above offend you, may you not interpret it so badly; besides, it appears as if he is afraid that you could have written me, and so he reported the above to me and put forth the pretense of friendship. P[eters].

1. This letter seemingly answers Beethoven's letter of June 26 (Anderson No. 1083), with further basis in his letter of June 5 (Anderson No. 1079). It surely crossed in the mails with Beethoven's letter of July 6 (Anderson No. 1085).

2. This passage is based on Nohl's paraphrase of the opening.

3. *Missa solemnis*, Op. 123.

4. On June 5, 1822 (Anderson No. 1079), Beethoven had offered Peters *Mit Mädeln sich vertragen*, WoO 90, *Prüfung des Küssens*, WoO 89, and the *Elegischer Gesang*, Op. 118. Items that Beethoven later sent Peters are identified by Anderson No. 1137 (letter of February 15, 1823) as *Opferlied*, Op. 121b, *Bundeslied*, Op. 122, and *Der Kuss*, Op. 128, for various vocal and instrumental combinations. Ultimately, the latter were published by Schott in 1825.

5. WoO 18, 19, 20 and 24.

6. Viennese publisher Sigmund Anton Steiner (1773–1838), with whom Beethoven's cordial relationship had cooled considerably by this time, largely because of financial disagreements.

7. Nohl gives the date as June 26 on p. 210 and as June 22 on p. 207.

8. Beethoven had been in Döbling off and on since early May.

Incipit (this excerpt): Sollten Sie inzwischen einen Theil. . . .

Sources: Nohl, *Neue Briefe* (1867), pp. 206–207, 210. The main portion of the letter is given on pp. 206–207, the contents of the enclosed sheet on p. 210. Mentioned briefly, with one sentence quoted, in Thayer-Deiters-Riemann, IV, 255, and Thayer-Krehbiel, III, 61.

295. *Carl Friedrich Peters to Beethoven*

Leipzig; July 12, 1822[1]

Sir,

You report to me in your honored letter of the 6th that the four marches,[2] the songs[3] and the Bagatelles[4] for piano are ready to be sent off, so I ask you to transfer them to me.

Since I do not know how long the Bagatelles are,[5] I can only see after their receipt whether I will issue them individually or together. Still, send me *several* of them and at the same time let me know *how many* such little pieces you possess. I would probably be able to take them all, so that you then need not enter into negotiations with another publisher.

Concerning the songs I rely entirely on your selection, but in doing so, at the same time I ask that you give consideration to those with a beautiful text. I would most prefer if I could receive a few *individual* songs on the order of your "Adelaide,"[6] "Schloss Markenstein [*sic*],"[7] etc. I would very much like to mark the beginning of our business relationship by receiving very beautiful things.

At the prices designated to me, that which you are now sending me comes to between 200 and 300 gulden at the *twenty* gulden rate. Since I cannot determine the amount exactly, however, you need only collect it from the banking firm of Meiss [Meisl] Brothers there upon presentation of the shipping bill and your receipt. I have notified these friends about it today. Otherwise it is all the same to me whether you collect this money now or later; from now on it is on deposit there ready for you, and thus is entirely at your disposal. In this manner, convenient for you, I shall have the fee paid every time I receive a manuscript from you.

I am not taking it into my head to bargain down [the price] that you demand, for I certainly cannot equate an artistic product with a commodity; on the contrary, I rely entirely upon your fairness, that you are setting for me prices at rates similar to those quoted to other publishers; thus I will not be burdened with this, for I have already been reproached several times that I pay too high a fee — I am certainly glad to pay the artist what I can, only no one needs to know (enough that I know it) how hard it is for me to procure the money that the many good works I print annually cost.

I do not blame you for setting your string quartet at a high price, but, as I just observed, I cannot bargain down,[8] and since the fee asked for it is too high for my abilities to pay, I had better hold off. Besides, I am not presently in the need for new string quartets, since I still have to print this year four new quartets by Spohr, one by B. Romberg and one by Rode, all of which are beautiful, excellent works.[9] Still, at a price that was more reasonable for me, I would gladly have taken yours as well, although if you receive more for it from another publisher, I shall do without it gladly and be happy that you profit from it.

Furthermore, note that *first of all* I did not wish to have a string quartet from you, but rather a quartet for *piano* and strings, and if you compose one sometime I shall welcome it. Then I ask, however, that it *not* be made *too difficult*, so that good dilettantes can enjoy playing it, for with the presently deteriorated tastes, one must lead amateurs back to better taste by means of works by *good* masters that are not too difficult, but rather are more pleasant. With works that are too difficult, good masters often open the way to superficial composers, for music lovers will be frightened off by difficult works and easily grasp at the bad ones. If, however, good artists take the trouble to write music that is not too difficult but is quite agreeable, then good taste will be preserved—as a publisher I can observe this quite often and can sympathize with the fact that they would gladly prefer the works of great masters if they were not always frightened off by so many difficulties.[10]

More next time; meanwhile I remain with true esteem

Your entirely devoted,

C. F. Peters

1. Answers Beethoven's letter of July 6, 1822 (Anderson No. 1085); partially answered on August 3 (Anderson No. 1092).

2. WoO 18, 19, 20 and 24.

3. See Peters's letter of July 3 (No. 294 above) and Beethoven's letter of June 5 and July 6 (Anderson Nos. 1079 and 1085).

4. Possibly Op. 119, Nos. 1–6 (Anderson No. 1079).

5. Peters uses the word "stark," translated as a term of length in Thayer-Krehbiel, III, 61, and Thayer-Forbes, 791. Beethoven had already said that some of the bagatelles were "von ziemlicher Länge" on July 6, so Peters may also have been referring obliquely to their difficulty here as well. The term could also refer to quantity, but a little later on Peters specifically asks "wie viel" such pieces Beethoven has. A veiled reference to difficulty would be consistent with the lecture on the subject that Peters gives Beethoven near the close of this letter.

6. Op. 46 for voice and piano, dating from 1795–1796.

7. It is not clear whether Peters is referring to the version of Beethoven's short 1814 song "Merkenstein" for one voice (WoO 144) or for two voices (Op. 100), both with piano accompaniment.

8. In his June 5 letter (Anderson No. 1079), Beethoven had asked 50 ducats for such a work, evidently conceived but not yet composed, possibly Op. 127. On June 15, Peters had said that it might exceed his ability to pay. Beethoven's letter of July 6 (Anderson No. 1085) indicates his reluctance to reduce his fee for this work, to which Peters here replies defensively.

9. During this period, Peters published the String Quartets, Op. 58, Nos. 1–3, by Louis Spohr (1784–1859) as well as Spohr's *Quatuor brillante*, Op. 61. Of the works by Bernhard Romberg (1767–1841), Peters likewise published the Quartet No. 8 (Op. 37) in 1822 or early 1823 and the Quartet No. 9, Op. 39, by early 1824. Although there is record of four Quartets, Opp. 11–14, by Pierre Rode (1774–1830) published in Vienna in 1822–1823, these do not seem to have appeared under Peters's imprint; even so, given the accuracy of his statements concerning Spohr and Romberg, there is little

reason to doubt that he was at least negotiating seriously with Rode at this time. (Whistling and Hofmeister, *Handbuch der musikalischen Litteratur, 1823*, p. 5; *1824*, p. 6.)

10. After reading similar pleas from George Thomson over the years, and given his sensitivity in artistic matters, Beethoven cannot have regarded this lecture kindly. Beethoven's letter of August 3 implies that, for the moment, he is sparing Peters an extensive retort.

Incipit: Ew. Hochwohlgeb. melden mir in Ihrem geehrten. . . .

Sources: Thayer-Deiters-Riemann, IV, 256–258, noting that the letter was in the collection of the artist Friedrich von Amerling (1803–1887), Vienna. Paragraph 4 excerpted in Max Unger, "Neue Briefe an Beethoven," *Neue Zeitschrift für Musik* 81, no. 28 (July 9, 1914), 411. Paragraphs 2–4 summarized in Thayer-Krehbiel, III, 61, and Thayer-Forbes, p. 791. Paragraphs 4–5 excerpted in Hilmar, *Musikverlag Artaria*, p. 36, noting that the autograph is now in the Bibliothek des Landes und der Stadt Wien.

296. Adolf Martin Schlesinger to Beethoven

Berlin; July 13, 1822

Honored Sir!

My most recent letter[1] will certainly be in your hands, and I look forward to your reply; likewise you will have received the Scottish Songs that are appearing.[2]

For the present, I only wanted to ask, concerning the second sonata[3] that you sent me, where the second movement has the superscription:

"Arietta"   adagio molto semplice
              e molto cantabile

if a third movement is not to be added, and the piece is thus ended,[4] and to whom you wish to make your dedications.

I very much request you to send or indicate this to my son in Paris, addressed: Mr. Maurice Schlesinger, Bookseller and Music Merchant, Quai Malaquais No. 13; or Rue de Richelieu, near the Boulevardes.[5]

In this expectation, signed with all esteem,

Your most devoted,
Ad[olf] M[artin] Schlesinger

1. Schlesinger's letter of July 2, 1822 (No. 292 above); Beethoven's reply is unknown.

2. Op. 108.

3. Piano Sonata, Op. 111. Actually this is the "third sonata" referred to in the Schlesingers' letters to Beethoven of July 2 and July 3 (Nos. 292 and 293 above).

4. Maurice Schlesinger had already asked Beethoven essentially the same question on July 3. The superscription quoted differs from the published manuscript known today.

5. Thayer (and Unger, possibly quoting him) transcribes the following variants in the address: "Ms.," "Malaquai," "Rive"; Kastner provides the variant "Boulevard." The Quai Malaquais, on the left bank of the Seine, remains a traditional site for bookshops. Across the river, extending from the Louvre north, is the Rue de Richelieu, which, at its north end, runs into or near several streets designated *boulevard.*

Incipit: Mein jüngstes Schreiben wird wohl. . . .

Sources: Thayer-Deiters-Riemann, IV, 248, transcribed from the original in the possession of Karl van Beethoven's widow, Caroline; Kastner (1910), pp. 684–685, with several corrections; Unger, *Beethoven und seine Verleger,* p. 96.

297. Ferdinand Piringer[1] to Beethoven, Oberdöbling

Vienna; July 25, 1822

Domine Generalissime!

Victoria in Döbling[2]—fresh troops are advancing! The wholesalers, Meisl Brothers, in the Rauhensteingasse, in their own building, 2d story, have received instructions from Herr Peters in Leipzig to pay several hundred gulden to Herr Ludwig van Beethoven.[3]

I hurry with Degen's wings[4] to report this happy news to *Illustrissimo* at once.

Today is the first sad day in the Viennese calendar, because yesterday was the last day of the Italian opera![5]

With greatest esteem,
Illustrissimi Generalissimi
humillimus servus
Ferd[inand] Piringer

1. Piringer (1780–1829), Viennese court official and amateur violinist and conductor, was a member of Beethoven's circle of friends. Beethoven enclosed this note with

his letter to C. F. Peters of September 13, 1822 (Anderson No. 1100). The composer's remarks indicate that his relationship with Piringer was rather cautious at this time because of his visits to Steiner's shop and the gossip exchanged there.

2. Beethoven lived in Oberdöbling through much of the summer of 1822. The military banter is typical of the Beethoven-Steiner circle.

3. In his letter of July 12 (No. 295 above), Peters had promised Beethoven just this method of payment. The composer's letter of September 13 seems to indicate some alarm over its swift delivery.

4. Jakob Degen (1756–1846), Swiss-born printer, clockmaker and aeronaut, active with his flying machines in Vienna by 1808. As indicated by his letters from Baden (where Degen evidently tried out his devices on a regular basis) in September 1813 (Anderson No. 432) and ca. September 1814 (Anderson No. 494), Beethoven maintained a continuing interest in his experiments. From at least the period of the Napoleonic Wars, aeronautics was viewed for its military potential; thus the reference to Degen is consistent with the tone of this letter.

5. Domenico Barbaja (ca. 1778–1841) had become director of the Kärntnertor Theater late in 1821 and on April 13, 1822, began a Rossini festival of six extraordinarily successful productions, with the Italian composer himself present. Beethoven and his circle of Austrians and Germans regarded the popular "Rossini fever" with some alarm, from both artistic and economic viewpoints.

Incipit: Victoria in Döbling—frische Truppen. . . .

Sources: Nohl, *Neue Briefe* (1867), p. 213; Kalischer, IV, 166; Kalischer-Shedlock, II, 209; Thayer-Deiters-Riemann, IV, 258, n.1; Kastner (1910), p. 690; Thayer-Krehbiel, III, 62; Thayer-Forbes, pp. 791–792.

298. *Franz Joseph Zips*[1] *to Beethoven, Oberdöbling*

Vienna; July 26, 1822

Dear Herr van Beethoven,

I hereby report to you that His Imperial Highness[2] is not well; therefore nothing will be done tomorrow. If it is agreeable to you, please come Wednesday, July 31, at 5:30, for his Imperial Highness will expect you.[3]

Now farewell; I am with all esteem

Your most devoted,

Zips

[Evidently on the exterior:]
    For Monsieur van Beethoven
    Oberdöbling, Alleegasse No. 135

1. Zips was a minor official in Archduke Rudolph's service; he is mentioned in Beethoven's letter to Rudolph, February 27, 1823 (Anderson No. 1146).

2. Archduke Rudolph.

3. At about this time, Beethoven wrote to his brother (Anderson No. 1086): "The Cardinal Archduke is here and I go to him twice a week." Rudolph must have remained in Vienna through the end of August before returning to Olmütz, judging from Beethoven's references here and in his letter to C. F. Peters, September 13, 1822 (Anderson No. 1100).

Incipit: Ich berichte Ihnen hiermit. . . .

Sources: Thayer-Deiters-Riemann, IV, 272, n.1; transcribed from the autograph, in the possession of Beethoven's nephew Karl van Beethoven's widow, Caroline; Kastner (1910), p. 687.

299. Prince Nicolas Galitzin[1] to Beethoven

St. Petersburg; November 9, 1822[2]

Monsieur Louis van Beethoven
Vienna

Monsieur!

As much a passionate amateur in music as a great admirer of your talent, I take the liberty of writing to you to ask if you would consent to compose one, two or three new quartets,[3] for which I would be pleased to pay you for the trouble what you judge appropriate. I shall accept the dedication with gratitude. Please let me know to which banker I ought to direct the sum that you wish to have. The instrument that I study is the violoncello. I await your reply with the most eager impatience. Please write your letter to me at the following address:

> To Prince Nicolas de Galitzin in St. Petersburg, in
> care of Messrs. Stieglitz & Co., bankers.

I ask you to accept the assurance of my great admiration and my high regard.

Prince Nicolas Galitzin

1. Prince Nicolas Borisovich Galitzin (December 8, 1794–October 22, 1866, old style), amateur violoncellist and promoter of cultural life in St. Petersburg. Galitzin commissioned and received the dedications to three of Beethoven's late String Quartets, Opp. 127, 130 and 132, but, owing to seeming financial reverses, made only a partial payment to the composer. The matter remained unresolved for three decades (see app. H, "The Later History of Prince Galitzin's Payments," Thayer-Forbes, pp. 1100–1102). Galitzin engineered at least two subscriptions for manuscript copies of the *Missa solemnis* and was influential in its April 1824 performance in St. Petersburg. For further information on the prince and his family, see Lev Ginsburg, "Ludwig van Beethoven und Nikolai Galitzin," *Beethoven-Jahrbuch* 4 (1962), 59–71; Ginsburg's similarly titled "Ludwig van Beethoven und Nikolai Fürst Golitzin," *Österreichische Musikzeitschrift* 19 (1964), 523–529; and Ernst Stöcke, "Golizyn," *MGG*, vol. XVI, cols. 504–506.

2. This letter was dated November 9 (new style) and postmarked October 28 (old style). Beethoven replied on January 25, 1823 (Anderson No. 1123 in the original French; MacArdle & Misch No. 347 in English translation).

3. On June 5, 1822, Beethoven had offered the possibility of a string quartet to C. F. Peters, which the Leipzig publisher had refused in his letter of July 12, 1822 (No. 295 above); thus Galitzin's letter here provided not only the opportunity but also the potential financial means for the composition of the late quartets. See also Johann van Beethoven's letter to Antonio Pacini, December 27, 1822 (No. 300 below).

Incipit: Aussi passionné amateur de musique. . . .

Sources: Nohl, *Beethoven's Leben* (1877), III, 357, 390, in French; citing Lenz, *Beethoven: Eine Kunststudie: Kritische Kataloge,* IV, 220. Nohl published a German translation in "Die Briefe Galitzins," *Allgemeine Deutsche Musik-Zeitung* 6 (1879), p. 1, col. 2. Thayer-Deiters-Riemann, IV, 324; Kastner (1910), pp. 699–700; Kalischer, V, 161–162; Kalischer-Shedlock, II, 389; Thayer-Forbes, p. 815 (the last in English). When Nohl and Thayer examined and made copies of them, the letters from Prince Galitzin were in the possession of Beethoven's nephew Karl's widow, Caroline, in Vienna. The autographs have since disappeared and are presumed lost.

300. *Johann van Beethoven*[1] *to Antonio Pacini,*[2] *Paris*

Vienna; December 27, 1822

Monsieur!

In response to your very estimable letter of June 22, I have the honor to tell you that I take care of my brother's affairs, and because I have spent several months on my estate, which is far from here, I am late in responding to a backlog of many letters.[3]

My brother was really moved by the plentiful praise that you gave him, and he is very charmed to have made the acquaintance of a man who loves and appreciates the arts.

You desire to have some quartets and quintets from him,[4] which might not yet have appeared; but at the moment it is impossible to favor you in this manner, since he is occupied with larger works, namely a new symphony,[5] an opera[6] and a grand mass,[7] the greatest work that he has composed until now in this genre, which is just finished, and which he intends to perform during this winter as an oratorio for his *Academie* [i.e., concert]. He will wish to have the manuscript of this mass presented to the grandest courts for a reasonable fee, but does not want it to be engraved for some years. You will oblige him very much if you would be able to indicate to him the means for having it reach the royal intendant of your court.

Out of special esteem for you, Monsieur, and to fulfill your desires as well, which is within his power, he will compose some quartets or quintets for you in the period of six months; but if you can make use of a new trio for two violins and a viola,[8] and a grand overture,[9] he is prepared to transfer to you the former for the price of 20 Louis and the latter for 30. If not, be so kind as to recommend these pieces to a good musical agent [i.e., publisher] in Paris, and agree upon the most equitable price, which you will then be willing to indicate to me.

I have the honor to be, with high regards, Monsieur,

Your very humble and obedient servant,

Jean van Beethoven[10]

Kothgasse No. 61, Vienna

Also you could be served
with six Bagatelles for
piano for the price of 15 Louis.[11]

I am engaged in procuring for you the catalogs of works engraved here in Vienna, and I should be pleased to have them sent to you by coach.

1. Beethoven's younger brother, Nikolaus Johann (1776–1848), pharmacist, entrepreneur and owner of a large estate at Gneixendorf, near Krems.

2. Antonio Francesco Gaetano Pacini (1778–1866), an Italian-born singer and manager, active as a music publisher in Paris from ca. 1806. Beethoven himself wrote to Pacini on April (May?) 5, 1823 (Anderson No. 1166; MacArdle & Misch No. 356, in English translation). The letter indicates no addressee, but Unger believed that it was written to the same recipient as that letter.

3. Beethoven evidently received Pacini's June 22 letter in Vienna, for, in his letter to Johann of July 22–26, 1822, he reported, "From Paris, too, I have received offers for my compositions." Beethoven's letters to his brother indicate that Johann had visited Vienna at least twice between July and December 1822 and that the composer was becoming vexed with him for not paying attention to the business matters he had presumably agreed to undertake.

4. Pacini's request for such works, especially those that would emerge as the late string quartets over the next several years, antedates Prince Galitzin's request of November 9, 1822 (No. 299 above). Beethoven's offer of a quartet to Peters on June 5 and his hint of still another work in this genre on July 6, 1822, seem to indicate that the *concept* for these works originated with the composer himself.

5. Symphony No. 9, Op. 125.

6. With *The Consecration of the House* (*Die Weihe des Hauses*), Op. 124, performed on October 3 and *Fidelio* revived on November 3, Beethoven may have seriously considered further dramatic works at this time, possibly Goethe's *Faust* (as reported by Rochlitz) or Grillparzer's projected *Die schöne Melusine*.

7. *Missa solemnis*, Op. 123. Beethoven, aided by Schindler as his secretary, began soliciting subscriptions as early as January 23, 1823, in a letter to the Royal Prussian Embassy (No. 303 below), among others.

8. Doubtless the arrangement of his early Variations on Mozart's "Là ci darem la mano," from *Don Giovanni*, for two oboes and English horn, WoO 28, also offered in more specific terms to C. F. Peters on December 20, 1822 (Anderson No. 1111).

9. *Consecration of the House*, Op. 124.

10. This letter's French text was written in another hand and signed (along with his own address) by Johann.

11. Doubtless six items from Op. 119, which the composer likewise (see n.8, this letter) offered to C. F. Peters at this time, although his negotiations for them with the Leipzig publisher had begun by June 5, 1822.

Incipit: En reponse de votre trés estimable. . . .

Sources: Max Unger, "Ein unbekannter französischer Brief Ludwig van Beethovens," (*Neue*) *Zeitschrift für Musik* 103 (April 1936), 415. The autograph was then in the Bibliothèque du Conservatoire, Paris, and has since been transferred to the Département de la Musique, Bibliothèque Nationale de France.

301. Royal Swedish Music Academy, Stockholm,[1] to Beethoven

Stockholm; December 28, 1822[2]

[Device: Muse with Lyre]

The Royal Swedish Musical Academy, which acknowledges its obligation to recognize and, for its improvement, to embrace unto itself persons who have, with success or in a distinguished manner, pursued praiseworthy music, has, as a declaration of its esteem and by election, named to its membership:

Herr Louis de Beethoven.

As further evidence hereof, it presents this open letter, which is confirmed by the Royal Academy's customary seal.

Stockholm, December 28, 1822

On behalf of the Royal Swedish Musical Academy,

[Seal]   A. J. Skjôldebrand[3]   Pehr Frigel
                 President   Secretary

1. In 1799, the academy had also named Joseph Haydn, Johann Georg Albrechtsberger and Antonio Salieri to honorary membership. They were the first foreign musicians so designated since the society's founding, twenty-eight years before (see Landon, *Haydn, Chronicle and Works,* IV, 462). Haydn's diploma has seemingly disappeared, but Landon reproduces an announcement in the *Wiener Zeitung,* April

13, 1799, that closely parallels the wording of the present diploma and that probably reflects the diplomas sent in 1799 as well.

2. Engraved diploma, oblong format, with a vignette by sculptor J. F. Martin at its head. Embossed seal. Beethoven's name and the date written in ink. For the accompanying letter, see the Academy to Beethoven, January 31, 1823 (No. 306 below). Concerning imperial permission to accept this honor from a foreign country, see Beethoven's draft letter of ca. April 8, 1824 (No. 354 below).

3. In the facsimile, the president's initials could possibly be read as "A.F." (as given by Frimmel).

Incipit: Kongl. Svenska Musicaliska Academien, Som råknar fôr en Skyldig-het. . . .

Sources: Theodor Frimmel, "Verzeichnisse," *Beethoven- Jahrbuch* 1 (1908), 111. Document then in the Bibliothek und Museum der Stadt Wien (Städtische Samm-lungen), but could not be located by Stadt- und Landesbibliothek staff in 1991. Facsimile (reduced in size) in Stephan Ley, *Beethovens Leben in authentischen Bildern und Texten* (Berlin: Bruno Cassirer, 1925), p. 104; and (further reduced) in Bory, p. 183. Both Ley and Bory cite the former Staatsbibliothek, Berlin, as the location of the document. Bory's photo is less distinct than Ley's; it may have been copied directly from Ley and the document's location cited without further verification. Sieghard Brandenburg, Beethoven-Archiv, Bonn, confirms that the location of the diploma is currently unknown.

302. Beethoven to Anton Diabelli

[Vienna; late 1822/early 1823][1]

Dear Diabelli!

I was so very busy that it has not yet been possible for me to serve you, but be assured that I shall show consideration for *you* more than anyone else—you are first of all receiving the Variations,[2] although I cannot yet specify the day and hour; also the 4-hand [sonata][3] as soon as possible. I shall visit you in a few days, when we shall discuss everything.

Your friend,

Beethoven

[Exterior:]
For Herr von Diabelli

1. Beethoven's equivocal language concerning the delivery date for the variations led Staehelin to date this letter, with some caution, as "around the turn of the year 1822/1823."

2. Variations on a Theme by Diabelli, Op. 120, which Beethoven had begun in 1819, and which were published by Cappi & Diabelli in June 1823. Late in 1822, Beethoven had been busy finishing the *Missa solemnis*.

3. For further references to such a sonata (never composed, but by then projected to be in the key of F), see Diabelli's letters to Beethoven of August 4 [7], 1824, and on or shortly after August 24, 1824 (Nos. 377 and 380 below).

Incipit: So sehr beschäftigt war es mir. . . .

Sources: Transcribed and edited by Martin Staehelin in Staehelin, "Unbekannte . . . Schriftstücke," pp. 77–79. Autograph in the Beethoven-Haus, Bonn, NE 123.

1823

303. Beethoven to the Royal Prussian Embassy, Vienna

Vienna; January 23, 1823[1]

The undersigned cherishes the wish to send his latest work, which he regards as the most successful product of his mind, to the Most Exalted Court of Berlin. It is a grand Solemn Mass for four solo voices with choruses and complete orchestra in score, which can also be used as a grand oratorio.

He therefore requests that the High Embassy of His Majesty the King of Prussia might graciously condescend to procure for him the necessary permission of your Most Exalted Court.

Since the copying of the score, however, entails a considerable expense, the undersigned does not think it excessive if a fee of 50 ducats in gold were fixed for it.[2]

The work in question, moreover, will not be published in the meantime.[3]

Ludwig van Beethoven

[Exterior:]

To the Exalted Royal Prussian Embassy, Vienna.

1. This item represents the form letter soliciting subscriptions for manuscript copies of the *Missa solemnis*, as the solicitation was first sent, written by Schindler and signed by Beethoven. In addition to the present example, the first group on January 23 went to the Electoral Embassy of Hesse-Cassel (Thayer-Deiters-Riemann, IV, 357; Thayer-Forbes, p. 822) and the courts of Baden, Württemberg, Bavaria and Sachsen-Weimar (Hans Schmidt, "Die Beethovenhandschriften des Beethovenhauses in Bonn," *Beethoven-Jahrbuch* 7 [1971], 154–155, No. 366). Probably the identical form was repeated "to the other ambassadors" on January 26.

By early February, some variants of order and wording had been introduced. These letters were sent to Mecklenburg and Hesse-Darmstadt (Prelinger No. 696; Anderson No. 1134) on February 5, to Copenhagen (presumably King Friedrich VI) and Nassau on February 6, to Tuscany on February 17 and to Paris on March 1.

The letter was also sent, with more minor variants, to Archbishop Alexander Rudnay of Esztergom on April 8 (MacArdle & Misch No. 335), to Prince Nikolaus Esterházy on ca. May 30, to the St. Petersburg Philharmonic Society on June 21

(MacArdle & Misch No. 365), to Czar Alexander I, probably in early May, and to the Musikverein in Frankfurt am Main, among others.

The Bavarian Embassy received a letter like the present one; its internal memos and machinations may be followed in Stainlein's letter of January 25, 1823 (see Nos. 304, 308 and 312 below). Various additional items of correspondence with Schelble (Frankfurt), Zelter (Berlin), Galitzin (St. Petersburg) and others are included in the present volume (Nos. 315, 309 and 310, respectively).

2. The list of subscribers ultimately included the czar of Russia, the kings of Prussia, France and Denmark, the elector of Saxony (Sachsen-Weimar), the grand dukes of Darmstadt and Tuscany, Prince Nicolas Galitzin, Prince Anton Heinrich Radziwill, and the Cäcilia Verein, Frankfurt (see Anderson No. 1452).

Beethoven has often been criticized in the literature for his allegedly unethical attempts at marketing the *Missa solemnis,* but by December 27, 1822, when such a scheme is first mentioned in his brother Johann's letter to Pacini in Paris (No. 300 above), Beethoven may have felt his health declining and with it the capacity to compose income-producing works on a scale comparable to the *Missa solemnis* and the Ninth Symphony. His possible suspicions ultimately proved correct since his final years were devoted exclusively to chamber works, with occasional sketches and projections for works on a larger scale, but little or nothing completed for forces greater than string quartet.

3. The *Missa solemnis* was, in fact, not published until four years later when it was issued by B. Schotts Söhne, Mainz, in March/April 1827, almost simultaneously with the composer's death.

Incipit: Der Unterzeichnete hegt den Wunsch. . . .

Sources: Elinore Barber, "Beethoven Writes to the Imperial Prussian Embassy in 1823, Concerning 'A Large Solemn Mass,'" *Bach* 7, no. 4 (1976), 23–25 (including facsimile). I made my translation in consultation with details apparent in the facsimile. In 1976, the autograph was then in the possession of Mrs. George Bickford, Cleveland.

304. Bavarian Ambassador Stainlein to King Maximilian Josef of Bavaria, Munich

Vienna; January 25, 1823[1]

Most Serene and Mighty King, Most Gracious King and Lord!

Subject: A musical work by Beethoven.

The famous composer Beethoven has requested me to inquire most humbly of Your Royal Majesty, if it would most graciously be permitted him to send your Supreme Highness his newest work, which he considers the most successful product of his spirit.

This work is a grand solemn Mass for 4 solo voices, with choruses and complete orchestra, in *score*. Since the copying of the *score* requires considerable expense, he believes that he might be allowed to fix upon it an honorarium of 50 ducats.

The above-mentioned work itself will not meanwhile be issued in print.

In most submissively requesting the delivery of your most gracious resolution, I remain in deepest respect,

Your Royal Majesty's

most humbly loyal and obedient

Stainlein

1. Forwards Beethoven's request in his form solicitation letter sent January 23, 1823 (No. 303 above), asking the court to subscribe to the *Missa solemnis*. The present memo largely paraphrases Beethoven. Its course of action is continued by Rumling to King Maximilian Josef, February 14, 1823, and Rechberg back to Stainlein, February 25, 1823 (Nos. 308 and 312 below).

Incipit: Der berühmte Compositeur Beethoven. . . .

Sources: Adolf Sandberger, "Beiträge zur Beethoven-Forschung," *Archiv für Musikwissenschaft* 2 (1920), 397–398, and "Zum Kapitel: Beethoven und München," in *Ausgewählte Aufsätze II* (Munich: Drei Masken, 1924; reprint, Hildesheim: Georg

Olms, 1973), pp. 258–260. When examined by Sandberger, the three documents in this sequence were in the Akta des Staatsministeriums des k. Hauses und des Äussern (Österreich M E 1913, F93/4), Munich.

305. Carl Maria von Weber[1] to Beethoven (Draft)

Dresden; January 28, 1823[2]

To Beethoven; *re Fidelio*

The performance of this mighty work, testifying to German greatness and depth of feeling, under my direction in Prague,[3] gave me an intimacy, as inspiring as it was instructive, with its[4] essence, through which I dare hope to present it to the public with its full effect here, where I have all possible means at my disposal.[5] Every performance will be a festival day, on which I shall be permitted to pay to your sublime spirit the homage that lives for you in my innermost heart, where veneration and love contend for preeminence.

1. Carl Maria von Weber (1786–1826), conductor and composer of *Der Freischütz* (1821), which was then taking Europe by storm.

2. Weber wrote to Beethoven on January 28, February 18, April 7 and June 5, 1823; Beethoven replied in letters received on February 16, April 10 and June 9. Weber's son, Max Maria von Weber, noted that the correspondence was lost except for this draft of the beginning of Weber's first letter.

On October 5, 1823, Weber visited Beethoven in Baden, accompanied by Tobias Haslinger and Julius Benedict.

3. Weber had performed *Fidelio* in Prague in 1814.

4. The word innern in the phrase "mit seiner innern Wesenheit" (with its inner essence) appeared in Max Maria von Weber's transcription but was omitted by Fürstenau. An examination of the autograph (facsimile in Lühning, p. 383) reveals that Weber's son must have misread "seiner" as "s. innern"; thus a correct reading contains no "inner" or "innern."

5. Weber received a copy of the score from Beethoven himself on April 10 and conducted *Fidelio,* with Wilhelmine Schröder-Devient in the title role, at the Royal Opera House, Dresden, on April 29, 1823. For related correspondence, see Könneritz's letter to Beethoven, June 26, 1823 (No. 325 below), and Beethoven's reply of July 17 (Anderson No. 1210).

Incipit (this abstract): Fidelio. Die Aufführung dieses. . . .

Sources: M. Fürstenau, "Zwei noch unbekannte Briefe Beethoven's," *Allgemeine musikalische Zeitung,* n.s., 1 (September 9, 1863), 633; Max Maria von Weber, *Carl Maria von Weber: Ein Lebensbild,* 3 vols. (Leipzig: Ernst Keil, 1864), II, 466; Nohl, *Briefe Beethovens* (1865), pp. 246–247; Nohl-Wallace, II, 129; Thayer-Deiters-Riemann, IV, 436; Thayer-Krehbiel, III, 129–130; Thayer-Forbes, p. 863; Kalischer (German), IV, 295; Kalischer-Shedlock, II, 271–272. Autograph in the Staatsbibliothek zu Berlin–Preussischer Kulturbesitz, Weberiana 1.11 A f 2,19; facsimile and transcription in Lühning, " 'Fidelio' in Prag," pp. 382–383.

306. Royal Swedish Music Academy, Stockholm, to Beethoven

Stockholm; January 31, 1823[1]

Monsieur!

The Royal Music Academy of Sweden . . . [invites you] to occupy a place among its foreign members . . . [further flattering prose and customary closing formulas].

Pehr Frigel
Perpetual Secretary of the Academy

1. Accompanied the society's diploma, dated December 28, 1822 (No. 301 above), naming Beethoven to honorary membership. Frimmel noted that the letter was "hardly important enough to be printed in its entirety" and provided only the excerpts and description translated here. Beethoven speedily replied on March 1, 1823 (Anderson No. 1149). He also used this occasion as an opportunity to write to King Karl XIV Johann of Sweden, the former French General Jean Baptiste Jules Bernadotte (1763–1844), who had visited Vienna while still in Napoleon's service, mentioning the academy's honoring him and soliciting the king's subscription for a manuscript copy of the *Missa solemnis* (Anderson No. 1150). The king did not subscribe.

Incipit: L'Académie Royale de musique de Swède. . . .

Sources: Frimmel, "Neue Beethovenstudien" (1895), p. 18. Autograph then in the collection of wholesale merchant Franz Trau, Vienna. Sieghard Brandenburg, Beethoven-Archiv, Bonn, confirms that the location of the letter is currently unknown.

307. Johann van Beethoven to (Domenico) Artaria[1]

[Vienna;] February 11, 1823

Herr von Artaria,
Famous Art Dealers
Vienna

The undersigned requests you herewith to inform Herr von Pacini[2] in Paris that as long as I have no reply from London, I can neither accept the 500 Francs, nor send him the desired two works.[3] As soon as a reply arrives from London, however, I shall write him *immediately.*[4] We are now resolved not to publish one single work more if it cannot be sold *simultaneously* in three Empires, namely, in *Vienna for all of Austria and the entire remainder of Germany,* in London for all of *England,* in Paris for all of *France.* Because of this I have also quoted Herr von Pacini a very cheap price, which will also be quoted to all the others.

Please accept the assurance of my esteem, with which I am

Yours truly,

Johann v. Beethoven
Estate owner

1. The letter does not specify to which member of the Artaria family it was directed, but a reference to "Herr Artaria" in Beethoven's letter of June 1, 1823 (Anderson No. 1188), provides evidence that the present addressee is Domenico Artaria (1775–1842).

2. Johann spells his name Paccini.

3. On December 27, 1822 (No. 300 above), Johann had offered Pacini the trio Variations, WoO 28; *The Consecration of the House* (*Die Weihe des Hauses*) Overture, Op. 124; and the Bagatelles, Op. 119, Nos. 1–6.

4. Ludwig's letter to Pacini of April 5, 1823 (Anderson No. 1166), may shed some further light on this projected transaction.

Incipit: Unterzeichneter ersucht hiemit. . . .

Sources: Theodor Frimmel, "Neue Beethovenstudien," *Neue Zeitschrift für Musik* 85 (1889), 549. The owner of this letter in 1889, Alexander Posonyi (Vienna), also possessed another letter in Johann's hand, not concerning Ludwig's affairs, but shedding some light on his own domestic situation. Addressed to the lawyer Weiss in Linz, on October 14, 1818, it reads, in part: "I would have answered you immediately, but I lay in bed and was always surrounded, so that it was impossible for me to write if I didn't want to *completely* destroy peace in the household. . . ."

308. Baron Theodor von Rumling, Court Music Intendant, *to King Maximilian Josef of Bavaria*

Munich; February 14, 1823[1]

Most Serene and Mighty King, Most Gracious King and Lord!

The Royal Court Chapel at present possesses so many works composed in the church style by the most famous masters that only a part of them, because of their great numbers, can be brought to performance. For this reason, and in consideration of the high honorarium of 50 ducats demanded for the score of the newest musical work of Beethoven, it is impossible for the Royal Court Music Intendancy to cover from its administrative fund such an expense whose costs, with the addition of the copying out of parts, would render claim to a sum not less than 500 gulden. The *Kapelle*, therefore, can only await that point in time when this work will be given over, by its brilliant composer, for publication and will be issued in print.[2] Upon this event, which will take place in its own time, the Royal Court Music Intendancy hopes to be in a position to increase its present fine collection of classical church music with a new masterwork, and to purchase a *printed copy* of this Mass.[3]

In most obediently carrying out, through this dutiful report, the mandate of the most gracious Ministerial Assignee, received on the 8th of this month, the Royal Court Music Intendancy returns in the accompanying file the two documents imparted to it, and remains in profoundest awe,

Your Royal Majesty's
Most humbly loyal and obedient

Baron von Rumling

1. On February 6, 1823, the Ministry of Finance had forwarded Stainlein's January 25 request (No. 304 above) to the Court Music Intendancy, "for its obliging examination." The decision is reflected in Rechberg to Stainlein, February 25, 1823 (No. 312 below).

2. Schott in Mainz published the score of the *Missa solemnis* in March/April 1827.

3. Also bearing on this negative decision was the fact that the newly built Court Theater had burned as recently as January 14, 1823, thereby creating financial and emotional distress among the Bavarian monarchy and cultural officials.

Incipit: Die königliche Hofkapelle besitzt. . . .

Sources: Adolf Sandberger, "Beiträge zur Beethoven-Forschung," *Archiv für Musikwissenschaft* 2 (1920), 397–398, and "Zum Kapitel: Beethoven und München," in *Ausgewählte Aufsätze II* (Munich: Drei Masken, 1924; reprint, Hildesheim: Georg Olms, 1973), pp. 258–260. When examined by Sandberger, the three documents in this sequence were in the Akta des Staatsministeriums des k. Hauses und des Äussern (Österreich M E 1913, F93/4), Munich.

309. Karl Friedrich Zelter to Beethoven

Berlin; February 22, 1823[1]

On the 15th of this month, my highly admired friend, I received your letter of the 8th, and if, in deepest sorrow, I sympathize with your continuing infirmity, my admiration is all the greater since, in spite of your condition, you enrich the world with a great new work[2] from your masterful hand.

I have acquainted my circle [of colleagues] with your undertaking and, along with all of your admirers, must wish you undivided success.[3]

And yet it will be as if nothing were done [on your behalf] if persons of great means and equal goodwill do not join in [this endeavor].

Concerning our *Singakademie,* you know them from your own experience. They appreciated you already about 25 years ago during your visit here, which remains unforgettable to me.[4] If they now no longer strive for the heights, I dare say, however, that they have not regressed [in their abilities]. Far over half of the society now consists of wives, daughters, youths and children—a significant part of whom are also exempt from the modest dues. To unite such a society (especially a musical one) now for a fund-raising project is an unusual task, and whoever asks much of them can only hope to get the desired results.[5]

This notwithstanding, I am considering purchasing a copy of your noble work for the specified price of 50 ducats if you, worthy friend, will agree to the following proposition.

You know that, in our *Singakademie,* only a capella works (without instrumental accompaniment) are rehearsed. Now, it says in your letter that your Mass *could almost be performed by the singing voices alone.*[6] Therefore it should give you only slight trouble to arrange the copy destined for me in such a manner that the work will be immediately useful for us.

There would not only be the advantage for your continuing fame that must result from our studying such a piece anew four or five times, year in and year out, but you would [also] thereby make your work usable by all similar societies, of which there are a significant number in Prussia alone, since in towns smaller than Berlin instrumental forces always prove to be meager.[7] As for us, you would be able to count on 4 to 8 good soloists, selected from a chorus of 160 ringing voices who gather twice weekly for rehearsal. And as for performance, I will, on my part, seek to do everything that I have always felt obliged to do for a fellow artist like you.

Send me an affirmative word on this matter soon. The money will then be transferred to you immediately. With fervent admiration,

Your,

Zelter

1. Answers Beethoven's letter to Zelter, February 8, 1823 (Anderson No. 1135).

2. *Missa solemnis,* Op. 123, to which Beethoven had invited Zelter to subscribe for a manuscript copy on behalf of the *Singakademie.*

3. In his letter of February 8, Beethoven suggested that Zelter intercede with such people as the king of Prussia and Prince Anton Heinrich Radziwill on his behalf.

4. Beethoven spent some time in Berlin in June 1796 during his tour and visited rehearsals of the *Singakademie.*

5. Zelter here adapts the proverb "Wer viel fragt, erhält viel Antwort" (Many questions, many answers) for his purpose.

6. Indeed, Beethoven wrote, "With slight alterations it could even be performed by voices alone," although he did add: "Still, the more that voices are doubled and multiplied and supported by instruments, the more powerful should be the effect" (as translated in Anderson No. 1135).

7. Zelter is speaking of his *Liedertafel* movement, an extension of the *Singakademie* concept, in which male choruses and mixed choruses were founded all over northern Germany after 1809. Another of Beethoven's sometime correspondents, Hans Georg Nägeli, was largely responsible for the similar *Liederkranz* movement, which at the same time was spreading from German Switzerland throughout southern Germany.

Incipit: Ihren Brief vom 8. d. . . . .

Sources: "Drei Briefe, zwischen Beethoven und Zelter gewechselt [in der Berliner Musik-Zeitung (Verlag von Bock) durch Herrn Dr. Ruitel mitgetheilt]," *Nieder-rheinische Musik-Zeitung* 5 (1857), 22–23; Nohl, *Briefe* (1865), pp. 224–225; Johann Wolfgang Schottländer, "Zelter und die Komponisten seiner Zeit," *Jahrbuch der Sammlung Kippenberg* 8 (1930), 178, 205–207.

310. Prince Nicolas Galitzin to Beethoven

St. Petersburg; February 23, 1823

Monsieur,

Your letter of January 25[1] did not reach me until yesterday. It filled me with joy by making me hope that I shall soon enjoy a new product of your sublime genius. I have given an order to my banker M[onsieur] Stieglitz for 50 ducats for the first quartet. I shall have another 100 for two others transferred immediately.[2]

From my impatience to relish your masterpieces, I take the liberty of entreating you to send me the first quartet as soon as it is finished, even before it is delivered to the press. I promise you not to communicate it to anyone, so that you may have all possible advantages in sending it to the printer, and so that I should not be an obstacle to the price that he will offer you.

The ordinary channel of transportation can sometimes be slow; thus I should recommend that you entrust this music either to the Russian Legation in Vienna or to the Ministry of Foreign Affairs, to be sent to the Legation of Austria in St. Petersburg. These two means are prompt and certain, considering the frequent communications between the two courts. Furthermore, if M[onsieur] Henikstein[3] wishes to take responsibility for the dispatch himself, I shall regard this means as more trustworthy yet.

I leave this entirely to your choice, convinced that you will want to satisfy the impatience of one of your most passionate admirers, who has enjoyed very pleasant moments in devoting himself to the creations of your spirit.

Please believe me, Monsieur, with all the admiration that I have for you,

Your very humble servant,

Prince Nicolas Galitzin

1. Replies to Beethoven's letter of January 25 (Anderson No. 1123, in the original French; MacArdle & Misch No. 347, in an English translation).

2. Nominally Opp. 127, 130 and 132, although not delivered until years later.

3. A Viennese banker and sometime musical patron.

Incipit: Votre lettre du 25. Janvier. . . .

Sources: Thayer-Deiters-Riemann, V, 552–553. The autograph was then in the possession of Beethoven's nephew Karl's widow, Caroline, Vienna, and has since disappeared.

311. *Count Moritz Dietrichstein*[1] *to Count Moritz Lichnowsky*[2]

Vienna; February 23, 1823[3]

Dear Friend!

It would have been my duty long ago to reply to the good Beethoven, since he came to me so trustfully. But after I had spoken with you, I decided to break silence only after I received definite information on the subject in question. I can now tell you with certainty that the post held by the deceased Teyber—who was not Chamber, but rather Court Composer—is not to be filled again.[4] I do not want to write this to Beethoven because I do not want to disappoint a man whom I so sincerely respect, and therefore I beg you to let him know, when the occasion presents itself, and then to inform me when and where I may meet him, since I have forgotten where he lives.

I am also sending you herewith the score of a mass by Reutter[5] that Beethoven wished to see. It is true that H.M. the Emperor is fond of this style, but Beethoven, if he writes a mass, need not adhere to it. Let him follow only the bent of his genius and take care merely that the mass not be too long or too difficult to perform; that it be a *tutti* mass and have only short soprano and alto solos in the voices (of which I have two fine singing boys) — but no tenor, bass or organ solos, and especially not for tenor, because then Barth[6] would sing. As for instruments, he could include a violin, oboe or clarinet solo if he wished.

His Majesty is very fond of fugues, appropriate, well developed, but not too long; the *Sanctus* and *Osanna* should have as little break as possible, so as not to delay the Transubstantiation, and — if I might add something on my own account — the *Dona nobis pacem* should be connected with the *Agnus Dei* without perceptible interruption, and performed softly. In two masses by Handel (put together from his anthems), two by Naumann[7] and by Abbé Stadler,[8] this makes a particularly beautiful effect. In brief, these are the things that — as the results of my experience — are to be kept in mind, and I would consider myself, the court and art fortunate if our great Beethoven were soon to set his hand to the task.

Please be so kind as to send me a brief receipt for the score, which was obtained from the Court Music Archives. I shall take the first free moment to renew in person my old and constant friendship for you.

Your devoted friend,

Moritz Dietrichstein

1. Count Moritz Dietrichstein-Proskau-Leslie (1775–1864), *Hofmusikgraf* (1819–1826), court theater director (1821–1826) and one of Beethoven's staunchest admirers. Dietrichstein writes to Lichnowsky using the familiar *du*.

2. Count Moritz Lichnowsky (1771–1837), brother of Prince Carl Lichnowsky. The count was also a longtime friend and, in 1823, precipitated the canon "Bester Graf, Sie sind ein Schaf," WoO 183.

3. Partially responds to Beethoven's letter to Dietrichstein of ca. January 1, 1823 (Anderson No. 1121); see also Dietrichstein's letter to Beethoven, March 10, 1823 (No. 314 below).

4. Anton Teyber (or Tayber), 1756–1822, had died the previous November 18, and Beethoven sought his position, which was, indeed, never filled again. Beethoven had thought that Teyber was I.R. chamber composer, a misconception clarified here. Schindler notes that the actual chamber composer was Franz Krommer. When Krommer died in 1831, his position likewise went vacant, further indicating to Schindler that, "at the imperial court, interest in music in general was dead."

5. Georg von Reutter (1708–1772), who in 1735 succeeded his father, the elder Georg (1656–1738), as *Kapellmeister* of St. Stephan's Cathedral. Reutter was the teacher of Beethoven's own teacher Haydn, thus a possible reason for this request.

6. Joseph Barth (1781–1865), I.R. court singer.

7. Johann Gottlieb Naumann (1741–1801), *Kapellmeister* at the Dresden court from 1776 until his death.

8. Maximilian Stadler (1748–1833), composer and abbé, who lived in Vienna off and on before moving there permanently in 1815.

Incipit: Schon längst wäre es meine Pflicht. . . .

Sources: Full text in Schindler, 3d. ed. (1860), pt. 2, pp. 30–31; Schindler-MacArdle, pp. 249–250; Thayer-Deiters-Riemann, IV, 393–394. Abridged versions in Schindler-Moscheles, pp. 85–86; Thayer-Krehbiel, III, 115–116; Thayer-Forbes, pp. 840–841. Autograph in the Staatsbibliothek zu Berlin–Preussischer Kulturbesitz, Mus. ms. autogr. Beethoven 35, 45a; listed in Kalischer, "Beethoven-Autographe," p. 49, and Bartlitz, p. 131.

312. Count von Rechberg, Royal Minister, to Ambassador Stainlein, Vienna

Munich; February 25, 1823[1]

At His Majesty the King's most high command:

According to the declaration of the Court Music Intendancy, the Royal Court *Kapelle* already possesses so many works composed in the church style by the most famous masters that only a part of them, because of their great numbers, can be brought to performance. Therefore no proposal is made at this time concerning the acquisition of the newest solemn Mass by the famous composer Beethoven;[2] which will be imparted to Ambassador von Stainlein concerning his report on this matter made on January 25.

Count von Rechberg

1. Concludes a surviving sequence of documents begun by Stainlein to King Maximilian Josef, January 25, 1823, and continued by Rumling to King Maximilian Josef, February 14, 1823 (Nos. 304 and 308 above).

2. This was not quite the directive received from above: Rumling did advise the purchase of a copy when the *Missa solemnis* became available in a less expensive *printed* edition. Then, as now, details of intent and meaning get lost from one bureaucratic level to another!

Incipit: Nach der Äusserung der Hofmusik-Intendanz. . . .

Sources: Adolf Sandberger, "Beiträge zur Beethoven-Forschung," *Archiv für Musikwissenschaft* 2 (1920), 397–398, and "Zum Kapitel: Beethoven und München," in *Ausgewählte Aufsätze II* (Munich: Drei Masken, 1924; reprint, Hildesheim: Georg Olms, 1973), pp. 258–260. When examined by Sandberger, the three documents in this sequence were in the Akta des Staatsministeriums des k. Hauses und des Äussern (Österreich M E 1913, F93/4), Munich.

313. Carl Friedrich Peters to Beethoven

Leipzig; March 4, 1823[1]

Herr von Beethoven
Vienna

I have received the manuscripts sent me through Herr Meisl, but upon their receipt, I was really troubled, for I have so openly and amicably obliged you, and have offered you in myself a publisher with whom you ought to be entirely satisfied, because unselfishness, solidity and order are the foundations upon which I do business; consequently, everyone must be satisfied with me, only I clearly see that my wishes were in vain, in that *you* have complied with them too little.

In August of last year I paid you the fee for three kinds of works,[2] which you offered me then and declared to be *finished,* which cannot have been the case, however, since now, after half a year, I still do not possess all of these works. The *endless* paperwork about this subject, and the fact that it was not settled punctually, was already very unpleasant to me, a stickler for punctuality. Nonetheless, I would still have let it pass quietly, if the manuscripts now sent to me had not forced me to express my dissatisfaction.

We have struck a bargain for the following manuscripts of yours:

1. Four marches for military band.
2. Three songs with piano accompaniment in the size [i.e., length] of *Adelaide,* consequently none too small, rather large enough that *each* can be published *separately.*[3]

3. Bagatelles for piano.[4]

I have negotiated and paid for these pieces, even up to the point where the songs and bagatelles cost me more. While I have fulfilled my obligations, you, however, now deliver to me:

1. Instead of four marches, only one march and three *Zapfenstreiche*. Perhaps Zapfenstreiche can find enthusiasts in Vienna, but I cannot use them at all since I have no public for them. Furthermore, at least the first Zapfenstreich that I presently hold in my hands must be a composition that you already wrote years ago, for the *oboe* carries the melody in it, while that has not been the custom in military bands for several years. In short, I absolutely do not know what to do with Zapfenstreiche, especially with such instrumentation.[5]

2. Instead of three larger-scale, developed[6] songs with piano, you send me only one arietta and two songs with orchestra accompaniment, and a piano version at the same time. I did not request songs with orchestra, because I already have many fine items of similar nature. I prefer not publishing them, though, because such pieces are usually not extensive enough to serve as large-scale individual vocal works. Certainly, I could omit the instrumental accompaniment and issue them only for piano, but since both songs are with *choruses*, they failed to meet the purpose that I had for them.[7]

In regard to the marches as well as the songs, you have sent me pieces other than those we had agreed upon, and since the shipment did not suit me, I cannot accept it. I am conscientious about the fulfillment of this [condition], for where would it lead if I did not hold my many obligations strictly in this manner?

3. Now I come to the bagatelles—at which I was very surprised. I have had several of them played, but *not one person* wants to believe me that these are by *you*. To be sure I wished to have small pieces,[8] but really, these are entirely too small. Besides, the majority are so easy that they are not suitable for somewhat better players, and for beginning players there are, now and again, passages that are too difficult. Furthermore, I confess that the effect was entirely contrary to my expectations: Nos. 1, 3 and 5 appealed to me somewhat, but the others not at all. It is possible that I expected too much, for I imagined having cute little pieces that, without having great difficulties, are quite genial and *appealing*—short pieces where the artist would show that he could write little pieces that would also be effective. So as not to

be misunderstood, I do not want to say anything further about it, except that I shall never print the small pieces; I would rather lose the fee paid for them. This declaration will perhaps shock you, but please just consider my *reasons,* and you will see that my actions are based on them, and in no way on whim. The first reason is that I do not want to risk the danger of being suspected of having committed a fraud by placing *your name* falsely in front of those *small pieces,* for few will believe these little works are by the *famous* Beethoven.

A second reason is that I do not want just to print compositions of yours; rather I want to have *exceptionally good* pieces of yours.

My customers are used to receiving excellent works from me, and it will be a real novelty if now, after many works by our most prominent artists have appeared from my press, I also publish the works of Herr v[on] Beethoven. But if I begin this undertaking with Zapfenstreiche and Bagatelles like these, it must appear as if I merely had taken what you had sought out for me and dispatched from among your older and neglected compositions. That such was the case with the Zapfenstreiche and small pieces is unmistakable; but I do not want just to have manuscripts of yours; rather I want to have exceptionally *successful* works, in return for which I shall even pay a *higher* fee, so that the amount that I offer is justly proportionate to the works that I request.

You will be angry at me—but I cannot help myself. I do not like circumlocution; rather I prefer to speak and do business openly and honorably, and say what I think. In the end, one gets further this way than by beating around the bush. Thus, no offense—I did not want to find fault with the manuscripts sent to me, only they are not suitable for me, for if I *appear* with Herr v[on] Beethoven's works, I also want to appear *properly,* and not to begin with Bagatelles and Zapfenstreiche; rather, if I bring out only small works now, they should be beautifully appealing pieces. Otherwise I would prefer to refrain from it altogether.

If you want to send me something else for piano in place of the small pieces, I shall acknowledge it gratefully. Such [a substitute] may consist of whatever you want, only it must be *pretty* and appealing, and I shall gladly pay in addition whatever *more* it costs; if you do not want to, however, I must put up with losing the fee; for I would rather forfeit the money than print the small pieces, because it is too painful to me to think that anyone could believe that I used your name falsely.

Concerning the Zapfenstreiche and the two songs with instrumental accompaniment, however, I must and can insist upon and demand that you send me marches instead of the former and two through-composed songs with piano instead of the latter. This much is to be negotiated between us. If you have no such marches and songs, report to me now what you *really* have *finished,* so that I may choose something else, for I wish to see this matter settled. It is bad enough that I sent you the money already in August, and now must experience such unpleasantness.

I wrote you last year that I would take your Mass, and you [wrote that] you would deliver the work to Herr G. Meisl on August 15.[9] Even today this still has not happened, and because of it my plans have become very frustrated, for I had made preparations for this great work. Since I now see how reliable you are with the delivery of your manuscripts, and [since] you write me that you were also engaged with two other masses, I release you from your promise regarding the Mass, and have no objection if you now give it to another [publisher].

I know quite well that you are a good man, and if I were in *Vienna* we would get along with each other *extremely well.* Because of our distance, however, it will not succeed. As a businessman, I see this quite well, and you, too, will concede this in silence; at least our *first* business gives evidence to this effect. What sickens me the very most about it is that, in order to torment me and only to be rid of the manuscripts for which we negotiated, you finally collected pieces for me, a few of which you perhaps had never published, and at least the Zapfenstreiche *prove* that they are old compositions. After my unselfish offer, however, I surely did not deserve this; rather, since I specified *no price* and set out to you my wishes for very excellent works so clearly, one after another, you ought to have provided for me very carefully as well, for this first business dealing should indeed serve as entry to further, even greater dealings. If the first [deal] is not to turn out according to my wish, however, I shall still always remain inclined to future dealings, but shall no longer engage in the written pursuit of the same; rather I am postponing such until my proposed journey to Vienna. Then we will want to deal with each other personally, if you are so inclined, for it will go better speaking *in person,* since the *Viennese* publishers also get along better with you in this manner. With them there cannot be the unpleasantness such as has now befallen me, since they are right there and can converse with you.

This letter will be disagreeable to you as an artist, and you will be angry at me. But do *not* do this, and do not take my frankness badly. Rather consider that I am a merchant and do business as such. I would never permit myself to place any kind of blame against a great artist such as you. What I blame now, however, concerns not the artist but instead the business deal that he has made with me; consequently the discussion above also in no way concerns the artist, but instead the artist taken solely as *businessman,* and as such you cannot take it amiss on my part, and it would be painful for me if such were the case, for what has transpired has not destroyed my high esteem for you or lessened my wish for your affection.

The Zapfenstreich, the two songs with orchestra and the bagatelles are returned herewith, and I request in return the marches for which I had bargained, the developed songs with piano, and a work for piano alone, and if you do not have such, just send me as a settlement the 360 florins that I paid.[10] [Still, I request] other works, with which I can prove to the public that I always endeavor to publish the most excellent pieces possible, which I really do and avoid no costs thereby.

I hope that you will *appreciate this effort,* and consequently will now *excuse* me, and remain,

[C. F. Peters]

1. Answers Beethoven's letter of February 26, 1823 (Anderson No. 1145), with further references to his earlier letters to Peters and Meisl (Anderson Nos. 1137 and 1141). Schindler remarks that Beethoven had noted on his calendar (in Schindler's possession) that he had received Peters's letter on March 19, 1823. If this is true, then the dating of Beethoven's letter to Peters (Anderson No. 1158) as March 20 seems highly unlikely, given its still friendly tone; viewed in context, Anderson No. 1158 probably dates from *February* 20, rather than a month later. Beethoven's next communication with Peters after receiving this letter, then, seems to have been on December 12, 1824 (Anderson No. 1324), since, after twenty months, its tone remains understandably wounded.

2. Piringer's letter to Beethoven, July 25, 1822 (No. 297 above), as well as Beethoven's letters to his brother Johann of late July (Anderson Nos. 1086 and 1087) indicate that Peters had already forwarded the money by that time.

3. *Adelaide,* Op. 46, was 181 measures long.

4. Op. 119.

5. The March in D, WoO 24, composed for Franz Xaver Embel probably in early 1816 (see Embel's letter, No. 225 above, commissioning this work from Beethoven), is the composer's largest-scale essay in the form. The remaining works were surely the

Marches, WoO 18–20, evidently labeled *Zapfenstreich*, Nos. 1, 3 and 2, respectively, by Beethoven and written in 1809–1810. WoO 18 and 19 do not use oboe, while in WoO 20 the first oboe essentially doubles the first clarinet throughout. The versions sent to Peters may have had recently composed trio sections, but WoO 18 had been published in its original form (thirty-four measures) by Schlesinger in 1818/1819 and remains today a popular staple of German march literature under the title "Yorkscher."

6. Originally *durchgeführt*, a term that, in context, modern analysts might call through-composed.

7. The arietta was *Der Kuss*, Op. 128, a setting with piano accompaniment. The other two items were the *Opferlied*, Op. 121b, for soprano, chorus and orchestra, and the *Bundeslied*, Op. 122, for voices and wind instruments. The longest of these was not much over half the length of *Adelaide.*

8. Peters says he wanted *Kleinigkeiten*, but these are too *klein,* thus the terms *small pieces* and *small* in translation rather than *bagatelles* for the former, in order to preserve the wordplay.

9. *Missa solemnis*, Op. 123; Beethoven had indicated this in his letter to Peters on August 3, 1822 (Anderson No. 1092).

10. According to a receipt (see Unger), the money was returned to Peters, through S. A. Steiner & Co., Vienna, on December 7, 1825.

Incipit: Die durch Hr. Meisl. . . .

Sources: Max Unger, "Neue Briefe an Beethoven," *Neue Zeitschrift für Musik* 81 (July 9, 1914), 412–413; mentioned in Schindler (1860), pt. 2, pp. 44–45, and Schindler-MacArdle, p. 259. Copy in the C. F. Peters copybooks, presumably destroyed in World War II.

314. Count Moritz Dietrichstein to Beethoven

[Vienna;] March 10, 1823[1]

I am sending you here, my honored friend, three texts for the *Gradual* and a like number for the *Offertory,*[2] so you can choose from them to use in the mass that you are composing.[3] I infinitely regret having missed you, since you had the kindness to visit me with Count Lichnowsky. I shall attempt to meet you as soon as possible. Accept the assurance of my sincerest esteem.

Moritz Dietrichstein

[Beethoven's pencil annotation:]

† Treat the *gradual* as a *symphony* with song.
Is it after the *Gloria?*

1. Follows Dietrichstein's letter to Count Moritz Lichnowsky, February 23, 1823 (No. 311 above), and the attempted personal meeting suggested therein. Answered by Beethoven's letter of ca. April 1823 (Anderson No. 1170).

2. As parts of the Proper of the Mass, the texts for the Gradual and Offertory varied with the day, feast and season. For another mention of such potential settings by Beethoven, see Haslinger to Beethoven, ca. June 5, 1822 (No. 288 above).

3. The idea of another Mass in addition to the *Missa solemnis* had arisen with Beethoven's letter to Dietrichstein, ca. January 1, 1823 (Anderson No. 1121). Sketches for a *Dona nobis pacem* in a Mass in C♯ minor appear in sketchbook Landsberg 8, Bundle 1, dating from about this time (in the midst of sketches for the first movement of the Symphony No. 9), and possibly in sketchbook Autograph 11, Bundle 2, from the fall of 1824 to January 1825 (among sketches for movements 2 and 3 of the String Quartet, Op. 127). See Nottebohm, *Zweite Beethoveniana*, pp. 152, 541, 543; and Johnson-Tyson-Winter, pp. 290, 300.

Incipit: Ich übersende Ihnen hier. . . .

Sources: Thayer-Deiters-Riemann, IV, 394; Kastner (1910), p. 722; mentioned in Schindler (1860), pt. 2, p. 32; Schindler-MacArdle, p. 250; Thayer-Krehbiel, III, 115–116; Thayer-Forbes, pp. 840–841. Autograph in the Staatsbibliothek zu Berlin– Preussischer Kulturbesitz, Mus. ms. autogr. Beethoven 35, 45b; listed in Kalischer, "Beethoven-Autographe," p. 49, and Bartlitz, pp. 131–132.

315. Johann Nepomuk Schelble[1] to Beethoven

Frankfurt am Main; March 19, 1823[2]

Wellborn Sir,
Highly admired Master,

The letter with which you honored the *Musikverein* here proved a never-ending joy for the society and for me as its director.

The hope of receiving a new work from you, great master, inspired all the members and fires their musical zeal anew. Therefore, I request that you, as soon as it pleases you, have a copy of your new Mass sent to me.

Be assured that the *Verein* values the distinction with which you honor it; but I especially may be permitted to show the esteem and unlimited admiration with which I have the honor to continue, as long as I live, to be

Your most devoted admirer,

J. N. Schelble
Music Director of the Society

1. Johann Nepomuk Schelble (1789–1837) had conducted the Cäcilien-Verein (founded in 1818) since 1819. The society was patterned after Zelter's *Singakademie* and *Liedertafel* in Berlin. Beethoven had evidently sent them a copy of his form letter soliciting subscriptions for the *Missa solemnis* (for similar letters, see Anderson No. 1134; MacArdle & Misch No. 365; and No. 303 above).

2. The date is given as May 19 by Thayer (all editions), May 9 in Kalischer's letters (both editions), and March 19 in Kalischer's and Bartlitz's catalogs. In the autograph, the month (like Schelble's signature) is written in Latin script: *Maerz.* Elsewhere Schelble placed an umlaut over his Gothic cursive *y*, which is not present here, to read *May* (old spelling).

Incipit: Das Schreiben womit Euer Wohlgeboren. . . .

Sources: Thayer-Deiters-Riemann, IV, 375 (Thayer's copy received through Nowotny); Kalischer, *Briefe,* V, 56; Kalischer-Shedlock, II, 335. Brief excerpt in Thayer-Krehbiel, III, 105; Thayer-Forbes, p. 833. Autograph in the Staatsbibliothek zu Berlin–Preussischer Kulturbesitz, Mus. ms. autogr. Beethoven 35, 55; listed in Kalischer, "Beethoven-Autographe," p. 51, and Bartlitz, p. 135.

316. Ferdinand Georg Waldmüller[1] to Gottfried Christoph Härtel, Leipzig

Vienna; April 18, 1823

Dear Sir!

With the greatest pleasure I [shall] fulfill your wish that I prepare[2] the portrait of H[err] v[an] Beethoven, and report to you that yesterday, Herr van Beethoven promised to sit for me in several days, which puts me in the position of being able to send you the portrait by around mid-May. Please indicate to me most kindly if it is to be sent to you by means of stagecoach or by another manner. I leave it to you to have a frame made, because it can be packed more securely.

My delayed answer to your kind letter of January is not my fault, since I just received it a few days ago. Concerning the painting of other portraits, you will find me ready at any time to satisfy you in the best possible way.

1. Waldmüller (1793–1865) was a respected genre and landscape painter of the Viennese Biedermeier period. His portrait of an irritated Beethoven for Breitkopf und Härtel, completed hurriedly after one sitting, has a rather pancake-flat appearance. After providing a detailed account of Waldmüller's solitary session with Beethoven, Schindler pronounced the portrait "further from the truth than any other." Slightly later, when he probably could invest more time in its preparation, Waldmüller made a copy for the Leipzig publisher Friedrich Kistner; this version shows two buttons on the right lapel, where Härtel's has three. More important, however, a portrait resembling the Kistner copy displays more three-dimensional aspects than its earlier counterpart. Comini vociferously defends the Waldmüller portrait, as sent to Härtel, for its accuracy; she does not discuss the copy for Kistner. The Härtel version (damaged beyond repair during World War II) has been widely reproduced; for the Kistner copy (which survives), see *Philips Music Herald* (Autumn 1969), cover (color reproduction) and pp. 12–13 (side-by-side comparison of the two versions). Most recently, the Kistner copy, described as a study for the Breitkopf und Härtel version, was depicted in color on the dustjacket and in black and white in pl. 21 of William Kinderman, *Beethoven* (Berkeley and Los Angeles: University of California Press, 1995). See also Waldmüller's letter to Härtel, May 3, 1823 (No. 318 below).

2. Waldmüller's verb is *verfertigen*, meaning "to make" or "to paint the portrait." *Incipit:* Ich erfülle mit grösstem Vergnügen. . . .

Sources: Wilhelm Lütge, "Waldmüllers Beethovenbild," *Der Bär* (1927), 35–41, plate; Elmar Worgull, "Ferdinand Georg Waldmüller . . . ," *Studien zur Musikwissenschaft* (*DTÖ*) 30 (1979), 134. Autograph in Breitkopf und Härtel's archive, presumably destroyed during the World War II bombings of Leipzig.

For further discussion, see Schindler-MacArdle, pp. 453–455, 510; Alessandra Comini, *The Changing Image of Beethoven* (New York: Rizzoli, 1987), pp. 65–67, 423; as well as Lütge and the *Philips Music Herald* (Autumn 1969).

317. Schwebel, French Embassy, to Beethoven

Vienna; April 21, 1823[1]

Monsieur de Beethoven

Monsieur,

I hasten to communicate to you the letter that the ambassador has just received from His Excellency, the Minister of the House of the King[2] about the gift that you desire to make to His Majesty of a copy of your new Mass set to music. I ask you, Monsieur, to be so kind as to supply me with the information that the Minister requests at the end of his letter, so that I may give it to the ambassador in order that he might forward it to the Minister.

I have the honor, Monsieur, to be

Your very humble and very obedient servant,

Schwebel
Secretary of the Embassy

[Enclosed:]
  [Copy]

Paris; April 10, 1823

His Excellency, the Marquis de Caraman
Ambassador of France to the
Court of Austria

Monsieur Marquis,

I hasten to inform you that the First Gentleman of the King's Chamber,[3] after having taken His Majesty's orders concerning the gift that Monsieur de Beethoven desires to make him of a copy of his new Mass set to music, has just informed me that the King will accept with pleasure the work of so distinguished a composer. I ask Your Excellency to be so kind as to inform Monsieur de Beethoven of this and request him to address the copy that he designates for His Majesty directly to the Duke de Blacas, who is responsible for presenting it to the King. As for the solicited subscription, I cannot instigate a decision in this respect until I know the price of the work. I shall be obliged to you, Monsieur Marquis, if you will have the kindness to give me the information that you may have in this respect.

Accept, Monsieur Marquis, the assurance of my highest esteem.

The Minister/Secretary of State
of the House of the King,
(signed) Monsieur de Lauriston

1. Replies to a form letter offering the *Missa solemnis*, similar to that sent to Grand Duke Ludwig I of Hesse-Darmstadt on February 5, 1823 (Anderson No. 1134), and other items in the present collection (see, e.g., No. 303 above). In January and February 1823, Beethoven and Schindler blanketed important government and music positions throughout Europe with them. Ley depicts the impression of the seal from Schwebel's letter. See also Schwebel's letter of April 4, 1824 (No. 353 below).

2. Louis XVIII.

3. The duke de La Châtre (see his letter of February 20, 1824, No. 343 below).

Incipit: Je m'empresse de vous communiquer. . . .

Sources: Ley, *Beethoven als Freund*, pp. 220–221, taken from the Sammlung von Breuning.

318. Ferdinand Georg Waldmüller to Gottfried Christoph Härtel, Leipzig

Vienna; May 3, 1823[1]

Dear Sir!

Although I am busy almost to next year, and have commissions reserved, I [shall] nevertheless fulfill your wishes with pleasure, and if you are in no great hurry for the portraits to be painted and if the price of 12 ducats in gold seems acceptable to you for a half-length portrait. Your present wish to have the portrait of Herr van Beethoven already half completed is unacceptable to me, but as you know, it is not my fault, due to the delayed letter, and I believe, on the other hand, that I am doing you a favor by painting the portrait quickly, because Herr van Beethoven is soon going to the country in any case.

1. Härtel must have replied to Waldmüller's letter of April 18 (No. 316 above) and seemingly pressed the artist either to hurry unduly with Beethoven's portrait or even to send it without the finishing touches. Beethoven's single sitting for Waldmüller must have been a trying experience for all concerned and may account for the artist's somewhat vexed tone here. See the notes to the April 18 letter for further details, especially about the later copy that Waldmüller prepared for Kistner.

Incipit: Obschon ich beynahe bis künftiges Jahr. . . .

Sources: Wilhelm Lütge, "Waldmüllers Beethovenbild," *Der Bär* (1927), 35–41, plate; Elmar Worgull, "Ferdinand Georg Waldmüller . . . ," *Studien zur Musikwissenschaft* (*DTÖ*) 30 (1979), 134–135. Autograph in Breitkopf und Härtel's archive, presumably destroyed during the World War II bombings of Leipzig. See also Waldmüller's April 18, 1823, letter (No. 316 above).

319. Prince Nicolas Galitzin to Beethoven

St. Petersburg; May 5, 1823[1]

Monsieur,

You ought to have received through M[onsieur] Henikstein the sum of 50 ducats, the fee set for the first quartet.[2] I hope that you will not delay in allowing me to enjoy a sublime product of your spirit. I have indicated to M[onsieur] Henikstein the means by which I wish the dispatch to be sent to me, and I have given him my address. When you have done so, you may immediately sell your work to a music publisher, because it is not my intention to act against your interests: I ask for myself only the dedication and a manuscript copy as soon as you have finished. Please begin the second quartet,[3] and notify me of it; then I shall send you 50 more ducats at once. Although I am not sufficiently strong in the German language to write it, I understand it sufficiently to desire that you should reply to my letter in German and in your own hand, so that I would have the pleasure of having an autograph letter in your hand![4]

Accept, Monsieur, the assurance of my admiration and esteem.

Your very humble servant,

Prince Nicolas Galitzin

1. Galitzin had most recently written to Beethoven on February 23, 1823 (No. 310 above), and may not have received a reply. The prince evidently wished to be a more regular correspondent than Beethoven did, especially since the composer was obviously waiting until the *Missa solemnis* and the Symphony No. 9 were sufficiently secure before working seriously on Galitzin's commission.

2. Op. 127.

3. Ultimately, Op. 132.

4. As can be seen in Beethoven's letter to Galitzin, January 25, 1823 (Anderson No. 1123; MacArdle & Misch No. 347, in English translation), Beethoven's French-language letters were often written by a third party and only signed by the composer himself. For the most part, Beethoven seems to have continued that practice.

Incipit: Vous devez avoir reçu par M. Henikstein. . . .

Sources: Thayer-Deiters-Riemann, V, 553; one sentence in Nohl, *Beethoven's Leben* (1877), III, 891. When Thayer and Nohl copied it, the autograph was in the possession of Beethoven's nephew Karl's widow, Caroline, Vienna. It has since disappeared and is presumed lost.

320. *Prince Nicolas Galitzin to Beethoven*

St. Petersburg; May 28, 1823[1]

I have received, Monsieur, your friendly letter,[2] which gave me much pleasure, and has increased, if possible, all of the interest that I bear for you. — I have sent your letter on to its exalted destination, and when I know the answer that is made to it, I shall hasten to communicate it with you. An idea has occurred to me that may be useful to you in a very profitable and very easy manner: that is to have the Society here subscribe to your Mass. But I did not want to do so without your authorization.[3] If this is agreeable to you, please send me a subscription prospectus, with which I shall seek some subscribers, who will be easy to find and who will bring you some money that you could [otherwise] not have counted upon. I hope that you will soon satisfy my extreme impatience by making me the possessor of a new masterpiece of your fertile and sublime genius.[4]

Accept, Monsieur, the expression of my high regard.

Prince Nicolas Galitzin

1. Galitzin's original is dated May 16/28, using old style/new style dating. Western Europe, of course, was on the new (Gregorian) calendar; thus the letter falls in the present chronology as dating from May 28.

2. No letter to Galitzin from Beethoven between January 25, 1823, and this date seems to have survived. From the context, Beethoven's letter to which Galitzin refers must have been written in early May 1823. It doubtless contained, as well, the composer's form letter to the heads of Europe (this time addressed to the czar of Russia), soliciting a subscription to the *Missa solemnis* for 50 ducats.

3. Beethoven sent an official request to the St. Petersburg Philharmonic Society, probably through Galitzin, on June 21, 1823 (MacArdle & Misch No. 365; not in Anderson, who gives the earlier prototype as No. 1134). Galitzin replies in part on August 3 (No. 333 below).

4. A reference to his earlier commissioning of one to three quartets, beginning with Op. 127 (see Galitzin's letter of November 9, 1822, No. 299 above). Eventually Opp. 132 and 130 were also applied to Galitzin's commission.

Incipit: J'ai reçu, Monsieur, votre aimable lettre. . . .

Sources: Thayer-Deiters-Riemann, V, 553–554. The autograph was then in the possession of Beethoven's nephew Karl's widow, Caroline, Vienna, and has since disappeared.

321. Beethoven to Anton Wocher,[1] Vienna

[Hetzendorf; ca. May 29–31, 1823][2]

Dear Sir!

Since I am glad to find opportunity to thank you for the many favors that you have already shown me, and for your friendly cooperation, I turn immediately again, however, in the event, to ask you for a new one, although you also appear just as obliging here. Thus I ask you to stand by your recent decision and to give Prince E[sterházy] the enclosure, although one should probably not start thinking about a completely different course of action, as desirable as it might be, until it is perceived how this will be received.[3] As soon as I have things fairly well in order here, I shall fetch you hither at once. It is understood, not without previous inquiries, that I shall likewise be very happy to see Gaal[4] here in your company. The surrounding regions are beautiful and can produce beautiful poetic images in him. Unfortunately, in my sickly condition, I am, in addition, still suffering with *my eyes,* and

I almost cannot read and write at all. For me it is worse than *exorcism* and *excommunication.* There are no longer people who drive out devils, and surely these are nested in my eyes. Meanwhile, I hope to be free from them soon by means of fresh air, and be able to view everything with good eyes again. As soon as this is the case, I shall likewise sincerely hurry to meet you. With grateful devotion,

Your,

Beethoven

[Exterior:]

    For Herr von Wocher

1. Wocher was private secretary to Prince Paul Anton Esterházy (1786–1866), a member of the Austrian legation to London since 1815.

2. On June 1 (Anderson No. 1188), Beethoven wrote Schindler that he had already written to Wocher/Esterházy. Thus this letter probably dates from very shortly before June 1, 1823.

3. Conversations between Beethoven and Schindler, dating roughly from the period May 17–18, 1823, indicate that they planned to approach Prince Nikolaus Esterházy (1765–1833) about subscribing for a manuscript copy of the *Missa solemnis.* Schindler reported that the prince regularly purchased church compositions and that Wocher had informed him that the prince often had Beethoven's Mass in C, Op. 86, performed. Prince Nikolaus had commissioned Op. 86 from Beethoven for his wife Marie's name day in 1807 and was seemingly disappointed with it; in any case, memories of Beethoven's defensive reaction to the reception at Eisenstadt may have lingered. Although Prince Nikolaus had recently returned from a journey, Wocher advised waiting until the younger Prince Paul returned from London in June, when he (Prince Paul) and Princess Marie could approach Prince Nikolaus and together persuade him to subscribe to the *Missa solemnis* (see Köhler et al., *Konversationshefte,* III, 284, 289–290, 293–294, 315).

Presumably after the conversations of ca. May 17–18, Beethoven asked Schindler (Anderson No. 1185) for the subscription form so that he could adapt a solicitation for Esterházy. This letter, then, accompanied the solicitation that Beethoven's nephew Karl hand carried to Wocher in Vienna. Prince Esterházy, however, never subscribed to the *Missa solemnis.*

4. Georg von Gaal (1783–1855), Prince Nikolaus Esterházy's librarian in Vienna since 1811. Gaal had poetic proclivities, and Beethoven possessed a copy of some of his verses, published in Dresden in 1812.

Incipit: Indem ich mich freue Gelegenheit. . . .

Sources: Transcribed and edited by Martin Staehelin in Staehelin, "Unbekannte . . . Schriftstücke," pp. 79–84. Facsimiles of the first page in Staehelin and the final page in Hans Schneider, *Musikalische Seltenheiten: Eine Auswahl . . .* (Tutzing: Hans Schneider, 1981). Autograph in the Beethoven-Haus, Bonn, NE 122.

322. *Prince Nicolas Galitzin to Beethoven*

St. Petersburg; June 2, 1823

I hasten to tell you, Monsieur, that your letter has been delivered to His Majesty, and that he has deigned to concede to the request that you made of him.[1] The orders will be given to the Ministry of Foreign Affairs to notify you of H.M.'s decision through our legation in Vienna.[2]

Accept the expression of my high esteem.

Prince Nicolas Galitzin

1. See Galitzin's letter to Beethoven of May 28, 1823 (No. 320 above). In late April or early May, Beethoven had evidently sent Galitzin one of his form letters requesting a subscription to the *Missa solemnis,* addressed to the czar of Russia (Alexander I), and seemingly forwarded by Galitzin. Beethoven triumphantly noted this acceptance in his letter to Archduke Rudolph, July 1, 1823 (Anderson No. 1203).

2. Anton Schindler wrote from Vienna to Beethoven in outlying Hetzendorf on July 9 (No. 329 below), proudly proclaiming the arrival of the 50-ducat fee from Russia.

Incipit: Je m'empresse, Monsieur, de vous. . . .

Sources: Thayer-Deiters-Riemann, IV, 370–371, and V, 554 (with minor differences in spelling, punctuation and format); summary in Thayer-Krehbiel, III, 102, and Thayer-Forbes, p. 829. When Thayer copied it, the autograph was in the possession of Beethoven's nephew Karl's widow, Caroline, Vienna, and has since disappeared.

323. *Beethoven to Johann Schickh,*[1] *Vienna*

[Hetzendorf; June 5 or 6, 1823][2]

Perhaps I shall ask you while I live here among the trees. . . . [The text continues with Beethoven's offer to correct the proofs of "Edel sei der Mensch" before publication.]

1. A regular member of Beethoven's circle of friends, Schickh (1770–1835) was the editor of the *Wiener Zeitschrift für Kunst, Literatur, Theater und Mode,* which carried supplements in the form of fashion plates and musical numbers. Beethoven's canon "Edel sei der Mensch, hülfreich und gut," WoO 185, appeared as a supplement to the June 21, 1823, issue.

2. Schickh's annotation indicates "received from Hetzendorf on June 6, 1823"; this undated letter was probably written on that day or the day before.

Incipit: Vielleicht werde ich sie bitten während ich hier nur unter Bäumen lebe. . . .

Sources: Drouot Rive Gauche, *Autographes Musicaux,* auction catalog (Paris, June 20, 1977), item 9. Quoted briefly, with incipit added, in Helms and Staehelin, "Bewegungen . . . 1973–1979," p. 351. Location of autograph not indicated.

324. *Franz Schoberlechner*[1] *to Beethoven*

Vienna; June 25, 1823[2]

Highly honored Sir,
Great Master![3]

Encouraged by Herr Schindler,[4] but even more by the conviction that it always gives joy to noble-minded men to be of service to young people who, for the ennobling of their talent and the awakening of true feeling for art, wish to educate themselves further by going on tour, I take the liberty to ask you for letters of recommendation to Leipzig, Dresden, Berlin and other cities of northern Germany, and if possible also for Moscow, Warsaw, St. Petersburg. I am sure that your recommendations will surely be of very much use to me, and sign myself, respectfully and in anticipation,

Your
grateful and obliged servant,

Franz Schoberlechner

[On the reverse, Beethoven wrote:]
"A competent fellow needs no other recommendation[s] than those from good houses to others like them."[5]

1. Schoberlechner (1797–1843) was a young Viennese pianist and composer who had studied with Johann Nepomuk Hummel and Emanuel Aloys Förster. For a

period he had been *Kapellmeister* to Duchess Maria Luise in Lucca, but he returned to Vienna in 1820. On April 6, 1823, Schoberlechner gave a well-attended concert, and, on June 29 (shortly after this letter was written), nephew Karl noted in Beethoven's conversation book: "I have to laugh at the confident expectations of Herr Schoberlechner, who wants to have no more than six letters of recommendation" (Köhler, *Konversationshefte*, III, 163, 345).

2. Beethoven seems not to have sent his immediate reaction to this letter, as annotated on the reverse. In one letter to Schindler (Anderson No. 1194), written soon after receiving Schoberlechner's flattering request, Beethoven gave a fuller opinion, beginning, "Surely it must have been clear to you that I would have nothing to do with this matter." Nonetheless, Beethoven may have moderated his initial reaction. In another letter (Anderson No. 1196), in which he warns Schindler, "do not pay any more calls at the Embassies which have subscribed [to the *Missa solemnis*]," he also concluded with: "I shall let you know about Schob[erlechner] tomorrow." Beethoven may ultimately have signed a letter for Schoberlechner, although penned by another hand. See July 23, 1823 (No. 330 below).

3. Full salutation translated here to set the tone for his request.

4. Beethoven's friend and secretary Schindler made the following marginal note: "That is not so; I merely answered Schoberlechner's question in this case that he might seek it [a recommendation] from Beethoven. One can see his reply on the cover of this letter. Beethoven's letter about it to me [Anderson No. 1194], no less characteristic than the reply to Herr Schoberlechner, may be found among his letters written to me."

5. Although not sent, Beethoven's annotation has been published separately as Anderson No. 1193.

Incipit: Aufgemuntert durch Herrn Schindler. . . .

Sources: Thayer-Deiters-Riemann, IV, 440; Kastner (1910), p. 738; Kalischer (German), IV, 270–271; Kalischer-Shedlock, II, 256–257. Autograph in the Staatsbibliothek zu Berlin–Preussischer Kulturbesitz, Mus. ms. autogr. Beethoven 35, 53.

325. *Hans Heinrich von Könneritz*[1] *to Beethoven*

[Dresden;] June 26, 1823[2]

To Herr *Kapellmeister* Beethoven in Vienna

Your opera *Fidelio* has now been performed here with decided success,[3] and while I am pleased to be able to report this to you, at the same time I gratefully add the fee of 40 ducats for it, concerning which I request that the enclosed receipt, provided by the R[oyal] Theater treasurer, be sent back to me.

1. Considerable confusion surrounds the identity and given names of Könneritz. Anderson No. 1210 identifies him as Hans Wilhelm Traugott von Könneritz, born in 1753, who served from 1819 to 1824 as *Kapellmeister* and director of the Court Theater in Dresden. John Warrack, *Carl Maria von Weber*, 2d ed. (Cambridge: Cambridge University Press, 1976), p. 204, confirms his dates of activity, but calls him Hans Heinrich von Könneritz and gives his position merely as *Intendant*, successor to the layman Count Heinrich von Vitzthum. Karl-Heinz Köhler, *Konversationshefte*, III, 491, likewise calls him Hans Heinrich. Volkmar Köhler, "Heinrich Marschner," *MGG*, vol. VIII, col. 1683 (and index), calls the *Intendant* Heinrich von Könneritz. Fürstenau, however, to whom this seeming abstract was first sent by *Generalmusikdirector* Otto von Könneritz (who died in May 1863), credited this letter to Otto. One Julius Traugott von Könneritz (1792–1866) was prime minister of Saxony, 1843–1848 (*Encyclopaedia Britannica* [1965], XX, 37); therefore the family name must have been common among the powerful of Dresden and its environs.

2. Beethoven replied on July 17 and 25 (Anderson Nos. 1210 and 1212).

3. *Fidelio* had been performed at the Royal Opera in Dresden, under Carl Maria von Weber's direction, on April 29, 1823.

Incipit (this draft): Ew. Wohlgeboren Oper Fidelio ist hier. . . .

Sources: M. Fürstenau, "Zwei noch unbekannte Briefe Beethoven's," *Allgemeine musikalische Zeitung,* n.s., 1, no. 36 (September 2, 1863), 618, quoting this seeming abstract from a copybook in the archive of the Royal Saxon Capelle (königliche sächsische musikalische Capelle) and Court Theater (Hoftheater), Dresden. Later printed in Thayer-Deiters-Riemann, IV, 437; Kalischer (German), IV, 295; Kalischer-Shedlock, II, 272; and Hans Volkmann, "Beethoven und die erste Aufführung des Fidelio in Dresden," *Die Musik* 15, no. 1 (December 1922), 183.

326. Anton Schindler to Beethoven, Hetzendorf

Vienna; July 3, 1823[1]

Greetings![2]

The enclosed letter is from Herr Schlösser in Paris.[3] A young painter by the name of Wüht[4] brought it yesterday, and indicated that Schlösser gave him instructions to get any necessary reply from you and to send it to him in Paris. He left his address with me for that purpose.

Yesterday at noon, Prince Hatzfeld[5] sent out with the serious question whether he should have received the Mass by now,[6] since the completion date has passed. He has been badgered so very much from Berlin on this account that the whole matter has already become a burden to him. You might, therefore, have the kindness to write to the Prince without delay, in your own handwriting, telling him when he will receive the work, so he can indicate such to Berlin. He lives in Penzing, No. 20, the fifth or sixth house on the left, as you go out into the village from Vienna.

About your brother and the people dear to him, I shall confine myself to telling you as much as *circumstances now allow.*

He is weak, unfortunately a far too weak man, though greatly to be pitied. He is *your* brother, and consequently worthy of all your attention. This illness was and is like Touchstone's,[7] in that he has two vipers[8] at his side. Since I visited him three or four times daily, as long as he lay [ill], and entertained him for hours on end, I had the opportunity to observe these two persons closely.[9] Thus I can assure you upon my honor that these persons, despite their[10] most venerable name, are worthy of being locked up, the older woman[11] in prison, the younger[12] in a correction house. How they can treat a husband and father in such a manner during his illness can only be imagined among barbarians; only such people could do that. This illness came at just the right time for both of them to get into unconstrained mischief. They would have let him rot, these beasts, if others had not often taken care of him. A hundred times he might have died, while the one would be in the Prater or in Nussdorf[13] and the other at the baker's,[14] without their even looking in on him. Thus he remained, in the hands of the domestic servants who often left him alone, even though he could not move a limb for several weeks. There was no alternative but that he hire himself a private nurse, even though there are three women in the house. Since the nurse is unfortunately very hard of hearing, however, she still does not serve him fully. He often wept over the behavior of his family, and once, completely consumed in grief, he begged me to report to you how he is being treated, so that you might come to him and give these two the beating that they deserve. Out of fear for his well-being I almost did not tell you all of what has happened. Last Friday, I came to him again, as usual, and met the doctor there. He had already complained to the doctor about how he had to lie the previous night entirely without help because the nurse slept so soundly the whole night through that he could not awaken her, which is no wonder since she had not slept for two weeks. The others, however, lay in the next room and let him call out. At that I could no longer hold back my displeasure, and broke out in a loud curse to the doctor. Quite naturally, the old lady was very indignant that I raised the devil about it.

It is most unnatural, though, and more than barbaric, when the wife, while her husband lies ill, leads her lover into his room to [meet] him, gets herself all gussied up like a sleigh horse in his presence, then goes driving with him [the lover] and leaves her sick husband languishing at home. She has done this very often. Your brother himself called my attention to it, and is a fool for having tolerated it so long. Either his hands must be tied, to tolerate this boyfriend, or his conduct, in this matter as always, is a complete riddle to me. I was with him yesterday for the first time since the last incident on Friday, for only his person and his circumstances compel me not to leave him, and to entertain him for a few moments each day, because otherwise *not one* of his many friends visits him.[15] I have just heard that he is worse again today. As soon as it is possible for him to venture out without danger, I ask you, for his sake, to take him to stay with you. He himself said to me recently that he would gladly go to you for a short time if his condition permitted it. Dr. Saxinger is his physician. He is a very strict man and treats him well.[16]

Enough on this subject for the present, although much more could be said about it. I implore you, however, for your brother's sake and mine, to do nothing right now, because it would only make the matter worse. The fact remains, and you can make use of it at the appropriate time. For now, ignore everything; otherwise I could under no circumstances enter your brother's house again, which, however, is not advisable at present. Also, any anger would only harm your brother, for he has indicated to me that he is always worse after each of these crude scenes. Also the physician has strictly forbidden him to get irritated. Even so, it [the situation] cannot be allowed to become any worse than it already is.

Do write a few lines to the Russian Chargé d'affaires Obreskow.[17] There are always many Russians traveling to St. Petersburg. Perhaps someone could take the package safely and quickly in this manner. It goes very slowly through business houses: in 1819, I myself sent a package of books through Geymüller to Riga, which only arrived in Riga after fifteen months, for it went by way of Warsaw to Danzig, from there back to Lübeck and only from there to Riga. Everywhere it lay there for several months.[18] The fastest route is still via Hamburg to St. Petersburg. Concerning the 30-kreuzer postage for the letter carrier, you yourself are to blame if you unduly indulge the letter carriers. I recently heard at the small post office that letter carriers who deliver letters to you audibly brag that they would soon become rich if they could serve such *splendid* gentlemen exclusively. They joke about it to no end. You could just give them 6 kreuzer for every letter, but not 30 kreuzer. No prince pays that much.

I have just come from the police; the housekeeper was with me. An appointment has been made for the landlord together with me tomorrow afternoon at 5 o'clock.[19] The Director of Police and Herr Ungermann[20] send compliments to you, and indicate in advance that the matter will be concluded as you wish it. Concerning the lighting fee, however, you ought not to regard the 6 florins as an affront on the [landlord's] part.[21] I am preparing myself for tomorrow, for I am sincerely inclined to read him the riot act, and it is just as well that it take place before the authorities. I shall report the result to you immediately.

Otherwise I am, in deepest *submission*,

Your unalterably loyal,

A. Schindler

1. Answers Beethoven's letter of July 2 (Anderson No. 1205); prompts Beethoven's draft letters of July 4 or 5 (Nos. 327 and 328 below) and Beethoven to Schindler, July 4, 1823 (Anderson No. 1186); partially answered by Beethoven's letter of shortly after July 9 (Anderson No. 1206) and possibly by Anderson No. 1247.

2. Schindler uses the salutation "Gott zum Gruss!"

3. Louis Schlösser (1800–1886), from Darmstadt, arrived in Vienna in the spring of 1822 to study with Ignaz von Seyfried, Joseph Mayseder and Antonio Salieri. In November 1822, he heard a revival of *Fidelio* and, shortly thereafter, met Beethoven. Schlösser left Vienna for Paris in May 1823, taking with him letters from Beethoven to Luigi Cherubini and Moritz Schlesinger (see Anderson No. 1176). Schlösser's letter seems not to have survived.

4. Nothing is known of this *Mahler* (painter), whose name Schindler may have spelled phonetically.

5. Prince Franz Ludwig Hatzfeld (1756–1827) had been Prussian envoy in Vienna since 1822 (Anderson No. 1508).

6. Beethoven had solicited a subscription to the *Missa solemnis* from the Prussian embassy on January 23, 1823 (No. 303 above).

7. In Shakespeare's *As You Like It*, the character Touchstone is in love with the country wench Audrey, reputed to be a slut.

8. *Schlangen*, "snakes" or "false creatures."

9. Johann lived in an apartment in the Kothgasse (Oberepfargasse) No. 61, a building owned by his brother-in-law, master baker Leopold Obermayer. While Beethoven was away in Hetzendorf, Schindler occupied the composer's apartment in the building next door, No. 60.

10. The autograph reads *ihres* (lowercase), "their." Thayer-Krehbiel translates it as "your" (requiring uppercase); not indicated in Thayer-Deiters-Riemann. Someone, possibly Schindler, crossed out the phrase "despite their most venerable name" in the autograph, seemingly at some later date.

11. Johann's wife, Therese (née Obermayer).

12. Therese's illegitimate daughter, Amalie Waldmann (born in 1807).

13. Popular recreational areas.

14. Therese's brother, Amalie's uncle, master baker Leopold Obermayer (see n.9, this letter).

15. About seven largely illegible words have been crossed out here.

16. Dr. Joseph Saxinger, member of the medical faculty of the University of Vienna, was married to Therese van Beethoven's sister Agnes (née Obermayer). See also Beethoven's draft letter to his brother Johann, July 4 or 5, 1823 (No. 327 below).

17. Beethoven's letter to Obreskow (unlocated) accompanied his letter to Anton Schindler of shortly after July 9, 1823 (Anderson No. 1206). Schindler recalled that the package contained the *Missa solemnis* for Prince Galitzin.

18. Thayer-Deiters-Riemann gives this word as "Wochen"; the autograph clearly reads *Monathe*. Geymüller was a partner in the Viennese wholesale firm of Ochs, Geymüller & Co.

19. Judging from his correspondence, Beethoven had been squabbling with Johann Ehlers, his landlord at Kothgasse (Oberepfarrgasse) No. 60, for some time. The composer's contentions are best summarized in his letter to Schindler, July 2, 1823 (Anderson No. 1205).

20. Thayer-Deiters-Riemann reads "Der Polizeidirector (etc.?) Hr. Ungermann." Although the autograph reads "Der Polizeidirector Hr. Ungermann," the verb that follows is plural, indicating two individuals. Anton Ungermann was commissioner of police (see Anderson No. 1048), a position evidently distinct from that of director of police. Beethoven's letter to Schindler, July 4, 1823 (Anderson No. 1186), confirms this supposition. See also Beethoven's draft letter to the police (?), July 4 or 5, 1823 (No. 328 below).

21. On Michaelmas, September 29, 1826 (see No. 438 below), Beethoven paid Mathias Mann 12 florins for his house lighting at the Schwarzspanierhaus for the next year. Thus the fee mentioned here was probably for a half year's lighting. Beethoven's letter to Schindler, July 4 (Anderson No. 1186), indicates that he would send the 6 florins.

Incipit: Der beigefügte Brief ist von H. Schlösser. . . .

Sources: Essentially complete text, except for the first paragraph, divided in three places in Thayer-Deiters-Riemann, IV, 358, 577–579, 444–445. Excerpts concerning Johann's family in Thayer-Krehbiel, III, 132, and Thayer-Forbes, p. 866. Autograph in the Staatsbibliothek zu Berlin–Preussischer Kulturbesitz, Mus. ms. autogr. Beethoven 36, 75; listed in Kalischer, "Beethoven-Autographe," p. 61, and Bartlitz, p. 176.

327. Beethoven to Johann van Beethoven, Vienna

[Hetzendorf; probably July 4 or 5, 1823][1]

Now you have gotten into a fine mess; I am informed of everything that Schindler has observed at your house. He was useful to me, so that I can learn about you and also help you.

You see *how right I was* to hold you back from *this,* etc.[2] Come to me and stay with us; I want nothing from you. How terrible if you would have to give up the ghost in such hands! If you want to come, then come *alone,* for I do not want her.[3] [Having] Dr. Saxinger instead of Dr. Smetana—this also does not please me.[4]

The Czar of *Russia* also subscribes—between us, just like Prince Galitzin.[5] Several more subscribers . . . [Radz]iwill, also[6] . . . [illegible word] asked to send some an invitation to subscribe.[7]

I advise you to come out and stay here, and later to *live with us* all the time. How much more happily you could live with an excellent youth like Karl, and with me your brother. Truly you[8] would have heavenly bliss on earth.

1. Prompted by Schindler's letter to Beethoven of July 3, 1823 (No. 326 above), reporting the misconduct of Johann's wife, Therese. This draft, jotted in Hetzendorf, is found on leaves 5r–6r in Conversation Book 35. It is followed immediately by a continuation, seemingly a draft for a letter to the Viennese police. This letter could

also have been drafted on July 5, if Beethoven waited until the landlord's hearing had taken place (on July 4) to open further contentious questions.

2. In 1812, Beethoven had tried unsuccessfully (even enlisting the aid of the authorities) to break up Johann's relationship with Therese; to outmaneuver him, they simply married.

3. The original reads "sie," a reference to Johann's wife, Therese, possibly plural if Beethoven means Therese's daughter as well.

4. Dr. Joseph Saxinger, a member of the medical faculty of the University of Vienna, was Johann's physician. Saxinger was also married to Therese van Beethoven's sister Agnes. Dr. Karl von Smetana (or Smettana), 1774–1827, had operated on Beethoven's nephew Karl in 1816, had treated Beethoven himself on occasion and was consulted again when young Karl attempted suicide, probably on August 6, 1826 (see Köhler et al., *Konversationshefte*, x, 84–95).

5. Prince Nicolas Galitzin's letter of June 2, 1823 (No. 322 above), had informed Beethoven that Czar Alexander I had consented to subscribe to the manuscript sales of the *Missa solemnis*.

6. Prince Anton Heinrich Radziwill, a friend of Prince Galitzin's (see n.2 to Galitzin's letter, April 8, 1824, No. 355 below).

7. A strip of paper has been torn from this leaf in the conversation book. The ellipses indicate portions lost. Schindler went over much of this material in pen, rendering some of it differently, some of it illegible. The word *baten* (asked) could also be read *baden,* possibly indicating some scheme to induce guests at spas to subscribe to the *Missa* (although such a meaning is unlikely). Several of Beethoven's letters from the remainder of July, however, indicate that he was redoubling his efforts to get various European courts to subscribe.

8. Instead of "you," Beethoven originally wrote "we."

Incipit (this draft): Endlich hast du Schöne Erfahrungen gemacht. . . .

Sources: Köhler et al., *Konversationshefte,* III, 347–348, 486 (© Deutscher Verlag für Musik, Leipzig). Autograph in the Staatsbibliothek zu Berlin–Preussischer Kulturbesitz.

328. Beethoven to the Police, Vienna (?)

[Hetzendorf; probably July 4 or 5, 1823][1]

What a disgrace, that the mother leads the daughter herself to clandestine love, as the watch-guard during her fleshly pleasures.[2] Meanwhile, however, I still have Schindler observing there[3] — she had quickly gotten up from the sofa in order to straighten herself up in front of the mirror. You see then that the daughter would still hold back. First thing tomorrow morning, have an earlier witness of her unsavory behavior called,[4] since he[5] is very timid and weak. She would[6] —— [draft ends].

    1. Like the previous draft, jotted immediately before it, this was prompted by Schindler's letter to Beethoven of July 3, 1823 (No. 326 above), reporting the misconduct of Beethoven's brother Johann's wife, Therese, and occupies leaves 6v through the first entry on 7v. Schindler's later reinforcements often blur the correct reading. The "earlier witness" mentioned here might be the "unnamed person" cited in the undated Beethoven letter to Schindler (Anderson No. 1247). This letter could also have been drafted on July 5, if Beethoven waited until the landlord's hearing had taken place (on July 4) to open further contentious questions.
    2. Schindler wrote in the margin: "This happened often."
    3. Because of Schindler's reinforcements, this passage is unclear.
    4. Schindler clarified in the margin: "in the morning have the daughter called."
    5. Schindler clarified: "the brother."
    6. There follows an illegible beginning of a word.
Incipit (this draft): welche Schändlichkeit, die Mutter führt. . . .
Sources: Köhler et al., *Konversationshefte,* III, 348–349, 486 (© Deutscher Verlag für Musik, Leipzig). Autograph in the Staatsbibliothek zu Berlin–Preussischer Kulturbesitz.

329. Anton Schindler to Beethoven, Hetzendorf

[Vienna;] July 9, 1823

I take pleasure in reporting to you herewith, that by command of the Emperor of all the Russias, 50 armored horsemen have arrived here as the Russian contingent, to do battle under your banner for the Fatherland. The leader of these crack troops is a Russian Court Councillor.[1] Herr Stein, piano maker, has been commissioned by him to arrange quarters for them with you.[2] Nothing new about our neighbors so far.[3]

Fidelissimus Papageno[4]

    1. The message announces the arrival of 50 ducats as the fee for the subscription to the *Missa solemnis* from the czar of Russia. Prince Nicolas Galitzin's letter of June 2, 1823 (No. 322 above), had told Beethoven that the subscription was forthcoming.

2. Matthäus Andreas Stein (1776–1842) had evidently been entrusted with the money on Beethoven's behalf.

3. This sentence was written in French and refers to Beethoven's brother Johann and his family (see Schindler's long letter to Beethoven, July 3, 1823, No. 326 above).

4. Most faithful Papageno; one of Beethoven's jesting names for Schindler, an allusion to the garrulous character in Mozart's *Die Zauberflöte*. Beethoven often warned Schindler against talking excessively and inappropriately.

Incipit: Ich mache mir das Vergnügen. . . .

Sources: Thayer-Deiters-Riemann, IV, 371; English translation in Thayer-Krehbiel, III, 102; Thayer-Forbes, p. 830. Autograph in the Staatsbibliothek zu Berlin–Preussischer Kulturbesitz, Mus. ms. autogr. Beethoven 36, 74; listed in Kalischer, "Beethoven-Autographe," p. 61, and Bartlitz, pp. 175–176.

330. Beethoven to an Unknown Person

Vienna; July 23, 1823[1]

[Fragment ending:] may . . . ,[2] then the same [person?] would be able to predict the auspicious result for his fame as well as for his fortune.

Ludwig van Beethoven[3]

1. Although place and date are indicated, this letter fragment is in another hand and merely signed by Beethoven.

2. Only the auxiliary verb *dürfen* remains at the end of this clause; the primary verb, coming first in German word order, is not included in this fragment.

3. The wording of this fragment indicates that it may be torn from a letter of introduction or recommendation. Franz Schoberlechner had written to Beethoven on June 25, 1823 (No. 324 above), asking for such a letter or letters to gain him entry in "Leipzig, Dresden, Berlin and other cities of northern Germany." Beethoven's initial reaction was negative, but it seems that members of his circle tried to moderate his refusal. A letter such as this one, authored by another (possibly Schindler) but signed by Beethoven, may have been the result.

Incipit: Unknown.

Sources: Stargardt, *Autographen aus allen Gebieten: Katalog 618* (Marburg, November 27–28, 1979), p. 213, item 711, closing portion only, with facsimile of Beethoven's signature. Quoted briefly in Helms and Staehelin, "Bewegungen . . . 1973–1979," p. 352. Auctioned in 1979, the autograph went into private possession in Germany.

331. Beethoven to Prince Anton of Saxony, Dresden (Draft)

[Vienna; ca. July 24–25, 1823][1]

Perhaps it is still possible that three new pieces be added, not so much only to fulfill that which one can demand, on the contrary far more to show the reports to Griesinger, etc.[2] . . . since he would make the proposal to someone to whom I, however, would gladly have shown the request, for which reason I have rejected it out of hand.

1. The letter, for which the phrases translated here were a draft, was enclosed with Beethoven's letter to Könneritz, July 25, 1823 (Anderson No. 1212). This draft's fragmentary nature makes an exact interpretation difficult, not assisted greatly by Anton's reply, dated September 12, 1823 (No. 335 below). Following this draft in the conversation book is a list of subscribers to manuscript copies of the *Missa solemnis*, Op. 123: "[Prince] Radziwill, King of France, King of Prussia, Czar of Russia, Hessen-Darmstadt, Frankfurt's [Cäcilia] Verein." Beethoven also notes his intentions to write to Gregor von Kudriavsky (of the Russian legation in Vienna) and Carl von Odelga (local representative of Nassau and Tuscany) as well as his own lawyer, Johann Baptist Bach.

2. Georg August Griesinger, councillor in the Saxon legation, Vienna.

Incipit: Vieleicht ist es noch mögl[ich]. . . .

Sources: Köhler et al., *Konversationshefte*, III, 381–382, 493 (© Deutscher Verlag für Musik, Leipzig). Autograph in the Staatsbibliothek zu Berlin–Preussischer Kulturbesitz.

332. Archduke Rudolph to Beethoven, Hetzendorf

Vienna; July 31, 1823[1]

Dear Beethoven!

I shall be back in Vienna on Tuesday, August 5, and then remain there for several days. I only wish that your health will also allow you to come into the city then.[2] I am usually at home from 4 to 7 o'clock in the afternoon.

My brother-in-law, Prince Anton,[3] has already written to me that the King of Saxony is expecting your fine Mass.

Concerning Drechsler,[4] I have spoken to our most gracious monarch as well as to Count Dietrichstein.[5] Whether this recommendation will be of any use I do not know, since there will be a competition for this position, where everyone who wishes to obtain it must demonstrate his capability. I would be glad if I could be of use to this skilful man whom, with pleasure, I heard play the organ in Baden last Monday, the more so since I am convinced that you would not recommend anyone unworthy.

I do hope that you have written out your canon,[6] and beg you, if it could adversely affect your health by coming into the city, not to exert yourself prematurely out of attachment for me.[7]

Your amicable pupil,

Rudolph

1. Answers Beethoven's letters to Rudolph, late July 1823 (Anderson Nos. 1214 and 1215), followed in turn by several letters to Rudolph from later in the summer.

2. Beethoven was staying in Baron Müller-Pronay's villa in Hetzingen, about four miles southwest of Vienna.

3. Prince Anton (1755–1836) was the younger brother of King Friedrich August III (1750–1827); he became king after the latter's death. He himself was an accomplished amateur composer. (See Prince Anton's letter to Beethoven, September 12, 1823, No. 335 below.) Beethoven had invited the king to subscribe to a manuscript copy of the *Missa solemnis.*

4. Joseph Drechsler (1782–1852), composer and church musician, had conducted at the Josephstadt Theater since 1822 and was seeking the position of second court organist. Beethoven enthusiastically discusses his background in Anderson No. 1214. Drechsler did not get the appointment he sought here. Probably because he was still alive in 1840, Schindler merely identified him as "D . . . . r" in his transcription of this letter.

Drechsler composed a cantata for the opening of Vienna's new Jewish synagogue in April 1826. Beethoven had been approached about composing such a work as early as January or February 1825, but he ultimately turned down the commission. Perhaps he himself suggested to the Israelitische Kultusgemeinde (Jewish congregation) that they turn to Drechsler, who was also a Catholic.

5. Count Moritz Dietrichstein (1774–1864), among other things, organized the church music for the imperial court and was on friendly terms with both Beethoven

and Salieri (see his letter to Count Moritz Lichnowsky, February 23, 1823, No. 311 above). The emperor was Franz I.

6. The canon, "Grossen Dank für solche Gnade," Hess 303, is mentioned in Beethoven's letters to Rudolph, late July 1822 (Anderson Nos. 1214 and 1215). It seems not to have survived in fair copy, but it does appear as a sketch among sketches for movements 2 and 3 of the Ninth Symphony in sketchbook Landsberg 8, Bundle 2 (see Johnson-Tyson-Winter, p. 295). An excerpt is quoted in Nottebohm, *Zweite Beethoveniana,* p. 177.

7. Schindler comments in a footnote: "The kind Archduke was unnecessarily concerned. Even when Beethoven was completely well, he went only with reluctance to visit his exalted protector and pupil."

Incipit: Ich werde Dienstag den 5ten August. . . .

Sources: Schindler (1840), pp. 140–141; Thayer-Deiters-Riemann, IV, 442–443; Nohl, *Neue Briefe* (1867), p. 238; Kalischer (German), IV, 300–301; Kalischer-Shedlock, II, 275; Kastner (1910), pp. 757–758. Autograph in the Staatsbibliothek zu Berlin–Preussischer Kulturbesitz, Mus. ms. autogr. Beethoven 35, 3; listed in Bartlitz, p. 118. Facsimile in Bekker (1911), p. 101.

333. *Prince Nicolas Galitzin to Beethoven*

St. Petersburg; August 3, 1823

Excuse me, Monsieur, if it has been some time since I replied to your last letter;[1] some sorrows at home, which are not yet passed, have been the reason for it. A cruel illness that for a month has threatened daily to carry off my only child has distracted me from all other occupation.[2]

You should already have received a letter from me[3] in which I told you that H[is] M[ajesty] had deigned to subscribe to your work.[4] In asking you to authorize me to find you some subscriptions within the Society,[5] I thought that you would change the subscription plan, because the musical amateurs[6] whom I know would not be in a position to pay 50 ducats for a written score. But I think that if you should decide to have your work printed, in fixing the price per copy at 4 or 5 ducats, one might possibly find fifty or so subscriptions, which would be easier than finding 4 or 5 persons who would consent to making an outlay of 50 ducats [each]. All that I can do is request you to place me among the number of your subscribers, and to send me a copy as soon as you can, in order that I might have it performed in a concert for the [benefit of] widows of musicians that takes place every year around Christmas.

I am infinitely grateful to you for having thought of sending me your two latest works for the piano;[7] my wife who studies this instrument, and who is also one of your great admirers, is delighted with them, even beforehand.

Adieu, Monsieur; accept the assurance of all my wishes for your health and your prosperity.

Your very devoted servant,

P[rince] Nicolas Galitzin

1. Beethoven must have replied, sometime in June, to Galitzin's letter of May 28 (No. 320 above). Beethoven's letter seems not to have survived.

2. That child seems to have died shortly after this letter was written (see Galitzin's letter of October 3, No. 336 below). Galitzin's wife, Elena Alexandrovna (née Saltikova), would give birth to another child, Juri Nicolaievich, on December 11, 1823. This son would also become an accomplished musician and would survive until September 14, 1872. Juri, rather than Nicolas, is probably the Prince Galitzin depicted in Landon, *Beethoven: Documentary Study* (1970), p. 345.

3. Galitzin's letter of June 2.

4. *Missa solemnis,* in handwritten copies.

5. Galitzin had made this proposal on May 28, 1823 (No. 320 above), and Beethoven had followed up by sending the St. Petersburg Philharmonic Society a formal invitation to subscribe for 50 ducats on June 21 (MacArdle & Misch No. 365).

6. Or: music lovers.

7. Probably two works from among the Sonatas, Opp. 109, 110 and 111. Galitzin's letter of November 29, 1823 (No. 338 below), identifies the works offered as "sonatas."

Incipit: Excusez moi, Monsieur, si j'ai. . . .

Sources: Thayer-Deiters-Riemann, V, 554–555; mentioned, with brief excerpt translated, in Thayer-Krehbiel, III, 102–103; and Thayer-Forbes, pp. 830–831. The autograph was then in the possession of Beethoven's nephew Karl's widow, Caroline, Vienna, and has since disappeared.

334. *Charles Neate*[1] *to Beethoven*

London; September 2, [1823][2]

My dear Beethoven,

You are doubtless as offended as surprised not to have received my news since you wrote me your obliging letter. Permit me to assure you that if I had something satisfactory to send you, I would certainly not have lost a moment in doing so, but it is a very unpleasant task for me to say what I have to say. My intention was to ask some musical friends to join with me in purchasing the manuscript of your three quartets;[3] although I am not rich enough myself to undertake this venture alone, I am entirely ready to subscribe to my portion of the sum. I did not foresee any difficulties in making this arrangement, but I am sorry to say that I found more of them than I expected. Some say that they must be absolutely certain of the arrival of the manuscript; others claim that they do not want to deprive the public of them, etc. However, it appears that, finally, I have managed to get you the sum of £100 sterling; but I am sorry to add that this sum cannot be paid before the manuscript has arrived here, because I shall have to collect the funds for it, and I am certain that the friends to whom I addressed myself will hasten to fulfill their obligations as soon as the manuscript is here. There is still one other difficulty: they fear that the Quartets will have been copied in Vienna. I trust that you will take care to prevent this.

A thousand thanks, my dear friend, for the wishes for my happiness that you expressed to me. I have the satisfaction to tell you that my family is in perfect health. As for me, I was not well for more than six months, and was even so ill that I believed that I might not live long enough to have the pleasure of hearing your new quartets. This is one more reason that lessened my courage to write you on the subject. Thank God I have now recovered, and I hope again to hear and play a great number of your compositions. Nothing could give me greater pleasure than to receive your news soon, but when you write me, I request you to do so in French, or at least in German with French letters, for I cannot read German letters.

Believe me, my dear Beethoven, to be as much your friend as your most sincere and devoted admirer.

Charles Neate

24 Foley Place
London

1. For further information on this British pianist (1784–1877), see his letter of October 29, 1816 (No. 234 above).

2. The autograph clearly reads 1822, and Schindler believed that the letter dated from that year. This must have been a slip of either Neate's mind or his pen, however, because this letter surely replies to Beethoven's letter to Neate of February 25, 1823 (Anderson No. 1144), and refers to the quartets commissioned by Galitzin on November 9, 1822 (No. 299 above). Moreover, the postmark reads "F (9 2) 23," which seems to confirm the September 2, 1823, date adopted here.

3. The late string quartets commissioned by Prince Nicolas Galitzin, ultimately Opp. 127, 130 and 132. Early in their correspondence, Galitzin had expressly given Beethoven permission to dispose of the quartets elsewhere.

Incipit: Vous êtes sans doute aussi offensé que. . . .

Sources: Excerpt in original French with German translation in Schindler (1860), pt. 2, pp. 103–105; translated into English and annotated in Schindler-MacArdle, pp. 300–301, 354. Present version taken from the autograph, Staatsbibliothek zu Berlin–Preussischer Kulturbesitz, Mus. ms. autogr. Beethoven 35, 54; listed in Kalischer, "Beethoven-Autographe," pp. 50–51, and Bartlitz, p. 135.

335. *Prince Anton of Saxony*[1] *to Beethoven*

Dresden; September 12, 1823[2]

Mein Herr *Kapellmeister!*

I have received your letter along with the enclosure to the King, my brother, and I do not doubt that he will grant your wish, especially since I have spoken with him about it in the name of my brother-in-law, the Cardinal.[3] The new work of which you speak will certainly be a masterpiece, as are your others, and I shall surely admire it when I hear it. I ask you to give my best regards to my dear brother-in-law, and for your part be convinced of the sentiments with which I remain my life long

Your truly affectionate,

Anton

1. Prince Anton (1755–1836) was himself an accomplished amateur composer; he succeeded his brother, Friedrich August, to the throne in 1827.

2. Replies to Beethoven's letter to Anton, ca. July 25, 1823, which seemingly has not survived, although a fragmentary draft for it is included in the present collection (No. 331 above). The letter to the theater director von Könneritz, dated July 25, that accompanied it is Anderson No. 1212. The letter to Anton, in turn, contained a further letter to Friedrich August, which, likewise, seems not to have survived.

3. Beethoven must have applied to the king of Saxony to subscribe to a manuscript copy of the *Missa solemnis* in the first group of such "form letters," sent out in late January and early February 1823 (see Anderson No. 1134 and contemporary items in the present collection, e.g., No. 303 above). The king must have declined, with the result that Beethoven determined to employ multiple influences on him by enlisting the aid of Archduke (Cardinal) Rudolph, Prince Anton and Court Councillor von Könneritz. For further background, see Anderson Nos. 1204, 1210 and 1212 as well as Rudolph's letter to Beethoven, July 31, 1823 (No. 332 above). The fee from Dresden must have arrived a week or so later (see Beethoven to Schindler, ca. September 30, 1823, Anderson No. 1241).

Incipit: Ich habe Ihren Brief nebst. . . .

Sources: Thayer-Deiters-Riemann, IV, 362; Kalischer (German), IV, 338; Kalischer-Shedlock, II, 296; Kastner (1910), p. 775. Mention only in Thayer-Krehbiel, III, 97; Thayer-Forbes, p. 825. Autograph in the Staatsbibliothek zu Berlin–Preussischer Kulturbesitz, Mus. ms. autogr. Beethoven 35, 2; listed in Bartlitz, p. 117.

336. *Prince Nicolas Galitzin to Beethoven*

St. Petersburg; October 3, 1823[1]

I received today your letter of the 17th, and I hasten to reply to it, and to direct the house of Henikstein to deliver to you immediately the 50 ducats that I believed had long ago been placed at your disposal.[2] Only try to have it[3] sent to me as soon as possible, so that it can be performed here for Christmas.

I have arrived at this moment from a long journey in the southern provinces of Russia to restore a little my wife's health, greatly disturbed by the loss of her child that she has suffered.[4] Of all the losses with which one may be tried here below, that of one's child is surely the most acute. But, in the end, one is not in this world for pleasure, and God never takes away anything that He does not return a hundredfold in this life or the next.[5] I hope that the infirmities from which you suffer will receive considerable relief by the treatment of the baths at Baden, which I know well, having spent my childhood in Vienna from 1804 to 1806.

I enclose here a letter from Monsieur Henikstein, and ask that you let me know in what time frame you want the 150 ducats for the Quartets, and I shall send them directly.

Accept the assurance of my high esteem and sentiments of perfect devotion.

P[rince] Nicolas Galitzin

1. Or: September 23 (old style). Answers Beethoven's letter of September 17, which seems not to have survived. In it Beethoven apparently asked Galitzin to apply the 50 ducats on deposit with Henikstein, originally sent for the first of the commissioned string quartets, to the purchase of the *Missa solemnis.*

2. Galitzin's letter of February 23, 1823 (No. 310), indicated that he had initiated the transfer of 50 ducats from St. Petersburg to Vienna, and by May 5 (No. 319 above) he assumed that Beethoven had withdrawn the sum. The fact that Beethoven had not done so possibly indicates that he did not intend to accept the fee until he delivered the first quartet.

3. The *Missa solemnis,* ultimately performed on April 7, 1824.

4. Galitzin's letter of August 3 indicated that the child had already been seriously ill for a month.

5. The family's next child, Juri Nicolaievich, was born on December 11, 1823; thus Galitzin's wife Elena was already about seven months pregnant at the time this letter was written.

Incipit: Je reçois à l'instant. . . .

Sources: Thayer-Deiters-Riemann, V, 555–556; brief excerpt translated and background given in Thayer-Krehbiel, III, 103, and Thayer-Forbes, p. 831. When Thayer copied it, the autograph was in the possession of Beethoven's nephew Karl's widow, Caroline, Vienna. It has since disappeared.

337. Henikstein & Co. to Prince Nicolas Galitzin, St. Petersburg

Vienna; October 25, 1823[1]

Monseigneur,

We have the honor to acknowledge the receipt of Your Highness's gracious letter, dated the 3d of this month,[2] and to add, at the same time, receipt from

Monsieur L. v. Beethoven for 50 ducats in (real) gold, which we have paid him by order and on account of Your Highness as fee for the Mass, which we have dispatched through the High State Chancellery. We note, moreover, that as [each] one of the four Quartets [*sic*] is finished, Your Highness will have the amount paid to us, and pray that this will be suitable, etc., etc.

1. This letter accompanied Beethoven's receipt for 50 ducats, paid for a handwritten copy of the *Missa solemnis,* dated October 22, 1823 (original French in Anderson, p. 1431; for an English translation, see MacArdle & Misch No. 372).

2. Galitzin must have written to the banking house of Henikstein (sometimes given as Henickstein) on October 3, as he promised to Beethoven on that date (No. 336 above).

Incipit: Nous avons l'honneur d'accouser. . . .

Sources: Thayer-Deiters-Riemann, V, 556; mentioned and partially translated in Thayer-Krehbiel, III, 103, and Thayer-Forbes, p. 831.

338. *Prince Nicolas Galitzin to Beethoven*

St. Petersburg; November 29, 1823[1]

With inexpressible joy, Monsieur, I have received the Mass you recently composed, and although I have only been able to judge it up to now by an examination of the score, I have found in it that grandeur that distinguishes all your compositions and that makes your works inimitable. I am occupied in having this beautiful work performed in a manner worthy of him who composed it and of those who are creating a festival to hear it. Indeed, I believe that it would be difficult to find anywhere else the same resources for the performance of an oratorio as in St. Petersburg. The singers of the court who will perform the choruses and the solo parts are very numerous and certainly the best that one can hear, as much for the beauty of their voices as for their ensemble.[2]

I deeply regret not yet having received the piano sonatas that you told me about a long time ago.[3] I am anxious to have all that comes from you, and I possess all that you have composed up to now for the piano as well as for all other instruments. During my leisure moments, I even take pleasure in arranging some of your beautiful solo piano sonatas as [string] quartets, and since I do not play this instrument, I take pleasure in performing them with the quartet. I have, nonetheless, also heard all these pieces performed on the piano, for Monsieur Zeuner,[4] who has the good fortune to be acquainted with you, and who is one of your greatest admirers, frequents my house daily and I never permit him to leave until he has played me some piece of your composition. In this manner they have all become familiar to me, and I owe to this distinguished artist my taste for music, my acquaintance with your works, and above all my appreciation of them. The bad taste that reigns in Europe disgusts me, and the Italian charlatanry aggravates me.[5] But all this enthusiasm for Italian twittering will pass with the fashion, and your masterpieces are immortal.

I am very impatient to possess a new quartet by you,[6] but I beg you not to pay any attention to this, and to follow in that respect only your inspiration and the inclination of your mind, for no one knows better than I that one cannot command genius, rather must leave it alone, and we know moreover that in your private life you are not a man to sacrifice artistic for personal interest, and that you do not deal in music upon demand. I only ask that you remember me in your moments of inspiration.

I most sincerely wish that, in providing the restoration of your health, heaven may yet long preserve for us a life as precious as yours. Too young to have known the celebrated Mozart, and having been present only in the last years of Haydn, of whom I caught only a glimpse during my childhood in Vienna,[7] I rejoice in being the contemporary of the third hero of music, who can find his equal only in the first two, and whom one might properly proclaim the god of melody and harmony.

Accept, I pray you, the very sincere expression of the sentiments that I have dedicated to you.

Prince Nicolas Galitzin

1. Replies to Beethoven's shipment of the *Missa solemnis,* sent through the banker Henikstein in Vienna between October 22 and 25, 1823 (see Henikstein's letter to Galitzin, October 25, No. 337 above).

2. Originally projected for the Christmas season of 1823, the performance took place on April 7, 1824 (new style).

3. Beethoven must have mentioned them in a letter written sometime in June 1823, judging from Galitzin's reference to the "two latest works for the piano" in his letter to Beethoven of August 3 (No. 333 above). The designation *sonatas* here narrows the possibilities to two works from among Opp. 109, 110 and 111.

4. Karl Traugott Zeuner (1775–1841), Dresden-born pianist and composer, who studied with Muzio Clementi, settled in St. Petersburg and became the teacher of Glinka. In a letter of late July 1825 (Anderson No. 1405), answering Galitzin's question concerning a passage in the Andante of the String Quartet, Op. 127, Beethoven defended Zeuner's reading as "perfectly right" and called him "a capable artist." Zeuner was in Vienna in 1805 (as piano teacher to Princess Galitzin, presumably the present Prince Nicolas's mother) and may have met Beethoven then (see Karl Laux, "Zeuner," *MGG*, vol. XIV, cols. 1249–1250).

5. A reference to the epidemic of "Rossini fever" spreading throughout Europe.

6. Eventually resulting in Op. 127.

7. Born in 1794, Galitzin had spent from 1804 to 1806 in Vienna.

Incipit: J'ai reçu avec une joie inexprimable. . . .

Sources: Original French in Thayer-Deiters-Riemann, V, 556–557; German translations in Nohl, "Die Briefe Galitzins," *Allgemeine Deutsche Musik-Zeitung* 6 (1879), p. 2, cols. 1–2; Georges Humbert, "Ein unbekannte Brief Beethovens an den Fürsten N. von Galitzin," *Die Musik* 9, pt. 1 (1909), 16–21; and Brenneis, "Fischhof-Manuskript," pp. 77–80. Brief excerpts in German in Nohl, *Beethoven's Leben* (1877), III, 890; and Schindler, 3d ed. (1860), pt. 2, p. 106; the last translated into English in Schindler-MacArdle, p. 301. Another brief excerpt in English in Thayer-Forbes, p. 924. When Fischhof made his copy (Staatsbibliothek zu Berlin–Preussischer Kulturbesitz), the autograph must still have been in the hands of Beethoven's nephew Karl. By the time Thayer and Nohl copied it, the autograph was in the possession of Karl's widow, Caroline, Vienna. It has since disappeared and is presumed lost.

339. *Beethoven to Archduke Rudolph, Olmütz*[1]

Vienna; [December] 7, 1823[2]

Your Imperial Highness!

Yes, yes, I am a windbag, it is said, so it seems, and yet it is not so. In [my] head I have written Y.I.H. every day, but I admit that nothing has been put on paper. Pardon me, my most gracious prince; the spirit is willing, but the flesh is weak![3] I have indeed noticed the progress in Y.I.H.'s exercises, but also, unfortunately, that misunderstandings exist in them. For the present, the best course is to realize figured basses by good composers in 4 parts, and occasionally to compose a 4-part song, until I again have the good fortune to be near Y.I.H. Writing in 4-part style for the piano can also have a beneficial effect, although it is more difficult for just this reason, since one cannot manage the upward or downward motion of the parts as naturally as in a vocal piece. . . .

Now, once more, a request to Y.I.H., which lies very close to my heart: namely, Schuppanzigh,[4] who is here again, has requested me to ask Y.I.H. to do him the great favor of writing to Count Moritz Dietrichstein,[5] so that he might receive the position of the deceased Court Musician Menzel.[6] I need not mention to my sublime pupil that this position might be won in such a manner, even less that a single letter from Y.I.H. works wonders here. I also know (very confidently!!!) that this request on behalf of a deserving artist will not be denied me (no wonder, I am already a bit spoiled by Y.I.H.'s graciousness and kindness); at least I know how gladly you most sublimely help, and that one need not acclaim Y.I.H. with the beautiful words, "Hülfreich sei der Mensch." . . .[7]

My health is finally much better; I had to spend until October 13 in Baden, then came here where I moved into a new apartment,[8] which robbed me of much time and, in my great enthusiasm, used my health in this activity. These are also the reasons for my silence up to now. I know that Y.I.H. never doubts my warmest enthusiasm. Why are circumstances aligned in such a manner that Y.I.H.'s great talent must really suffer from them?! It ought not to be—

With the warmest and most reverent sentiments, I kiss my dear most gracious Lord's hands, and trust in [his] pardon and—indulgence. . . .

L. v. Beethoven

1. Since Beethoven writes from Vienna in this letter, Rudolph had presumably returned to his ecclesiastical and administrative duties in Olmütz. Even so, the archduke continued his composition studies as time permitted.

2. Sieghard Brandenburg, Beethoven-Archiv, Bonn, has examined the autograph and confirms that the first page of this letter clearly indicates the German equivalent of "Vienna, on 7th Novemb. 1823," not the "3rd," as previously reported. However, the violinist Menzel, mentioned in this letter as "deceased," did not die until November 19, 1823 (see n.6, this letter). Moreover, Beethoven, Schuppanzigh and Beethoven's nephew Karl had a candid conversation concerning Schuppanzigh's desire for the vacant post on ca. November 26–27, 1823, concluding that Beethoven should write to Rudolph on Schuppanzigh's behalf (Köhler et al., *Konversationshefte*, IV, 266, 268). Thus it is likely that Beethoven simply penned the wrong month and actually wrote to Rudolph on the "7th" of December.

3. This was not entirely an empty excuse: on ca. November 25, 1823, Beethoven had noted in a conversation book, "Ollmuz" — hence his intention to write Rudolph in Olmütz.

4. Ignaz Schuppanzigh (1776–1830), one of Vienna's finest violinists, had led string quartets for Prince Lichnowsky (1794–1799) and Prince Rasumovsky (1808–1816) and had served as concertmaster for Beethoven's concerts in 1813–1814. After the dissolution of the Rasumovsky Quartet, Schuppanzigh journeyed through Germany, Poland and Russia, eventually returning to Vienna in April 1823 (whereupon Beethoven wrote the canon "Falstafferel, lass' dich sehen!" WoO 184, dated April 26). Beethoven insisted that Schuppanzigh serve as concertmaster for his concerts in May 1824. After three years as a probationary applicant, the Falstaffian fiddler finally received an official court appointment on September 1, 1827.

5. Count Moritz Dietrichstein (1774–1864) administered musical activities for the imperial court. The wording in Beethoven's letter closely follows the sense of conversation book entries made on ca. November 26–27, 1823 (Köhler et al., *Konversationshefte*, IV, 266, 268).

6. Born on October 12, 1757, Zeno Franz Menzel had been a member of the violin section of both the Hofkapelle and Burgtheater for over three decades. His career had begun auspiciously: on April 10, 1784, Mozart (writing from Vienna) described him to his father, Leopold, in Salzburg as "a handsome and clever young fellow . . . a charming violinist, and . . . also a very good sight-reader. So far no one in Vienna has played my quartets so well at sight as he has. Moreover he is the kindest fellow in the world. . . . I had him in the orchestra at my concert." Several letters and mentions later, Mozart's opinion had changed by June 12: "Herr Menzel is, and always will be an ass" (Emily Anderson, trans. and ed., *The Letters of Mozart and His Family*, 3d ed. [New York: W. W. Norton, 1985], Nos. 508 and 515).

After making some musical tours (presumably starting in June 1784), Menzel joined the Hofkapelle on March 1, 1787. He played solos at Tonkünstler-Sozietät concerts in 1787, 1788 and 1795 but may have fallen into routine section playing thereafter. He joined the Tonkünstler-Sozietät in 1793 but withdrew in 1815 (Pohl, *Tonkünstler Societät*, pp. 62, 65, 90, 107).

Menzel died on November 19, 1823 (Ludwig von Köchel, *Die kaiserliche Hof-Musikkapelle in Wien, von 1543 bis 1867* [Vienna: Beck'sche Universitäts-Buchhandlung, 1869], pp. 90, 93; confirmed by Archiv Wien, Totenprotokoll 1823, M Fol. 41; quoted in Köhler et al., *Konversationshefte*, IV, 379, n.580).

7. "Helpful be Man," a reference to Goethe's poem *Das Göttliche*, from which Beethoven derived a *Stammbuch* entry for Baroness Cäcilie von Eskeles ("Der edle Mensch sei hülfreich und gut," WoO 151) on January 20, 1823, as well as a six-voice canon, "Edel sei der Mensch, hülfreich und gut," WoO 185, which Beethoven entered

in Louis Schlösser's *Stammbuch* on May 6, 1823, and then published in the *Wiener Zeitschrift für Kunst, Literatur, Theater und Mode*, no. 74 (June 21, 1823).

8. Suburban Landstrasse No. 323, at the corner of Ungargasse and Bockgasse (now Beatrixgasse).

Incipit: Ja, ja ich bin ein Windbeutel, wird's heissen. . . .

Sources: Substantial text, with ellipses noted, in Stargardt, *Autographen aus allen Gebieten: Katalog 601* (Marburg, February 20–21, 1973), p. 138, item 599; quoted briefly in Helms and Staehelin, "Bewegungen . . . 1973–1979," p. 352; partial quotation translated in Kagan, *Archduke Rudolph*, p. 33. The autograph had been in the estate of an official in the Imperial Royal High Chamberlain's Office, was auctioned by Stargardt in 1973 and again went into private possession in Austria. Susan Kagan kindly sent a copy of the Stargardt entry, and J. Rigbie Turner supplied the facsimile.

340. *Prince Nicolas Galitzin to Beethoven*

St. Petersburg; December 30, 1823[1]

I have just received, Monsieur, your letter of December 13, with the enclosure of the first page of the *Gloria*.[2] I was rather happy because the copy that I received was complete, and nothing seems to me to be missing. I would have perceived this a long time ago because I study the score every day, and without having heard this masterpiece I have a grasp of it.

The tempo indication that you believed not to be marked in the section "in gloria Dei patris" is also marked in the score, but instead of [allegro] "maestoso e moderato" it says "allegro ma non troppo e ben marcato"; they amount to nearly the same thing.[3]

Next Monday we will hold the first full rehearsal of the Mass with full orchestra, but it will possibly only be performed in the month of February, in Lent. I am devoting all my care so this masterpiece will be performed in a manner worthy of its celebrated author.

I await with impatience the letter that you promised me, as I do with all that comes from you.[4] Let me know if you need the 50 ducats for the first Quartet,[5] and I shall make them immediately available to you.

I would have desired also that you had sent me the tempo indications for all the sections of the Mass according to Maelzel's metronome, which will give us a more exact idea of the speed at which you want the movements to be taken. I urge you very much to perform this same operation yourself for all the works that you have composed, because I have frequently observed great variants in the manner in which your music is performed, and by settling the question and the differing opinions, you yourself would establish the speeds in which you desire all your compositions to be played.[6] Maelzel's metronome seems to me valuable for this communication.

Adieu, Monsieur; accept the very sincere assurance of my devotion and my unbounded admiration.

P[rin]ce Nicolas Galitzin

[P.S.]

I do not yet have the music that you told me you were sending.[7] But I have found at the Marchands de Musique[8] here your Op. 120, which is 33 Variations, etc.[9] This piece is a masterwork, as is all that comes from you; one may only admire the happy fecundity that the science of harmony inspires in you in this piece. I do not know the works that are found between the Sonata, Op. 111, and the aforesaid Op. 120. I have not been able to obtain them and I address myself to you to ask you what are the works that I lack, so that I may obtain them.

1. Answers Beethoven's letter of December 13, 1823 (French original in Anderson No. 1244; English translation in MacArdle & Misch No. 374), which in turn replied to Galitzin's letter of November 29 (No. 338 above).

2. As Beethoven explained in his December 13 letter, he thought that Galitzin's copy of the *Missa solemnis* might have been sent without this page, which he had cut out of the original to prevent theft or fraud on the part of the copyist. After some delay, the St. Petersburg performance took place on April 7, 1824.

3. Beethoven does indeed write "Allegro maestoso e moderato" in his December 13 letter; the designation in Galitzin's score, however, is consistent with that in the *Gesamtausgabe,* ser. 19, no. 203, p. 67.

4. On December 13, Beethoven had implied that a "newsy" letter would follow.

5. Ultimately, the String Quartet, Op. 127.

6. Beethoven had provided metronome markings for selected compositions as early as December 17, 1817, when he published such tempo indications in the *Allgemeine musikalische Zeitung* (Leipzig).

7. See Galitzin's letters to Beethoven of August 3 and November 29 (Nos. 333 and 338 above); he is probably referring to two of the piano sonatas from among Opp. 109, 110 and 111.

8. Music merchants, possibly the proper name of the business, since Galitzin is careful to capitalize, as above.

9. Thirty-three Variations on a Waltz by Diabelli, Op. 120.

Incipit: Je viens de recevoir, Monsieur, vôtre lettre du 13. Decembre. . . .

Sources: Thayer-Deiters-Riemann, V, 557–558; brief excerpt translated in Thayer-Forbes, p. 925. When Thayer copied it, the autograph was in the possession of Beethoven's nephew Karl's widow, Caroline, Vienna. It has since disappeared.

In the *North American Beethoven Studies* series